WORD PRO
in easy steps

Stephen Copestake

COMPUTER STEP

In easy steps is an imprint of Computer Step
Southfield Road . Southam
Warwickshire CV33 0FB . England

Tel: 01926 817999 Fax: 01926 817005
http://www.computerstep.com

Copyright © 1999 by Computer Step. All rights reserved. No part of this book may be reproduced or transmitted in any form or by any means, electronic or mechanical, including photocopying, recording, or by any information storage or retrieval system, without prior written permission from the publisher.

Notice of Liability

Every effort has been made to ensure that this book contains accurate and current information. However, Computer Step and the author shall not be liable for any loss or damage suffered by readers as a result of any information contained herein.

Trademarks

Word Pro is a registered trademark of Lotus Development Corporation. ViaVoice is a registered trademark of International Business Machines Corporation. Microsoft and Windows are registered trademarks of Microsoft Corporation. All other trademarks are acknowledged as belonging to their respective companies.

Printed and bound in the United Kingdom

ISBN 1-84078-041-X

Contents

1 Getting Started — 7

Starting Word Pro	8
The Word Pro screen	10
SmartIcons	12
Infoboxes – an overview	15
Launching Infoboxes	16
The Word Pro HELP system	17
Ask the Expert	19
Other HELP features	20

2 Working with Files — 21

Entering text	22
New document creation	23
Creating blank documents	24
Using SmartMasters	25
Opening files	26
Opening files from the Internet	27
Moving around in documents	28
Document views – an overview	30
Using views	31
Changing zoom levels	32
Undo	33
Multiple Undo's	34
Searching for text	35
Using Quick Find	36
Replacing text	37
Saving files	38

3 Working with the Web — 39

Web documents – an overview	40
Creating Web documents	41
Converting files to Web format	42

Inserting hyperlinks	44
Activating hyperlinks	45
Saving files to the Web	46

4 Text Formatting — 47

Formatting text – an overview	48
Changing the font and/or type size	50
Changing text colour	51
Changing font attributes	52
Indenting paragraphs – an overview	53
Indenting paragraphs	54
Working with tabs	55
Viewing tab stops	57
Aligning paragraphs	58
Specifying paragraph spacing	59
Line spacing – an overview	60
Adjusting line spacing	61
Paragraph borders	62
Fast Format	63
Adding drop caps	65
Bulleting and Numbering paragraphs	67
Numbering lines	69
Text columns – an overview	70
Applying newspaper columns	71
Applying parallel columns	72

5 Page Formatting — 73

Page formatting/layout	74
Working with headers	76
Working with footers	81
Inserting page numbers	86
Inserting and activating hyperlinks	89
Inserting and jumping to bookmarks	90
Specifying margins	91
Specifying page sizes	92
Customising page sizes	93

Bordering pages	94
Shadowing pages	95
Applying backgrounds to pages	96
Applying patterns to pages	97
Applying watermarks to pages	98
Inserting new pages	99
Page styles – an overview	100
Creating a page style	101
Applying a page style	102
Amending a page style	103
Page style management	104
Copying page styles	105
Using function keys with page styles	107
Page layouts – an overview	108
Inserting a new page layout	109

6 Text Styles — 111

Text styles – an overview	112
Creating text styles	114
Applying text styles	115
Amending text styles	118
Text style management	119
Copying text styles	120
Renaming text styles	122
Using function keys with text styles	123

7 Proofing Tools — 125

Proofing – an overview	126
Spell-checking – an overview	127
Spell-checking on-the-fly	128
Spell-checking after editing	131
Spell-check options – an overview	133
Customising spell-checks	134
Using the Thesaurus	139
The Grammar Checker – an overview	141
Using the Grammar Checker	142

Customising grammar-checks	145
SmartCorrect – an overview	147
Using SmartCorrect	148
Customising SmartCorrect	150
Using Check Format	152
Customising Check Format	154
Tracking revisions	155
Document versions	157

8 Working with Pictures — 161

Working with pictures – an overview	162
Brief notes on picture formats	163
Inserting pictures	164
Manipulating pictures – an overview	166
Rescaling pictures	167
Bordering pictures	168
Moving pictures	169
Using frame styles	170

9 Printing — 171

Printing – an overview	172
Print setup	173
Customised printing	174
Printing with Net-It Now! SE	176

10 Using ViaVoice — 177

ViaVoice – an overview	178
Microphone Setup	179
Enrolment	180
Launching ViaVoice	182
Dictating text	183
Correcting errors	184
Vocalising text	185
Customising ViaVoice	186

Index — 187

Getting Started

This chapter shows you how to start and close Word Pro. You'll learn about the Word Pro screen, and specify which screen components display. You'll also discover how to use and customise SmartIcons; how to use Infoboxes; and how to use the inbuilt Word Pro HELP system (including Ask the Expert, which allows you to enter questions in your own terminology).

Covers

Starting Word Pro | 8

The Word Pro screen | 10

SmartIcons | 12

Infoboxes – an overview | 15

Launching Infoboxes | 16

The Word Pro HELP system | 17

Ask the Expert | 19

Other HELP features | 20

Starting Word Pro

The standard method for starting Word Pro is as follows.

Click the Windows Start button on the Task Bar at the base of the Windows screen – note that your Task Bar may look slightly different to the illustration below, depending on which programs you've installed onto your system and which are currently operational. (If the Task Bar isn't currently on-screen, move the mouse pointer over the relevant screen edge to make it visible.)

Finally, carry out the following steps:

| Click here

HANDY TIP

To close Word Pro, press Alt+F4. Alternatively, click this icon:

🗙

in the top right-hand corner of the Word Pro window.

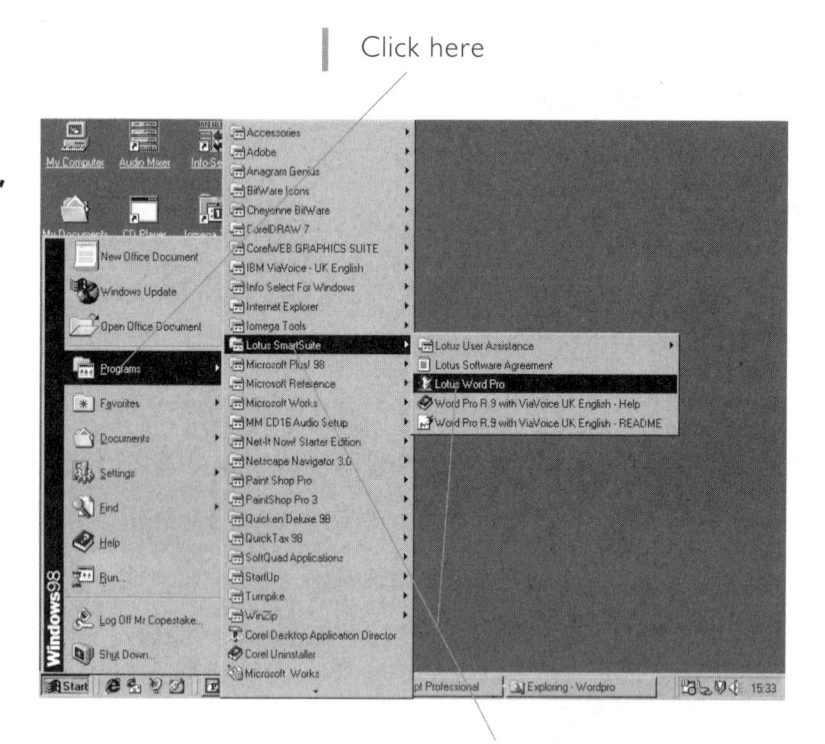

2 Click in both locations

Word Pro now runs.

8 Word Pro in easy steps

...cont'd

You can also use a special shortcut to launch Word Pro.

Using SuiteStart to launch Word Pro

If you installed SmartCenter as well as Word Pro, then SuiteStart is also installed by default. SuiteStart is a set of icons for SmartSuite programs which appears in the system tray, the section on the far right of the Windows Taskbar.

Refer to the Windows Taskbar (if it's currently invisible, make it visible by moving the mouse pointer over the relevant screen edge) and carry out the following step:

> **HANDY TIP** — **You can also use another method to launch Word Pro.** If SmartCenter is installed, activate the SmartSuite drawer. Click the Lotus Applications folder. Double-click the relevant icon.

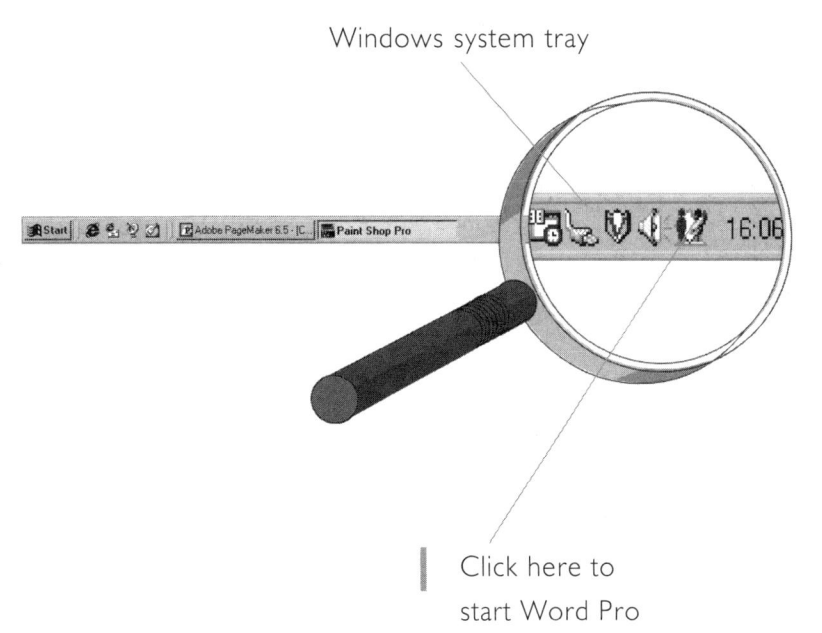

Windows system tray

Click here to start Word Pro

> **REMEMBER** — **Re step 1 – if you've installed other Word Pro programs, further icons will also appear.**

Word Pro now runs.

1 Getting Started

The Word Pro screen

Below is an illustration of the Word Pro screen.

Title bar — Menu bar — SmartIcons

REMEMBER

This screen is slightly different if ViaVoice is not installed – for how to use ViaVoice, see chapter 10.

REMEMBER

The Status bar displays information relating to the active document (e.g. what page you're on, the current typeface/ type size and the current text style).

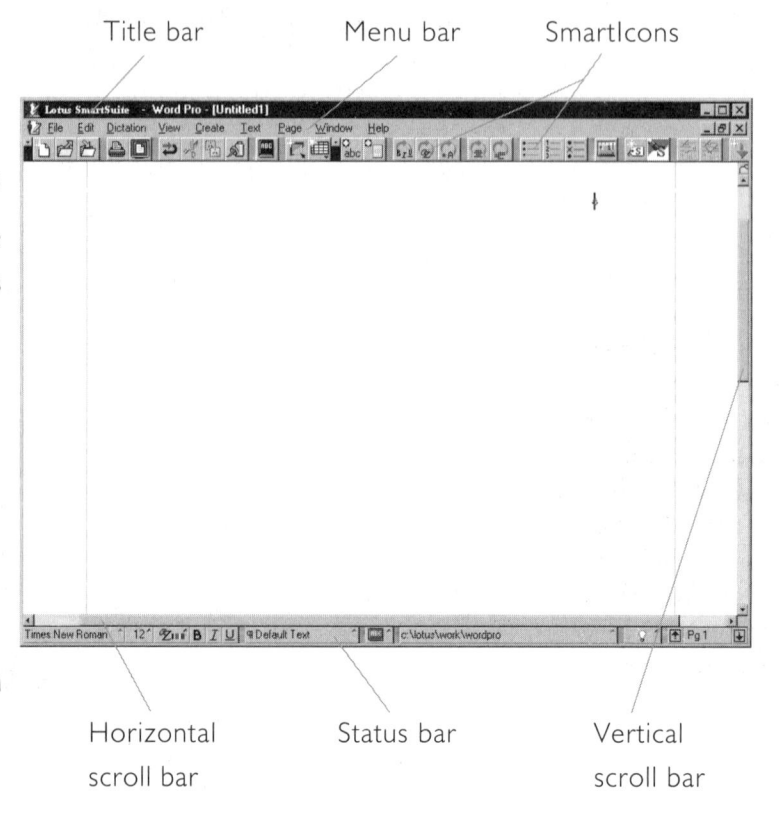

Horizontal scroll bar — Status bar — Vertical scroll bar

All of these – apart from the SmartIcons – are standard to just about all programs which run under Windows. A few of them can be hidden, if required – see page 11.

10 Word Pro in easy steps

...cont'd

Specifying which screen components display

Pull down the View menu. Carry out step 1 below. Then perform step 2 to hide or reveal a component, as appropriate:

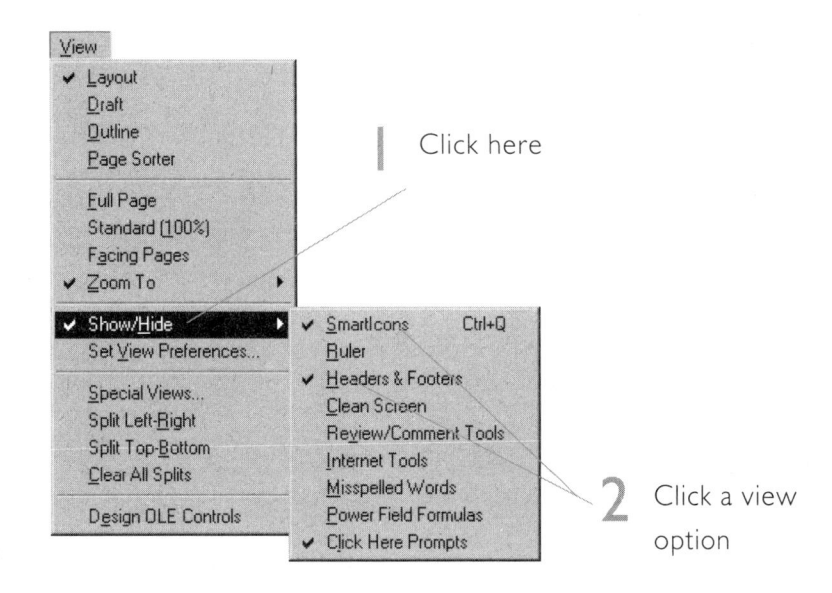

Click here

REMEMBER **The ✔ in the menu signifies that the item is currently visible. Clicking a ticked item hides it.**

2 Click a view option

Hiding *all* screen components

To hide all extraneous screen components (this increases working space), carry out step 1 above. In step 2, click Clean Screen.

To return to normal editing, click the following icon:

in the bottom right-hand corner of the screen.

SmartIcons

Word Pro provides access to a variety of SmartIcons. These are buttons you can click to initiate editing actions, and are contained in several on-screen bars. SmartIcons symbolise and allow easy access to often-used commands which would normally have to be invoked via one or more menus, or via Infoboxes.

> **HANDY TIP**
>
> **'Cycling' is a feature unique to Lotus SmartSuite applications.**
> **When you click a Cycle button repeatedly, Word Pro steps through associated options automatically until the correct one is activated.**

For example, Word Pro's Text and Universal SmartIcon bars let you:

- create, open, save and print documents;
- launch Infoboxes (see pages 15–16);
- cycle through alignment and/or indent options;
- cycle through typeface and/or type size options;
- cycle through text attribute options (**bold**, *italic* and underline), and;
- spell-check text;

by simply clicking the relevant button.

Hiding/revealing SmartIcons – the menu route

Pull down the View menu. Do the following:

> **HANDY TIP**
>
> **This method hides or reveals *all* currently visible SmartIcons.**
> **(To hide/reveal specific SmartIcon bars, see page 13).**

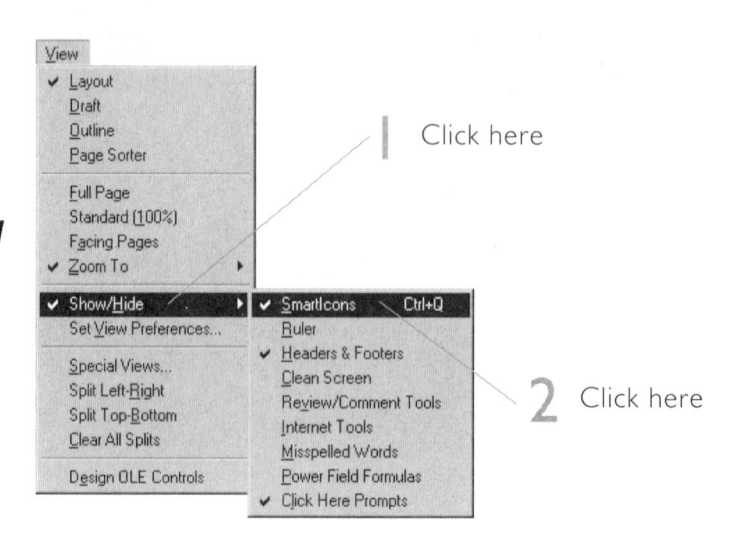

1 Click here

2 Click here

...cont'd

Hiding/revealing SmartIcons – an alternative

You can use another (and more versatile) method to control which SmartIcon sets (bars) display. (Just about any editing operation you can perform from within Word Pro menus can be incorporated as a SmartIcon, for ease of access.) Using this method, you can hide a specific set, or all sets.

Do the following:

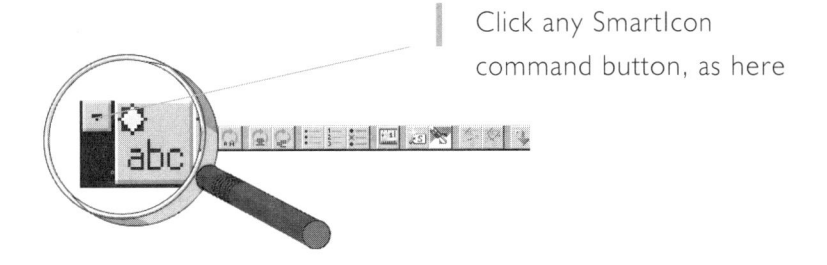

1 Click any SmartIcon command button, as here

| **HANDY TIP** | **Re steps 2 and 3 – this method only hides:** |

Now do either of the following:

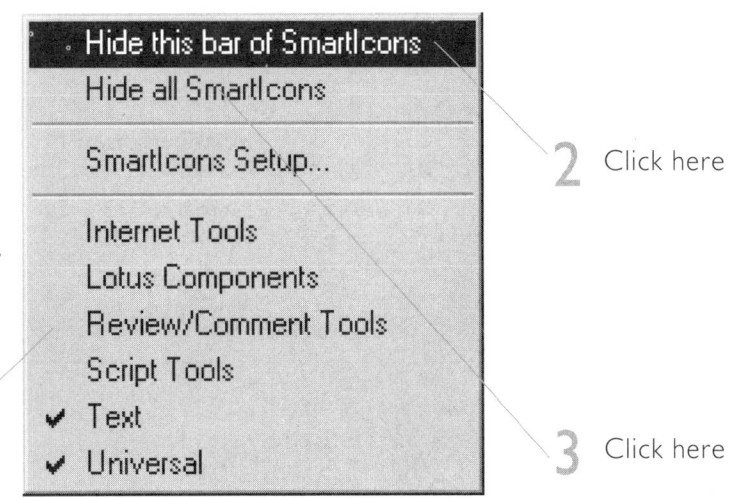

- the selected SmartIcon bar (step 2), and;
- all currently visible SmartIcon bars (step 3).

2 Click here

3 Click here

| **HANDY TIP** | **To hide/ reveal any other specific SmartIcon bar, simply click its entry in this section of the menu.** |

1 Getting Started **13**

...cont'd

Word Pro's Internet Tools SmartIcon bar is particularly useful:

- HTML options
- Open Web docs
- Save to the Web
- Hyperlink button
- Lotus home page
- Cust. support
- FTP server
- Web directory
- Web search
- Setup options
- **See tip below**
- Hide this bar

Click this button in the above bar to launch the Authoring Tools bar. Use this to:

- jump to Web addresses, and;
- launch the HTML Export Assistant.

Customising SmartIcons

You can:

- specify which SmartIcon bars display;
- add buttons to existing SmartIcon bars;
- remove buttons from bars, and;
- specify button size.

Click a SmartIcon command button (see page 13 for how to do this). In the menu that appears, click SmartIcons Setup.

Now carry out step 1 below to specify which bar displays. Follow step 2 to add a button to the bar, or step 3 to remove an existing one. Finally, carry out step 4:

3 Click a button; drag it off the bar

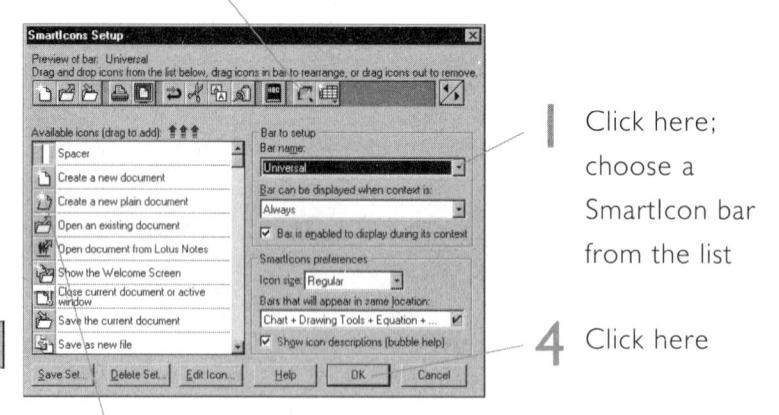

1 Click here; choose a SmartIcon bar from the list

4 Click here

2 Click the button you want to add; drag it onto the bar *in the dialog*

Adjusting button size

To adjust the size of SmartIcon buttons, click the arrow to the right of the 'Icon size' field; select the size you want from the list. Then follow step 4.

Infoboxes – an overview

Word Pro offers a feature which, until recently, had only been seen in top-of-the-range Desktop Publishing packages. You can use *Infoboxes,* which are collections of linked formatting features (called 'properties' in Word Pro), to make editing changes on-the-fly.

Below is the Text Properties Infobox:

To activate a different Infobox, click here; select the new Infobox from the list

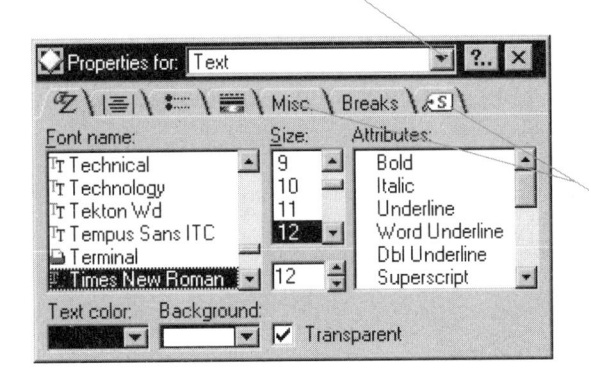

Tabs – click any of these for access to associated properties

Infoboxes provide the following advantages:

- If you want, you can have them stay open on-screen while you work (unlike dialogs, which close when you've finished with them). In this way, you can easily make multiple changes with the minimum of effort.

- You can use standard Windows techniques to move them to new locations on-screen.

- Changes you make within an Infobox are applied automatically, while you watch. (You don't have to click on OK or press Return to implement them.)

The following are some of the areas where Infoboxes are useful: text formatting, page layout, working with frames, working with headers/footers and columns.

1 Getting Started

Launching Infoboxes

In Word Pro, Infoboxes can be launched by clicking specific Infobox SmartIcons. Each contains a yellow star on a grey background:

HANDY TIP

You can also use a keyboard shortcut to launch the Infobox which is appropriate to the current context. Simply press Alt+Enter.

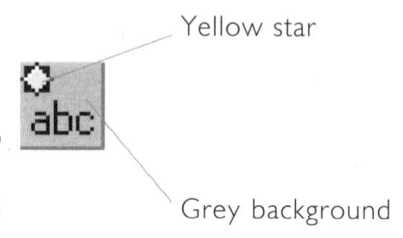

Yellow star

Grey background

The above is the SmartIcon which launches the Text Properties Infobox. Other Infobox SmartIcons include:

Page Properties Infobox

REMEMBER

Some of these icons only display in specific circumstances. For example, the Header Properties and Footer Properties icons only display when you've created or are editing a header or footer.

Frame Properties Infobox

Chart Properties Infobox

Header Properties Infobox

Footer Properties Infobox

16 Word Pro in easy steps

The Word Pro HELP system

Word Pro has comprehensive on-line Help facilities, organised under two broad headings:

- Contents (a list of topics and sub-topics)
- Index (an alphabetical list of topics)

Using Contents

Pull down the Help menu and click Help Topics. Now do the following, as appropriate:

REMEMBER **Press Esc at any time to close the Contents window.**

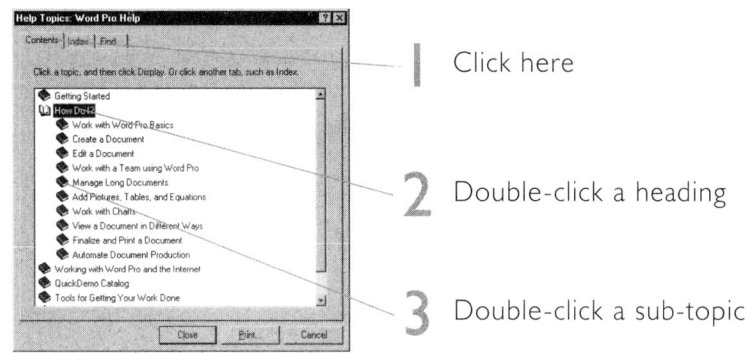

1. Click here
2. Double-click a heading
3. Double-click a sub-topic

After step 3, Word Pro launches a series of subheadings. Repeat until you find the topic you want information on (prefixed by [?]); double-click it to launch a HELP box.

Using Index

Pull down the Help menu and click Help Topics. Now do the following, as appropriate:

REMEMBER **Press Esc at any time to close the Index window.**

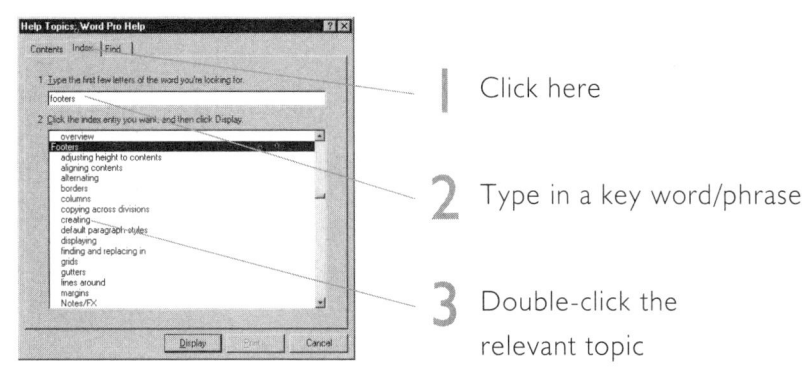

1. Click here
2. Type in a key word/phrase
3. Double-click the relevant topic

Getting Started **17**

...cont'd

When you've used the Contents or Index sections of HELP to pick the topic you want help with, Word Pro displays it as a separate window on top of the open document. Carry out steps 1 or 2 below, as appropriate. Alternatively, to access additional but related topics, perform steps 3–4:

1 Click here to access Contents

| HANDY TIP | **Click here: (when available) to display a useful HELP tip:** |

You can also reach the Frame InfoBox by choosing Frame - Frame Properties.

2 Click here to return to the previous topic (if applicable)

3 Click here for a list of associated topics

| REMEMBER | **To close any HELP window when you've finished with it, press Esc.** |

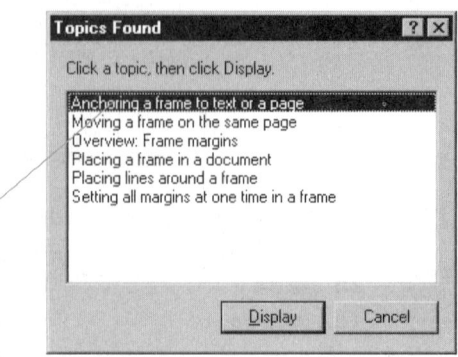

4 Double-click a topic to launch the appropriate assistance

18 Word Pro in easy steps

Ask the Expert

Often, when you invoke Word Pro's HELP system, you'll know more or less the question you want to ask, or the topic on which you need information. However, what happens if neither of these is true (for instance, if you don't know the name that Word Pro uses for a given feature)?

Word Pro offers a feature which resolves this: Ask the Expert. Its purpose is to allow you to enter questions in your own terminology. If you don't know the correct term for what you want to ask, you can simply express the question in your own words. Ask the Expert then supplies a list of related topics from which you can choose...

Launching Ask the Expert

Pull down the Help menu and click Ask the Expert. Do the following:

HANDY TIP **Re step 3 – if none of the visible topics are helpful, click this button:** More **for extra examples.**

3 Click a topic

1 Type in your question in Plain English

HANDY TIP **To close Ask the Expert, click the Done button.**

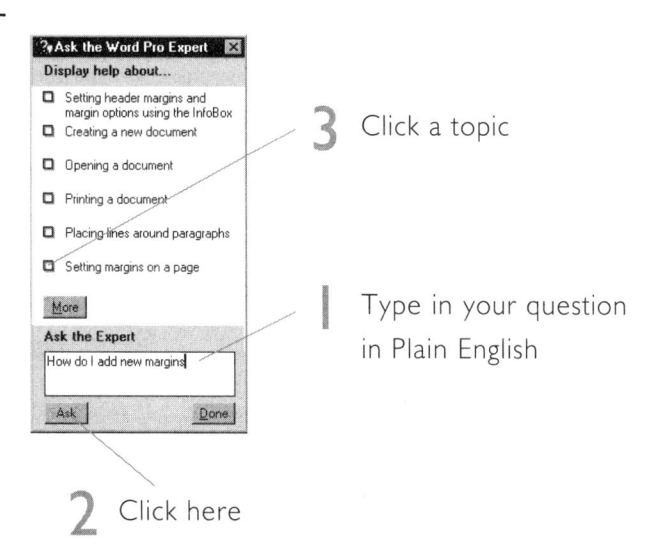

2 Click here

After step 3, Ask the Expert provides a relevant HELP window in the normal way.

Getting Started

Other HELP features

Bubble help
Whenever you move the mouse pointer over a SmartIcon and leave it there for a few seconds, Word Pro launches an explanatory HELP bubble:

Hold the mouse pointer over any SmartIcon to produce a helpful bubble

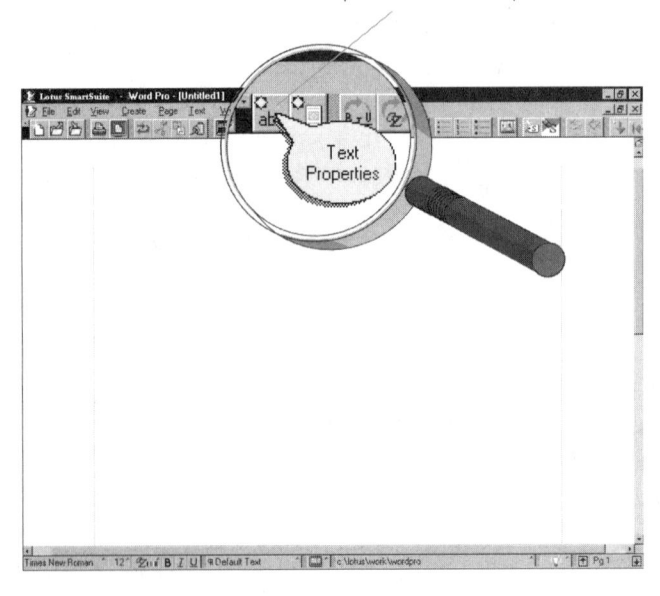

QuickDemos
Some HELP topics offer automated demonstrations of procedures. Do the following:

REMEMBER **After you've finished running the QuickDemo, carry out the demonstrated procedures yourself.**

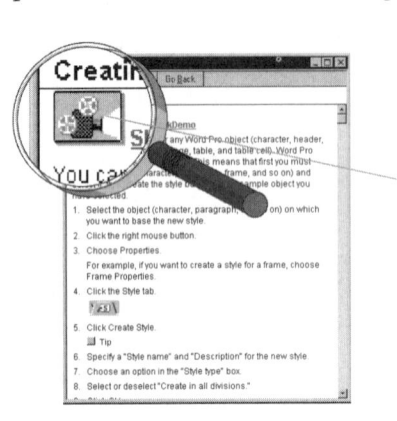

Click this icon, then follow the on-screen instructions

20 Word Pro in easy steps

Working with Files

Chapter Two

This chapter shows you how to begin to work with Word Pro. You'll enter text and move around in documents; create new documents; and open/save existing ones. You'll also change document views and zoom levels; undo multiple editing operations; and perform find-and-replace operations.

Covers

Entering text | 22

Creating new documents | 23

Opening files | 26

Opening files from the Internet | 27

Moving around in documents | 28

Document views | 30

Changing zoom levels | 32

Undo | 33

Multiple Undo's | 34

Searching for text | 35

Using Quick Find | 36

Replacing text | 37

Saving files | 38

Entering text

Word Pro lets you enter text as soon as you're presented with the basic editing screen. You enter text at the insertion point:

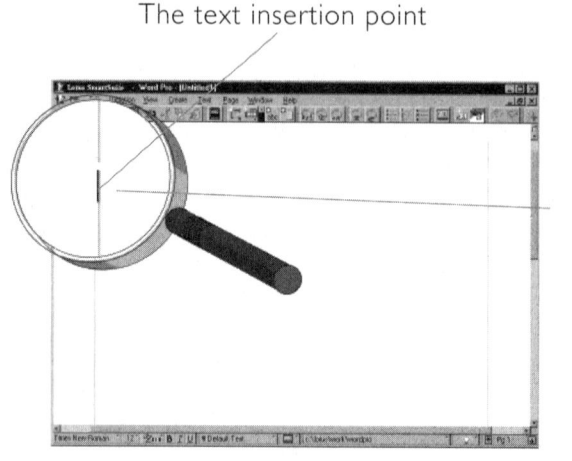

The text insertion point

Begin entering text here

HANDY TIP **Word Pro has automatic word wrap. This means that you don't have to press Return to enter text on a new line; a new line is automatically started for you, when required.**
   Only press Return if you need to begin a new paragraph.

Special characters

Most of the text you need to enter can be typed in directly from the keyboard. However, it's sometimes necessary to enter special characters (e.g. bullets like ☞, or ©). Word Pro lets you do this directly.

Place the insertion point at the correct location. Pull down the Text menu and click Insert Other, Symbol. Do the following:

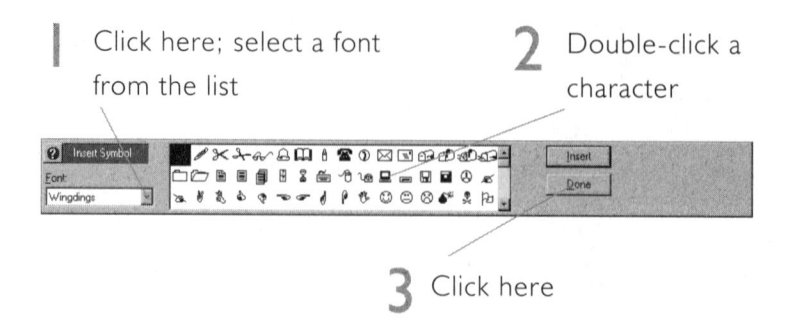

1 Click here; select a font from the list

2 Double-click a character

3 Click here

22 **Word Pro in easy steps**

New document creation

Word Pro lets you:

- create new blank documents, and;
- create new documents based on automated templates called SmartMasters.

REMEMBER — **See chapter 3 for how to create World Wide Web documents with SmartMasters.**

Creating blank documents is the simplest route to new document creation; use this if you want to define the document components yourself from scratch. This is often not the most efficient way to create new documents.

SmartMasters are special templates (document models containing preassigned formatting and/or text) which provide a shortcut to the creation of new documents. When activated, SmartMasters contain special 'click here' blocks which tell you where to insert relevant text. SmartMasters greatly simplify and speed up the creation of new documents, with highly professional results.

HANDY TIP — **To use a 'click-here' area, simply click it. Word Pro launches a help bubble which tells you what sort of text to insert:**

Click here to type Heading for your first article

(Type the text for your first article)

Documents created with the use of SmartMasters can easily be amended subsequently.

The illustration below shows the Newsletter SmartMaster which comes with Word Pro.

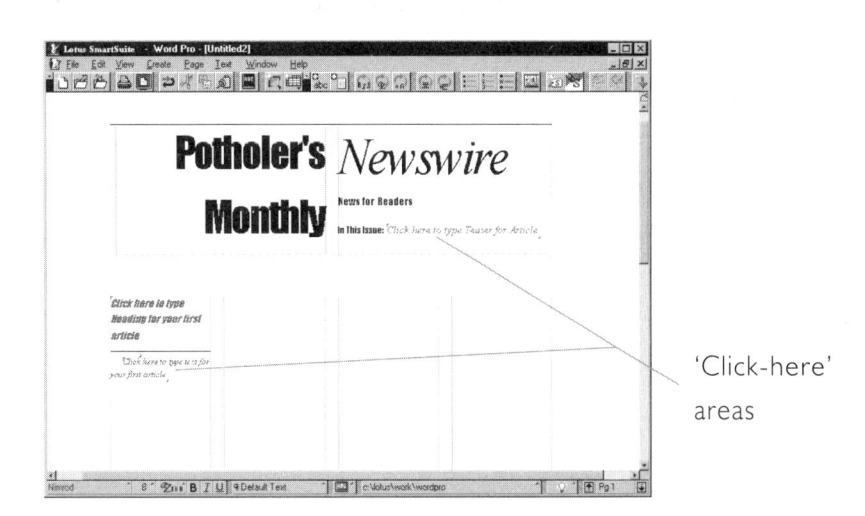

'Click-here' areas

2 Working with Files **23**

Creating blank documents

To create a new blank document, pull down the File menu and click New Document. Do the following:

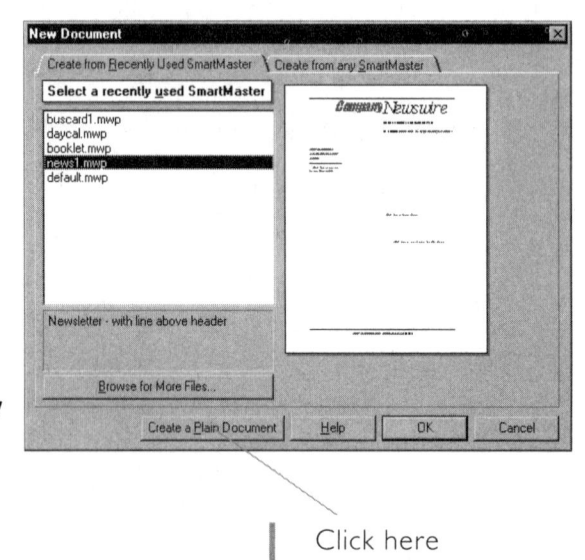

HANDY TIP **A version of the New Document dialog (called the 'Welcome to Lotus Word Pro' screen) also appears automatically whenever you launch Word Pro.**

Click here

Word Pro launches a blank document ready for editing:

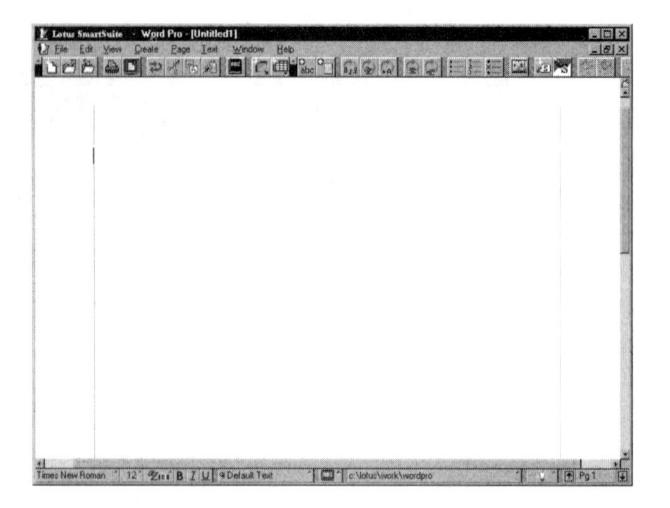

24 Word Pro in easy steps

Using SmartMasters

Word Pro provides a large number of SmartMasters. With these, you can create a wide variety of professional-quality documents. For example, you can create newsletters, calendars, faxes, labels, letters, memos, indices, tables of contents and Internet-specific documents, and more.

REMEMBER **You can also create Internet documents with SmartMasters – see chapter 3.**

Creating a new document with a SmartMaster

Pull down the File menu and click New Document. Perform steps 1–4:

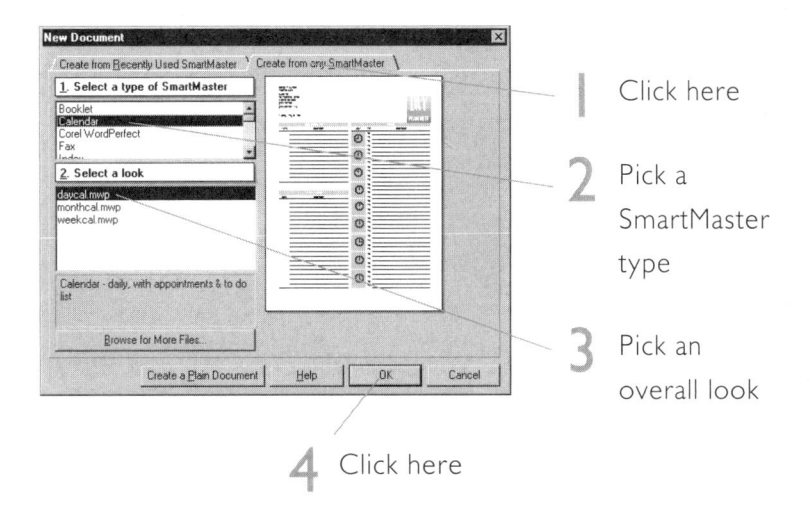

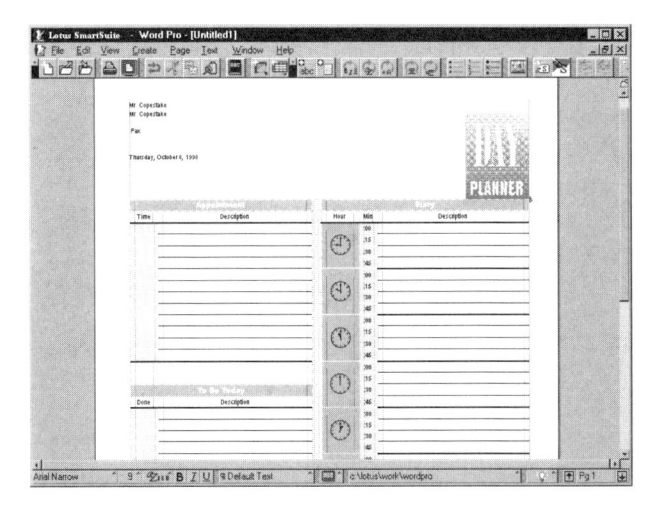

1 Click here

2 Pick a SmartMaster type

3 Pick an overall look

4 Click here

The final document – in this case, a calendar

2 Working with Files **25**

Opening files

You can open Word Pro documents you've already created.

HANDY TIP — **To open an existing file while in the process of launching Word Pro, double-click the file in the 'Select a document to open' section of the 'Welcome to Lotus Word Pro' screen. Alternatively, click this button:**

Browse for More Files...

Now perform steps 1–5, as appropriate.

Pull down the File menu and click Open. Now carry out the following steps, as appropriate:

2 Click here. In the drop-down list, click the drive which hosts the file

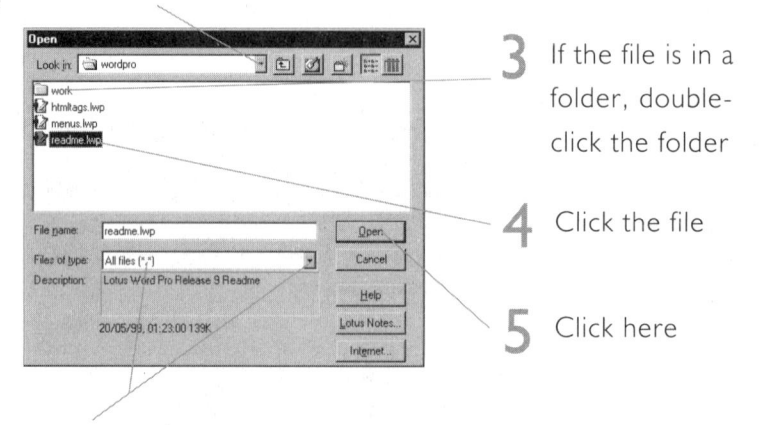

3 If the file is in a folder, double-click the folder

4 Click the file

5 Click here

1 Make sure All files (*.*) is shown. If it isn't, click the arrow and select it from the drop-down list

HANDY TIP — **You can also use the Documents section (available from the Windows Start menu) to open recently used Word Pro files – see your Windows documentation for how to do this.**

Third-party file formats

You can open documents created in other word processors directly from within Word Pro. To do this, simply follow steps 1–5 above.

When you perform step 5, Word Pro automatically converts the third-party file into its own format.

Opening files from the Internet

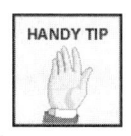

HANDY TIP **To open Internet files, you must have a live Internet connection. This means one of the following:**

- a modem attached to your PC (plus a live connection to a service provider);
- an ISDN line, or;
- a leased line.

HANDY TIP **Before you open a file on the World Wide Web or an FTP server, you may need to fine-tune your connection settings. To do this, click the Setup button before step 2.**
  Complete the dialog which launches – if you need any help doing this (or with any other aspect of connection) consult your service provider or network administrator.

From within Word Pro you can open documents directly from the World Wide Web or FTP (File Transfer Protocol) servers.

First, ensure your Internet connection is open. Launch the Open dialog (see page 26 for how to do this) and click this button: [Internet...] then carry out the following steps:

Web connections

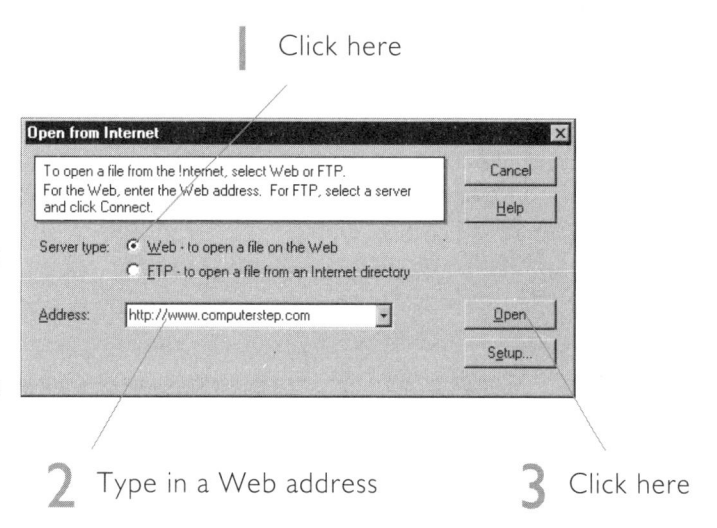

1 Click here

2 Type in a Web address

3 Click here

FTP Connections

To open a file from an FTP server, click 'FTP - to open a file from an Internet directory' in step 1. In step 2, select a server. Finally, click this button:

[Connect]

The dialog expands. Select the file you want to open and click:

[Open]

For information on creating and working with Internet files, see chapter 3.

Moving around in documents

REMEMBER **The following useful keystroke combinations are unique to Word Pro:**

- to move from an Infobox to the open document (and vice versa), hit Alt+Enter
- to go to the start of the next sentence, hit Ctrl+.
- to go to the start of the previous or current sentence, hit Ctrl+,
- to go to the start of the next paragraph, hit Ctrl+↑
- to go to the start of the current paragraph, hit Ctrl+↓

HANDY TIP **When you drag the box on the Vertical Scroll bar, Word Pro displays an indicator showing which page and section you're up to:**

Body ◆ 2

You can use the following to move through Word Pro documents:

- keystrokes;
- the vertical/horizontal scroll bars, and;
- the Go To dialog.

Using keystrokes

Word Pro implements the standard Windows direction keys. Use the left, right, up and down cursor keys in the usual way. Additionally, Home, End, Page Up and Page Down work normally.

Using the scroll bars

Use your mouse to perform any of the following actions:

Click anywhere here to jump to the left or right

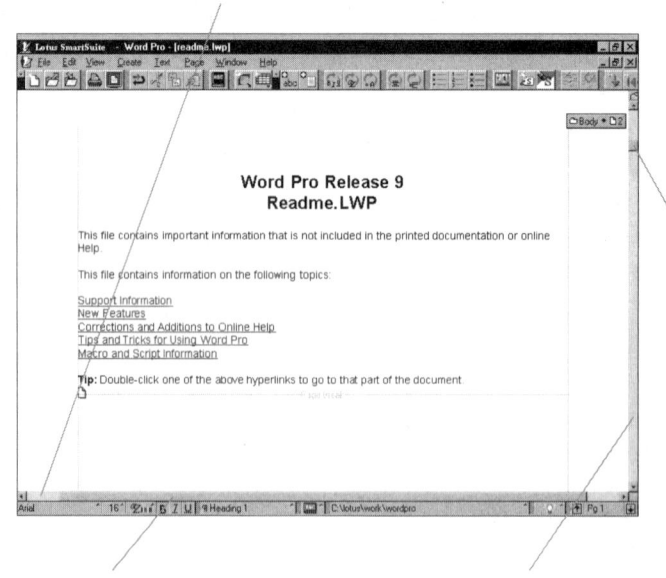

Drag this up or down to move through the active document

Drag this to the left or right to extend the viewing area

Click anywhere here to jump to another location in the document

28 Word Pro in easy steps

...cont'd

Using the Go To dialog
You can use the Go To dialog to navigate through the open document.

Pull down the Edit menu and click Go To. Now do the following:

> **HANDY TIP** — **You can use a keyboard shortcut to launch the Go To dialog: simply press Ctrl+G.**

1 Click here; select a document component from the list

4 Click here

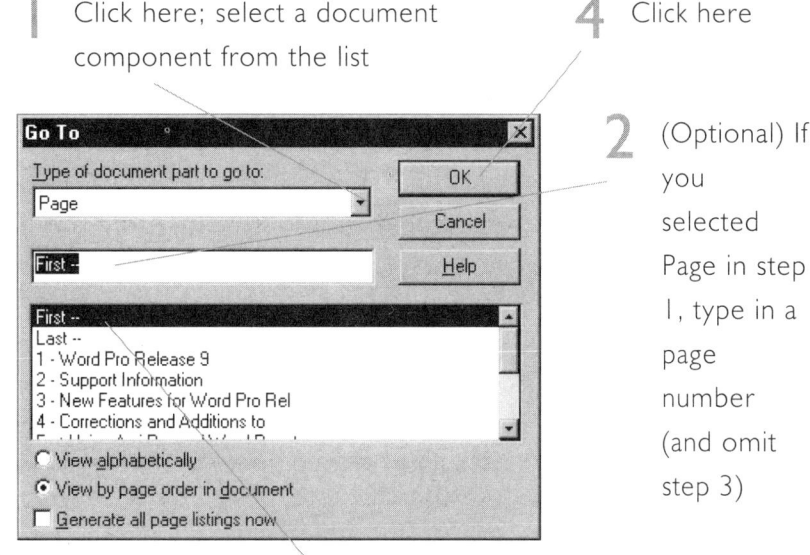

2 (Optional) If you selected Page in step 1, type in a page number (and omit step 3)

> **REMEMBER** — **Re step 2 – you can use an alternative technique to move to a specific page. Click any character-based page definition (see 'Refinements...' for more information). Then carry out step 4 after omitting step 3.**

3 Click First or Last, to determine direction of movement

Refinements...
Word Pro automatically creates definitions of each page within a document by noting the first few characters. As a result, if you select Page in step 1 above, you can opt to move to a specific page *based on recognition of the contents* – see the REMEMBER Tip in the margin for how to do this.

By default, Word Pro arranges these potted page descriptions in page order. If you want them organised in alphabetical order instead, click View Alphabetically in the dialog above.

2 Working with Files

Document views – an overview

Word Pro lets you examine your work in various ways, according to the approach you need. It calls these 'views'.

There are three principal views:

Draft

Draft View is used for basic text editing. In Draft View, most formatting elements are still visible; for instance, coloured, emboldened or italicised text displays faithfully. On the other hand, page breaks and headers/footers aren't shown. Certain kinds of inserted pictures display faithfully; others don't.

For these reasons, Draft View is quick and easy to use. It's suitable for bulk text entry and editing. It may not be suitable for use with graphics (for this, switch to Layout view – see below).

Layout

Layout view – the default – works like Draft view, with one exception: it's fully WYSIWYG (What You See Is What You Get), and the positioning of all items on the page is reproduced accurately. What you see is an accurate representation of what your document will look like when printed. Headers and footers are visible, and can be edited directly; margins display faithfully; and all pictures occupy their correct position on-screen.

In Layout view, the screen is updated more slowly. As a result, use it when your document is nearing completion, for final proofing. This suggestion is particularly apt if you're working with a slow computer.

Page Sorter

Page Sorter view is another Word Pro feature 'borrowed' from high-end Desktop Publishing programs. In Page Sorter view, documents are shown as 'thumbnails' representing individual pages (based on sections and page breaks).

Using views

REMEMBER — **The view that is currently active has a ✓ against it.**

Switching between views

Pull down the View menu. Click Draft, Layout or Page Sorter, as appropriate.

Using Page Sorter

In Page Sorter, you can:

- visually move pages or groups of pages, and;
- expand or contract groups of pages.

When you've launched Page Sorter, carry out step 1 below to move a page or page group. Or follow step 2 to expand or contract a group.

HANDY TIP — **You can edit text in the normal way within Page Sorter view.**

1. Click a page's title bar; drag it to a new location (the cursor becomes a page icon). Release the mouse button to confirm the move.

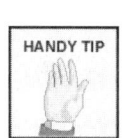

HANDY TIP — **Re step 2 – the lens shows a magnified view of the expand/contract control button. If - (rather than +) displays, clicking it contracts the group.**

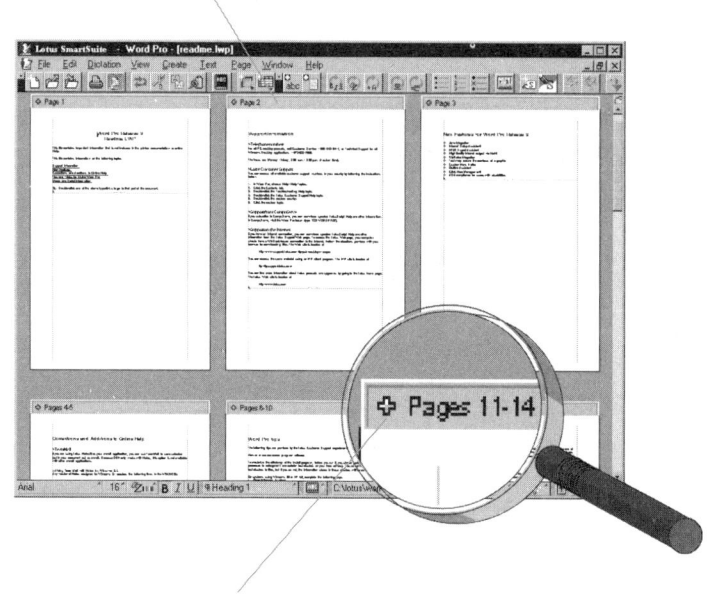

2. Click here to expand a page group

2 Working with Files

Changing zoom levels

The ability to vary the level of magnification for the active Word Pro document is often useful. Sometimes, it's helpful to 'zoom out' (i.e. decrease the magnification) so that you can take an overview; at other times, you'll need to 'zoom in' (increase the magnification) to work in greater detail. Word Pro lets you do either of these very easily.

You can do any of the following:

- choose from preset zoom levels (e.g. 100%, 75%);
- specify your own zoom percentage, or;
- choose a zoom setting excluding document margins.

Setting the zoom level

Pull down the View menu. Carry out step 1 below. Then, to apply a preset zoom percentage, follow step 2. Or follow steps 3–5 inclusive to customise the zoom level.

HANDY TIP — Re step 2 – to exclude margins from the view, select Margin Width.

HANDY TIP — Click Full Page to have an entire page display.

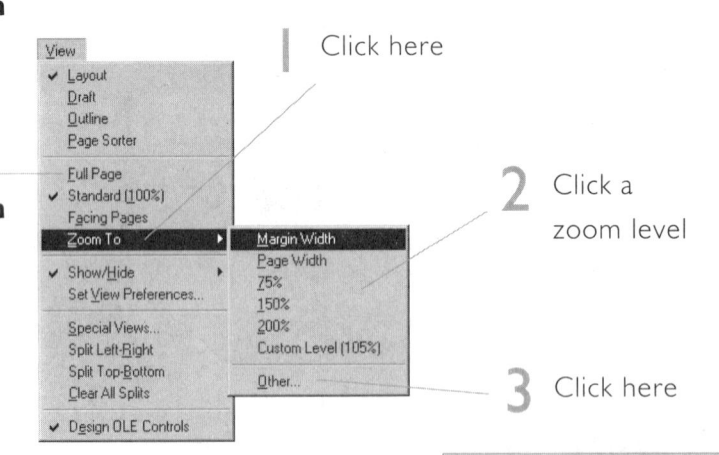

1 Click here

2 Click a zoom level

3 Click here

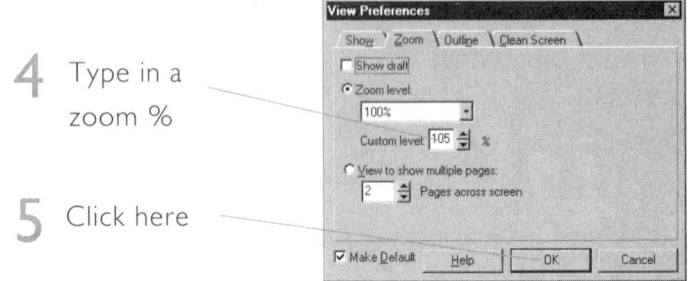

4 Type in a zoom %

5 Click here

32 Word Pro in easy steps

Undo

REMEMBER **To set the number of consecutive undos, pull down the File menu and click User Setup, Word Pro Preferences. In the Word Pro Preferences dialog, click the General tab. In the 'Undo levels' field, type in the number. Click OK.**

Word Pro lets you reverse – 'undo' – most editing operations.

You can undo the last editing action in the following ways:

- via the keyboard;
- from within the Edit menu, or;
- by using a SmartIcon.

Using the keyboard
Simply press Ctrl+Z to undo an action.

Using the Edit menu
Pull down the Edit menu. To undo an action, do the following:

BEWARE **Don't set too many undo levels – this can slow down your computer unacceptably (because Word Pro has to store details of editing actions in memory).**

Click here

REMEMBER **The precise text of the menu entry above depends on the action being undone.**

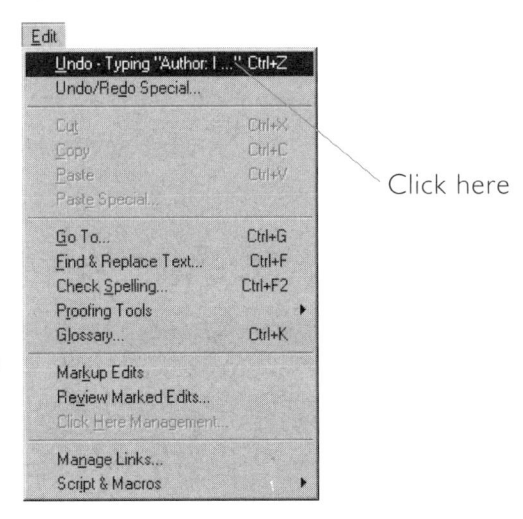

Using the Undo SmartIcon
To undo an operation, click the following SmartIcon in the Universal SmartIcon bar:

2 Working with Files **33**

Multiple Undo's

You can also carry out more than one Undo at a time. You do this with the help of a special dialog.

Carrying out multiple Undo's

Pull down the Edit menu and do the following:

1 Click here

HANDY TIP **You can also redo an action – this is tantamount to undoing an undo.**
Follow step 1. Then do the following:

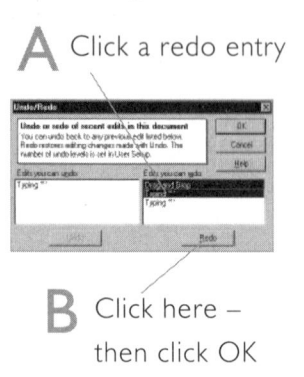

A Click a redo entry

B Click here – then click OK

2 Click an entry in the Undo 'tree' (all entries above it are also selected)

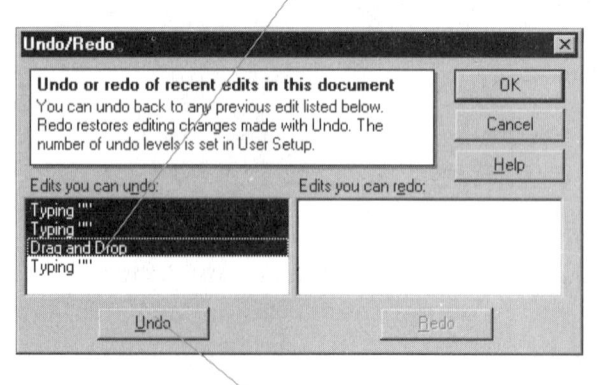

3 Click here – then click OK

34 Word Pro in easy steps

Searching for text

Word Pro lets you find specific text within documents.

HANDY TIP

When you've finished using the Find & Replace bar, click this button:

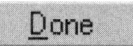

[Done]

You can also search for special characters. For instance, you can look for paragraph marks, tabs, carets (^) and wildcards (characters which stand for one or more others).

You can also:

- limit the search to words which match the case of the text you specify (e.g. if you search for 'Arm', Word Pro will not flag 'arm' or 'ARM'), or;
- limit the search to whole words (e.g. if you search for 'eat', Word Pro will not flag 'beat' or 'seat').

HANDY TIP

Re step 3 – click the left-pointing arrow to search backwards, or the right-pointing arrow to search towards the end of the document.

Initiating a text search

Pull down the Edit menu and click Find & Replace Text. Now carry out the following steps, as appropriate:

1 Type in the text you want to find

3 Click a search direction

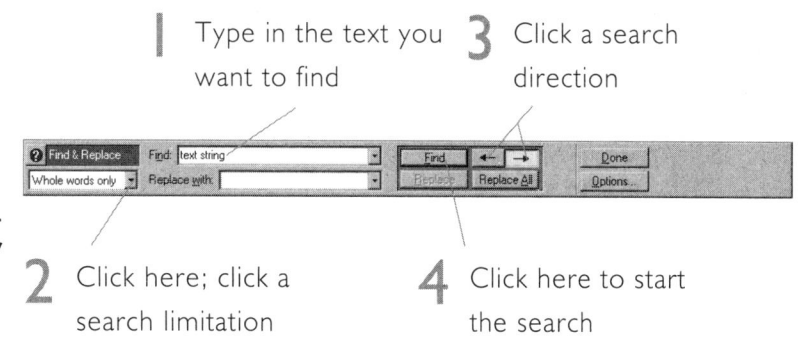

2 Click here; click a search limitation

4 Click here to start the search

REMEMBER

The Word Pro wildcards – '^?' and '^*' – are especially useful. (NB: ignore the quotation marks in this tip when entering wildcards.) For instance, searching for 'me^?t' would find 'meet' or 'meat'. Searching for 'le^*' would find 'lend', 'leap', 'lexicography', etc.

Entering codes

When you complete step 1, you can enter the following:

^t	Tab
^r	Paragraph mark
^^	^
^?	any one character
^*	any number of characters (to the end of the word)
^+	any number of characters (across multiple words)

2 Working with Files

Using Quick Find

Word Pro has a shortcut you can use to find simple text even more easily: Quick Find.

Launching Quick Find
Pull down the Edit menu and do the following:

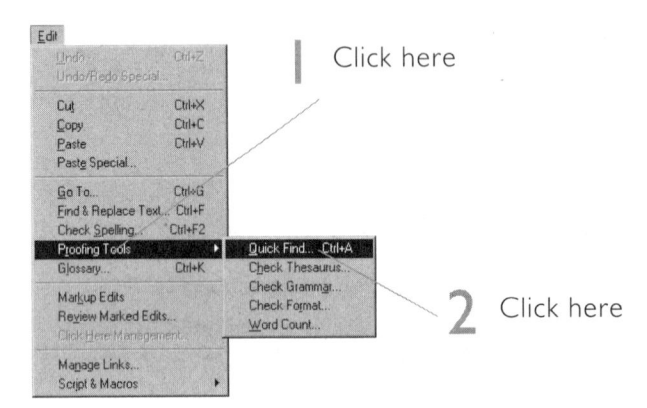

1 Click here

2 Click here

HANDY TIP

To find further instances of matching text, click:

`Next`

in the Quick Find bar.

NB: if you want to reverse the search direction, first click:

`←`

3 Type in the text you want to find

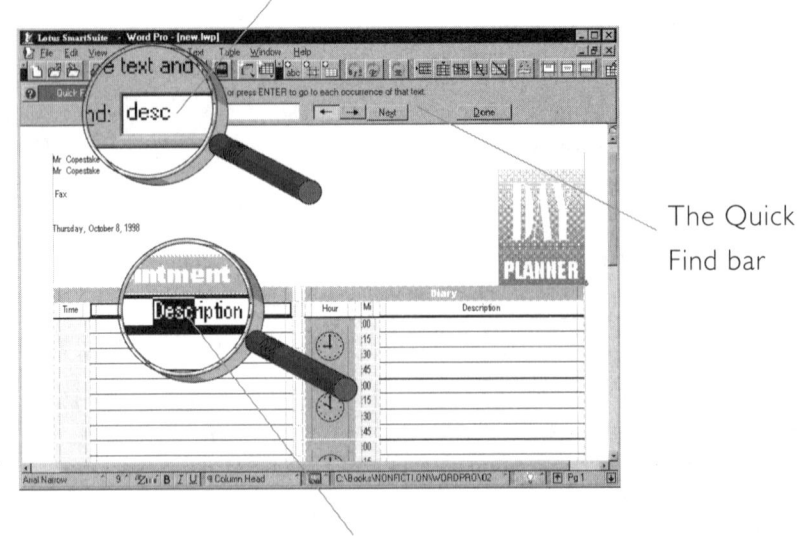

The Quick Find bar

REMEMBER

When you've finished with Quick Find, click:

`Done`

in the Quick Find bar.

After step 3, Word Pro automatically flags the first instance of matching text

36 Word Pro in easy steps

Replacing text

You can't use Quick Find to replace text.

When you've searched for and located text in the active document, you can have Word Pro replace it automatically with the text of your choice.

You can customise find-and-replace operations with the same parameters as a simple find operation. For example, you can make them case-specific, or only replace whole words. You can also incorporate a variety of codes (for how to do this, see page 35). For instance, you could have Word Pro locate instances of two paragraph marks and replace them with a single mark...

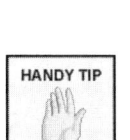

When you've finished using the Find & Replace bar, click this button:

There is, however, one way in which find-and-replace operations differ from find operations: wildcards can't be incorporated in replacement text.

Initiating a find-and-replace operation

First pull down the Edit menu and click Find & Replace Text. Now follow steps 1 and 2 below. Carry out steps 3 and 4, as appropriate. Finally, follow step 5 to perform all valid find-and-replace operations automatically (or see the REMEMBER tip):

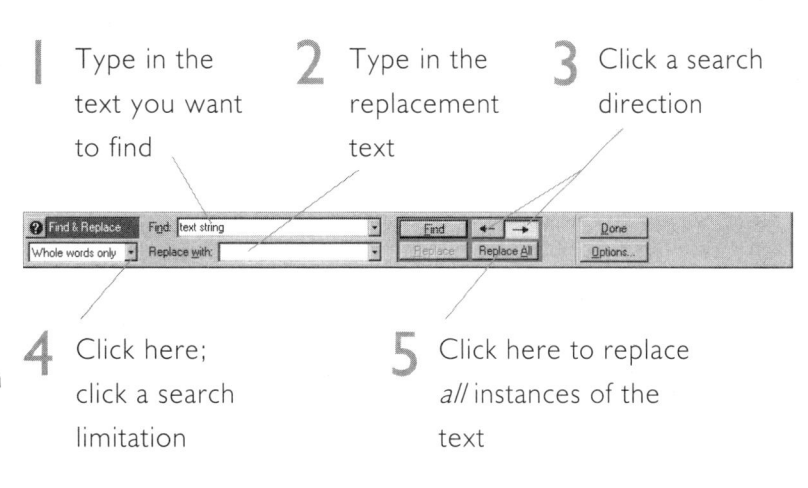

If you don't want all instances of the text replaced immediately, don't carry out step 5. Instead, click the Find button after step 4. When the first match has been found, click Replace. Repeat this as often as necessary.

1 Type in the text you want to find

2 Type in the replacement text

3 Click a search direction

4 Click here; click a search limitation

5 Click here to replace *all* instances of the text

2 Working with Files **37**

Saving files

It's important to save your work at frequent intervals, in order to avoid data loss in the event of a hardware fault or power interruption. Word Pro makes saving your work easy.

Saving a document for the first time

Pull down the File menu and click Save As. Now do the following:

HANDY TIP Page 46 shows you how to upload files to an Intranet or Internet server. Word Pro provides a special tool – the HTML Export Assistant – to help you convert them to HTML format before you do so.
   See pages 42–43 for how to use the HTML Export Assistant.

1 Click here. In the drop-down list, select the drive you want to host the document

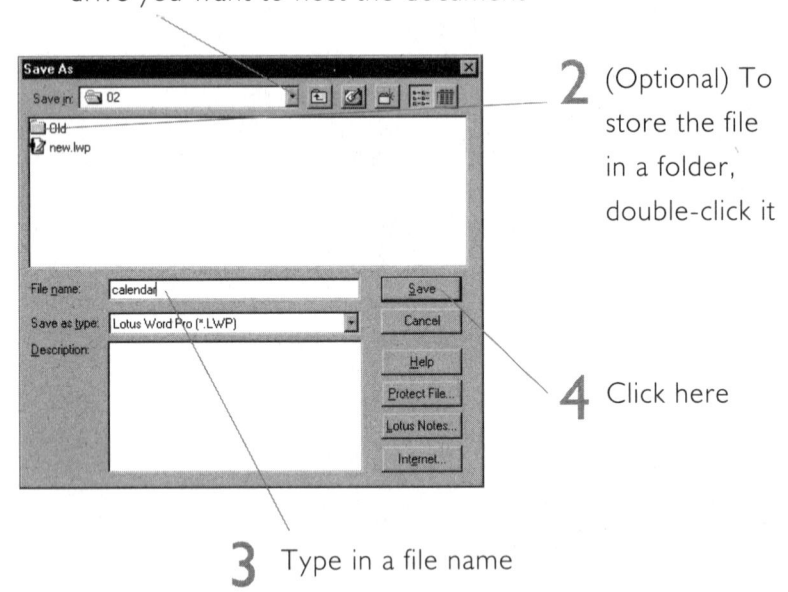

2 (Optional) To store the file in a folder, double-click it

3 Type in a file name

4 Click here

Saving previously saved documents

Pull down the File menu and click Save.

Word Pro saves the latest version of your document to disk, overwriting the previous one.

Chapter Three

Working with the Web

This chapter shows you how to use SmartMasters to create documents specifically designed for the World Wide Web. You'll also use the HTML Export Assistant to convert existing Word Pro documents into a format which can be used on the Web. Finally, you'll insert and activate hyperlinks, then upload your Web files to an Internet or Intranet server.

Covers

Web documents – an overview | 40

Creating Web documents | 41

Converting files to Web format | 42

Inserting hyperlinks | 44

Activating hyperlinks | 45

Saving files to the Web | 46

Web documents – an overview

With the widespread adoption and use of the Internet and Intranets, it's very useful to create your own Web documents. Word Pro lets you do this with the use of specialist SmartMasters. You can also:

- convert standard Word Pro documents into a Web-based format, and;
- upload finished Web files to Internet or Intranet servers.

You can create new Internet documents in the following categories:

Corporate

Within this category, the following 'looks' are available:

Catlog.mwp	a product catalogue
Cohome1.mwp	a corporate home page
Html.mwp	a blank Web page you can customise yourself
News.mwp	a corporate newsletter
Produc1.mwp	a product list

Personal

Bio1.mwp	an author biography
Favweb1.mwp	a lit of favourite Web sites
Home.mwp	a personal Home page (see over)
Kidpg1.mwp	a child's Home page

Once you've created Web pages in Word Pro, you can add hyperlinks to them.

> **HANDY TIP**
> See chapter 2 for how to create non-Internet documents with SmartMasters.

> **REMEMBER**
> 'Looks' customise the appearance and function of the Web document.

> **HANDY TIP**
> For how to further develop and refine Internet documents, see Web Page Design, also in the 'in easy steps' series.

> **HANDY TIP**
> See page 27 for how to open World Wide Web and FTP files.

Creating Web documents

Pull down the File menu and click New Document. Perform steps 1–4:

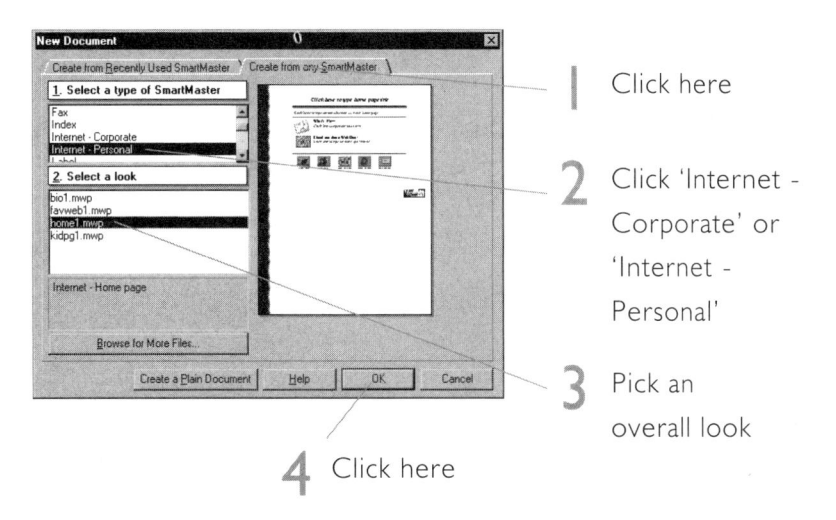

1 Click here

2 Click 'Internet - Corporate' or 'Internet - Personal'

3 Pick an overall look

4 Click here

You can now begin to replace the 'filler' text with your own, insert pictures and customise the Web page to satisfy your own visual style.

REMEMBER

This is the Web document created with Home.mwp.

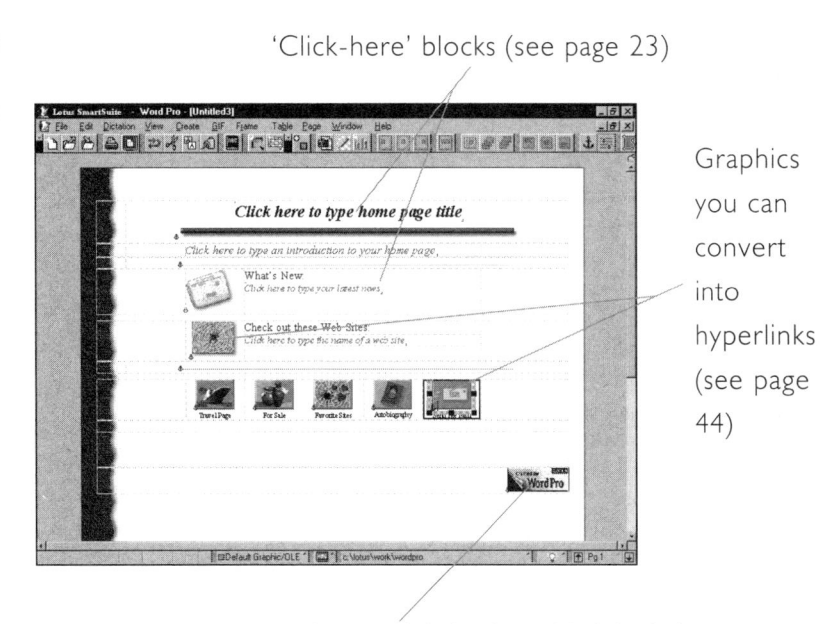

'Click-here' blocks (see page 23)

Graphics you can convert into hyperlinks (see page 44)

A pre-inserted hyperlink (to Lotus' Web site)

3 Working with the Web

Converting files to Web format

Beware Re standard Word Pro files – carry out steps 1–8 before you perform the procedures on page 46.

Word Pro also provides a special assistant which guides you through the process of converting existing, standard Word Pro documents into a format you can use on the Internet. This format is a simple text based mark up language called HTML (HyperText Markup Language).

Launching the HTML Export Assistant

Open the file you want to convert to HTML format. Pull down the File menu and carry out the following steps:

Remember You can also use Net-It Now! SE (if this was installed as part of SmartSuite) to convert Word Pro documents into a format which can be used on the Internet.

See chapter 9 for more information on how to use Net-It Now! SE.

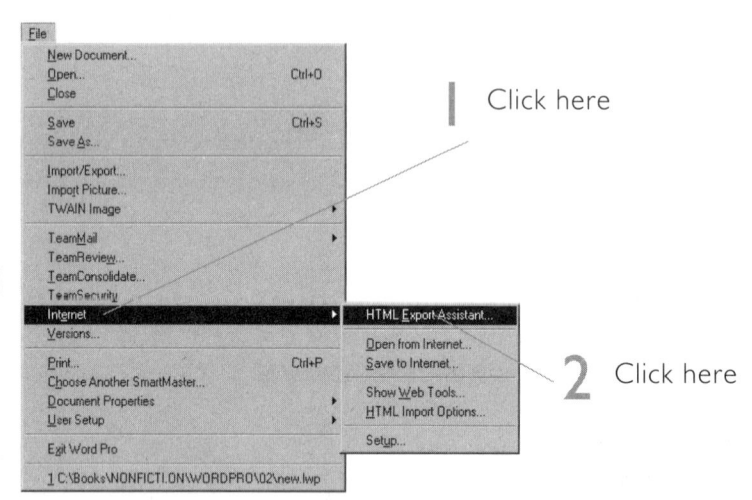

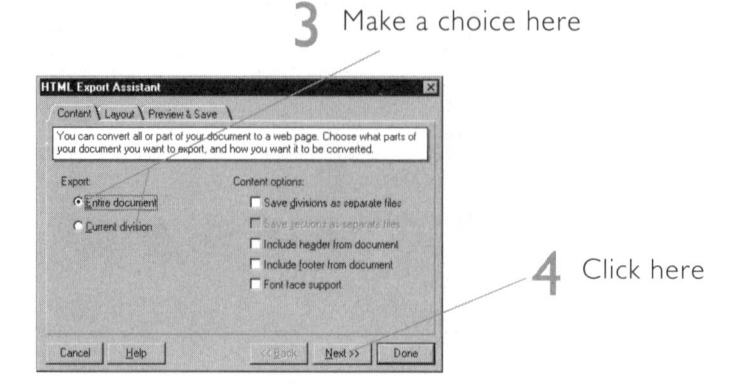

1 Click here

2 Click here

3 Make a choice here

4 Click here

...cont'd

REMEMBER: After step 7, use the Browse dialog to select the drive/folder combination to which you want to save your HTML files.

HANDY TIP: Re step 7 – if you want to save your HTML files directly to the Internet, click the Save to Internet button instead. Then complete the resulting dialogs. (For how to do this, see page 46.)

REMEMBER: By default, the assistant saves pictures to the JPEG format. If you don't want this, select PNG instead.
(See chapter 8 for more information on graphics formats.)

5 Optional – click here and type in Web address details

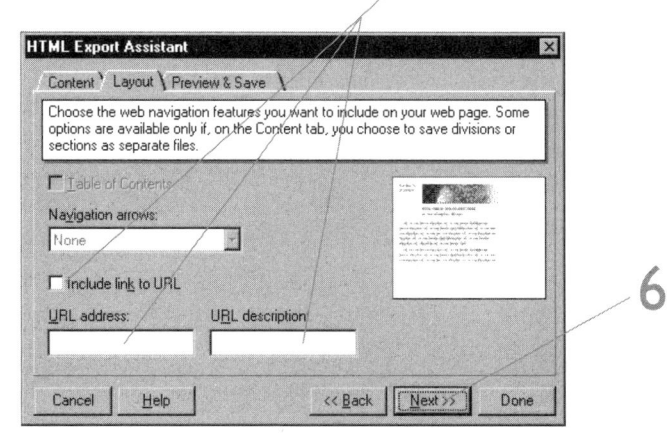

6 Click here

7 Click here

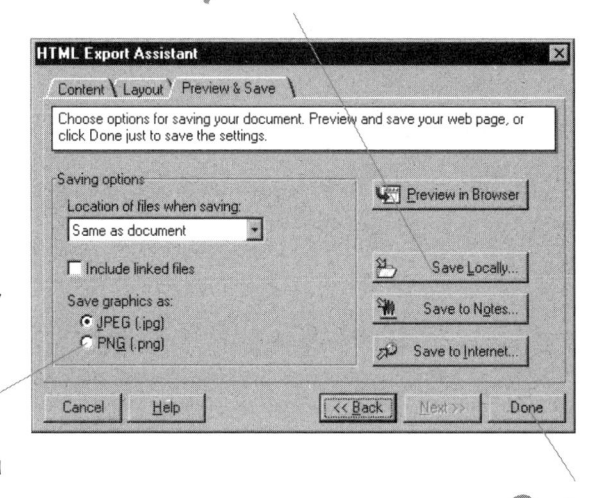

8 Click here

If you didn't follow the procedures in the HANDY TIP, carry out steps 1–3 on page 46 to save your Web files to the Internet.

3 Working with the Web   **43**

Inserting hyperlinks

You can insert hyperlinks into normal Word Pro or Web documents. Hyperlinks are text or graphics linked to:

- another location in the same document, or a different document on your local hard-drive (see page 90), or;
- a document on the World Wide Web or an Intranet.

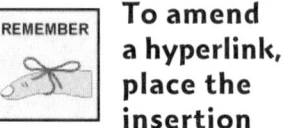

To amend a hyperlink, place the insertion point within it (for text hyperlinks) or select the graphic (for graphics hyperlinks). Pull down the Edit menu and click Edit Hyperlink. Complete the Edit Hyperlink dialog, then Click OK.

Creating a hyperlink

Select the text or graphic you want to be the source of the link. Pull down the Create menu and do the following:

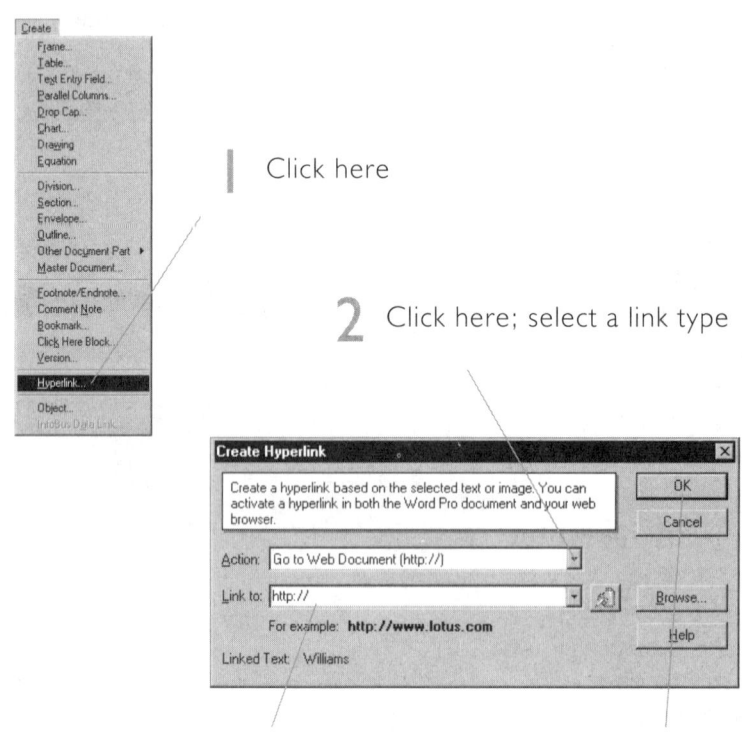

1 Click here

2 Click here; select a link type

3 Type in a Web document or bookmark address

4 Click here

To delete a hyperlink, place the insertion point within it (for text hyperlinks) or select the graphic (for graphics hyperlinks). Pull down the Edit menu and click Remove Hyperlink.

Activating hyperlinks

To jump to one of the following:

- a linked World Wide Web document, or;
- a bookmark in the active (or another) document,

do the following:

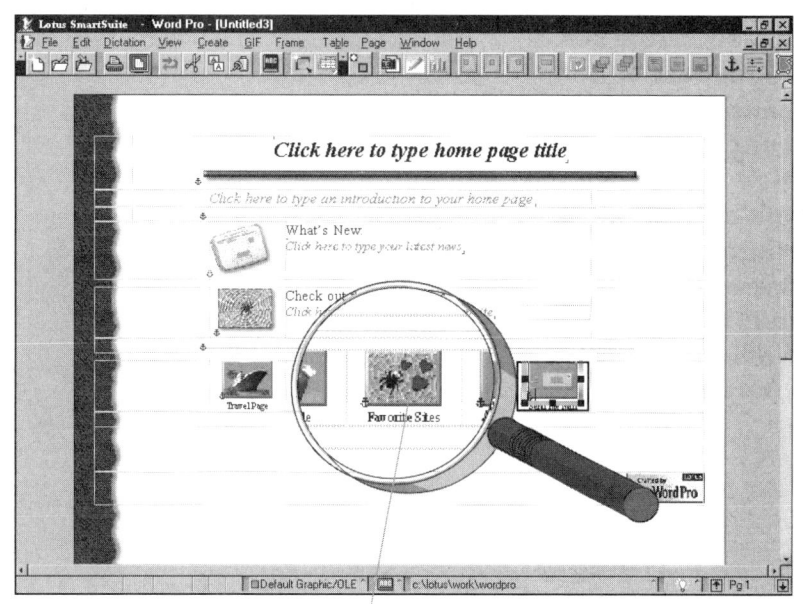

REMEMBER **To activate a hyperlink to a World Wide Web document, first ensure your Internet connection is live.**

REMEMBER **Here, a graphic inserted by the** Home.mwp **Internet SmartMaster has been converted to a hyperlink.**

The activation procedure is the same for a text hyperlink.

Double-click any hyperlink

REMEMBER **Note that inserted text hyperlinks are:**

- underlined, and
- coloured blue.

3 Working with the Web

45

Saving files to the Web

HANDY TIP

Before you save a file to an FTP server, you need to configure your FTP host settings. To do this, click the Setup button before step 2.

Complete the dialog which launches – if you need any help doing this (or with any other aspect of connection) consult your service provider or network administrator.

You can save files to an FTP server (but see pages 42–43 for how to convert them to a Web-based format first).

Ensure your Internet connection is live. Launch the Save As dialog – for how to do this, see page 38. Then do the following:

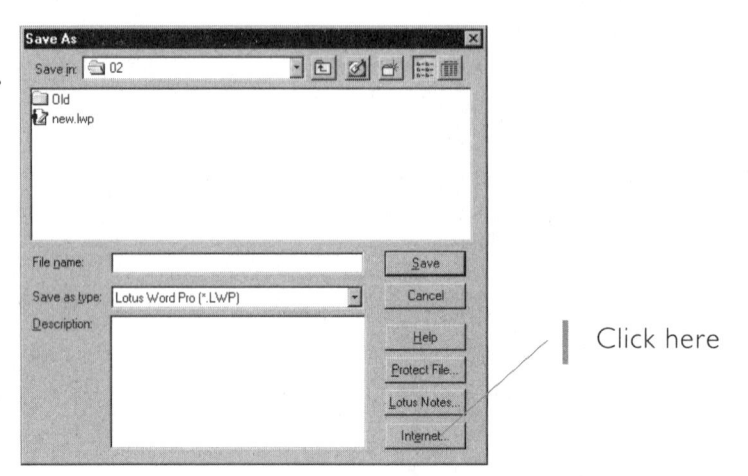

| Click here

REMEMBER

After step 3, the Save to Internet dialog expands:

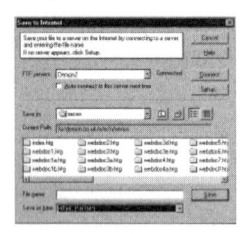

2 Click here; select a server in the list

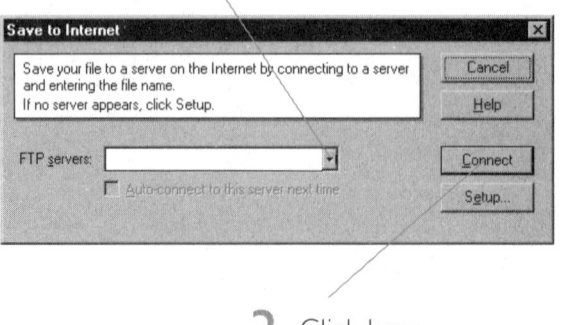

Complete this in the normal way. Finally, click Save to save your file to the selected FTP server.

3 Click here

46   Word Pro in easy steps

Chapter Four

Text Formatting

This chapter shows you how to apply formatting to text. You'll change typefaces, type sizes and font attributes; indent/align text; apply tabs; vary paragraph/line spacing; border paragraphs; insert drop caps; apply bullets/numbers to paragraphs; and number lines. Finally, you'll apply columns to text and use Fast Format to copy formatting between text segments with just a few mouse clicks.

Covers

Formatting text – an overview | 48

Character formatting | 50

Paragraph formatting | 53

Fast Format | 63

Adding drop caps | 65

Bulleting and Numbering paragraphs | 67

Numbering lines | 69

Text columns | 70

Formatting text – an overview

Word Pro lets you format text in a variety of ways. Very broadly, however, and for the sake of convenience, text formatting can be divided into two overall categories:

Character formatting

Character formatting is concerned with altering the *appearance* of selected characters. Examples include:

- changing the font;
- changing the type size;
- colouring text;
- changing the font attributes (bold, italic, underlining etc.), and;
- superscripting and subscripting text.

Character formatting is a misnomer in one sense: it can also be applied to specified paragraphs of text, or to parts of specified paragraphs.

REMEMBER

The distinction between character and paragraph formatting is sometimes blurred: for instance, both can relate to font appearance. When it comes to text styles, however, there is less confusion (see chapter 6 for how to use styles).

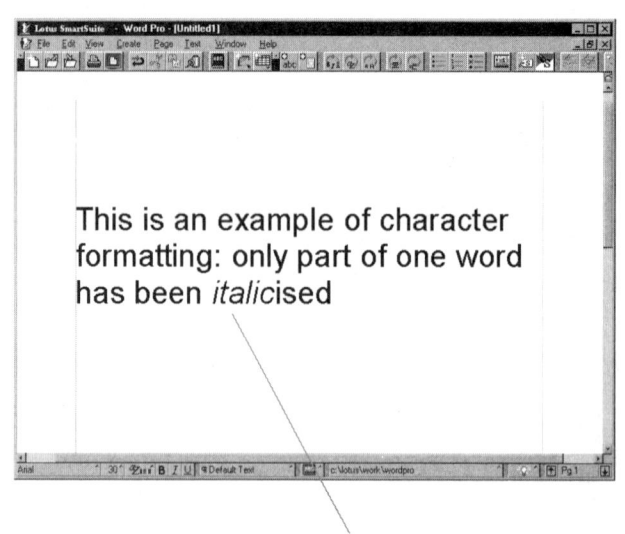

Character formatting in action

...cont'd

Paragraph formatting

Paragraph formatting has to do with the structuring and layout (as well as the appearance) of one or more paragraphs of text.

Examples include:

- specifying paragraph indents/tabs;
- specifying paragraph alignment (e.g. left or right justification);
- specifying paragraph and line spacing;
- imposing borders and/or fills on paragraphs;
- applying typefaces and type sizes;
- colouring text;
- applying bullets to paragraphs;
- applying numbers to paragraphs, and;
- applying drop caps to paragraphs.

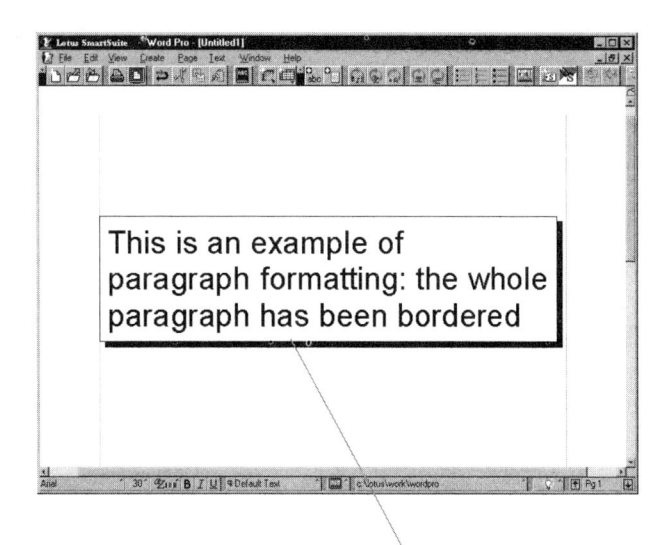

Paragraph formatting in action

Changing the font and/or type size

Character formatting can be changed in two main ways:

- from within the Text Properties Infobox, or;
- (to a lesser extent) by using 'cycling'.

Using the Text Properties Infobox

First, select the text whose typeface and/or type size you want to amend. Pull down the Text menu and click Text Properties. Now carry out these steps, as appropriate:

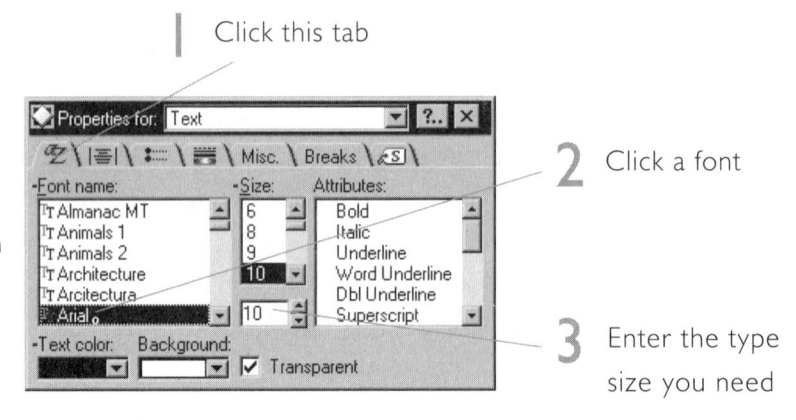

> **HANDY TIP** — **Word Pro uses standard Windows procedures for text selection. However, note the following Word Pro-specific techniques:**
>
> - To select a whole sentence, hold down Ctrl and click in it.
> - To select a whole paragraph, hold down Ctrl and double-click in it.

1 Click this tab

2 Click a font

3 Enter the type size you need

The changes you make are automatically applied to the selected text.

> **HANDY TIP** — **Re step 3 – as well as whole point sizes, you can also enter fractions (to 3 decimal places). For instance, Word Pro will accept 10, 10.6 or 10.879... This level of precision – rare in a word processor – is another feature borrowed from DTP packages.**

Using cycling

Select the relevant text and do either of the following:

Click here repeatedly to step up alphabetically through the fonts on your system, one by one

Click here repeatedly to step up through type sizes in increments of 2 (e.g. from 6 to 8 to 10...)

Changing text colour

You can change the colour of text:

- from within the Text Properties Infobox, or;
- by using the Status bar.

Using the Infobox

First, select the relevant text. Pull down the Text menu and click Text Properties. Now do the following:

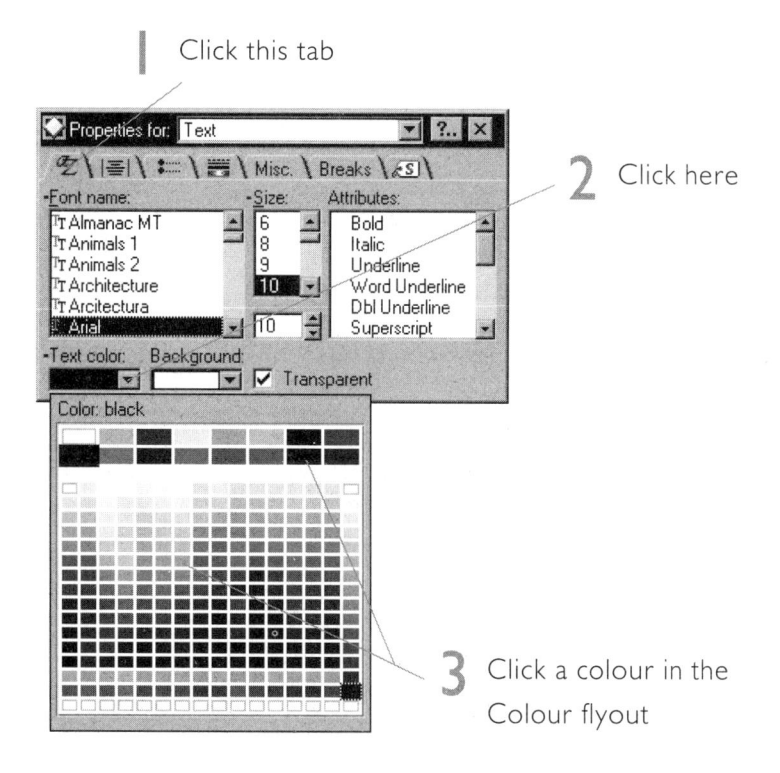

1 Click this tab

2 Click here

3 Click a colour in the Colour flyout

Using the Status bar

Select text. Carry out the action indicated below to launch the Colour flyout. Then follow step 3 above.

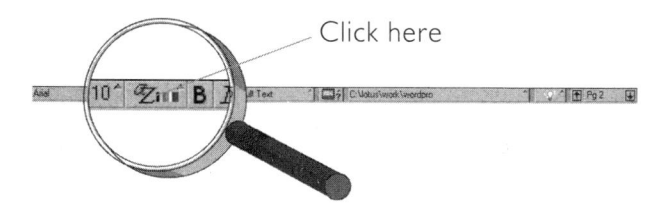

Click here

4 Text Formatting

Changing font attributes

In Word Pro, the principal typeface attributes you can apply are:

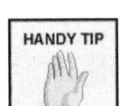

- Bold (**bold**) and Italic (*italic*);

- Word Underline (word underline) and Underline (underline);

- Strikethrough (~~strikethrough~~); Small Caps (SMALL CAPS); Superscript (^{superscript}) and Subscript ($_{subscript}$), and;

- Upper Case (UPPER CASE) and Lower Case (lower case).

You can use the Text Properties Infobox or a specific 'Cycle' SmartIcon to change font attributes.

Using the Text Properties Infobox

First, select the relevant text. Pull down the Text menu and click Text Properties. Now do the following:

1 Click this tab

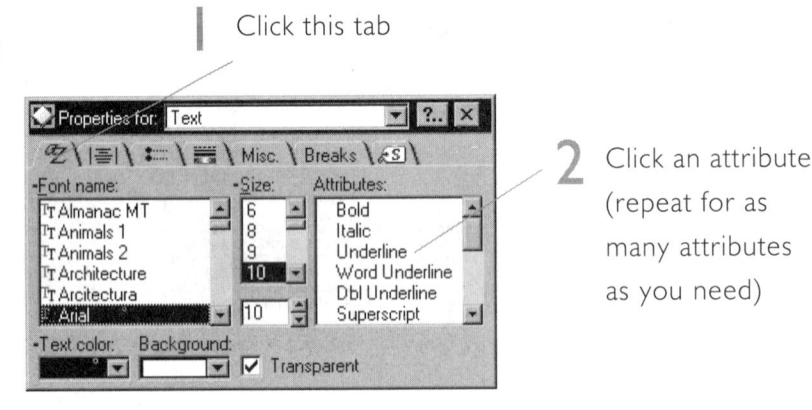

2 Click an attribute (repeat for as many attributes as you need)

Using cycling

First, select the relevant text. Then do the following:

Click here repeatedly to step up through the attributes, one by one

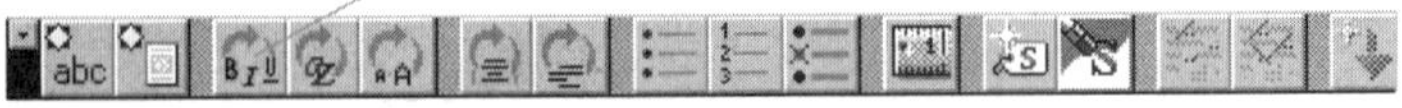

HANDY TIP

You can also use keyboard shortcuts:

- Ctrl+B to embolden text;
- Ctrl+I to italicise text;
- Ctrl+U to underline text;
- Ctrl+W to word-underline text (separating spaces are omitted), and;
- Ctrl+N to remove all attributes.

52 Word Pro in easy steps

Indenting paragraphs – an overview

REMEMBER

You can achieve a similar effect by using tabs (see pages 55–57).

However, indents are easier to apply (and amend subsequently).

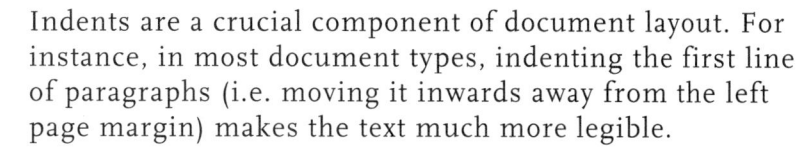

Indents are a crucial component of document layout. For instance, in most document types, indenting the first line of paragraphs (i.e. moving it inwards away from the left page margin) makes the text much more legible.

Other document types – e.g. bibliographies – can use the following:

- negative indents (where the direction of indent is towards and beyond the left margin);
- hanging indents (where the first line is unaltered, while subsequent lines are indented), or;
- full indents (where the entire paragraph is indented away from the left and/or right margins).

BEWARE

Don't confuse indents or tabs with page margins.

Margins are the gap between the edge of the page and the text area; indents/tabs define the distance between the margins and text.

Some of the potential indent combinations are shown in the (generic) illustration below:

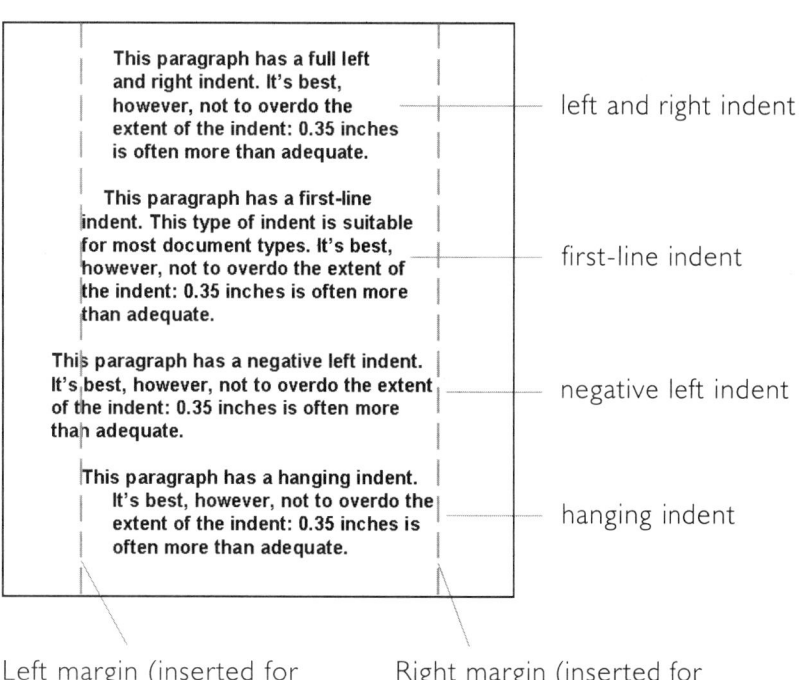

> This paragraph has a full left and right indent. It's best, however, not to overdo the extent of the indent: 0.35 inches is often more than adequate. — left and right indent
>
> This paragraph has a first-line indent. This type of indent is suitable for most document types. It's best, however, not to overdo the extent of the indent: 0.35 inches is often more than adequate. — first-line indent
>
> This paragraph has a negative left indent. It's best, however, not to overdo the extent of the indent: 0.35 inches is often more than adequate. — negative left indent
>
> This paragraph has a hanging indent. It's best, however, not to overdo the extent of the indent: 0.35 inches is often more than adequate. — hanging indent

Left margin (inserted for illustration purposes)

Right margin (inserted for illustration purposes)

4 Text Formatting

Indenting paragraphs

Paragraphs can be indented from within the Text Properties Infobox, or by using a 'Cycle' SmartIcon.

Using the Text Properties Infobox

First, select the paragraph(s) you want to indent. Pull down the Text menu and click Text Properties. Now do the following:

HANDY TIP

The Infobox indent buttons are:

- Left Indent
- First Line Indent
- Hanging Indent
- Full Indent

Click this tab

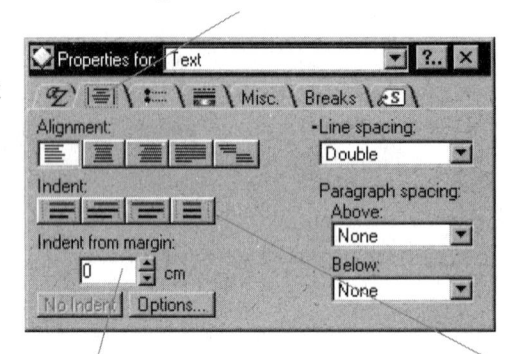

REMEMBER

Re step 3 – type in minus values for negative indents.

3 Type in the amount of indent

2 Click an indent button in the indicated row (see the HANDY TIP)

Using cycling

First, select the relevant text. Then do the following:

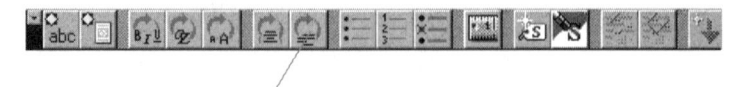

Click here repeatedly to step up through indent types, one by one

Note, however, that the Indent Cycle SmartIcon only applies Left Indent.

54 Word Pro in easy steps

Working with tabs

Tabs are a means of indenting the first line of text paragraphs. You can also use indents for this purpose (see pages 53–54) although tabs are probably more convenient for single paragraphs.

Never use the Space bar to indent paragraphs: spaces vary in size according to the typeface and type size applied to specific paragraphs, giving an uneven effect.

When you press the Tab key while the text insertion point is at the start of a paragraph, the text in the first line jumps to the next tab stop. This is a useful way to increase the legibility of your text. Word Pro lets you set tab stops with great precision.

By default, Word Pro (if you tell it to do so by selecting 'Evenly spaced every' in step 2 below) inserts tab stops every 0.635cm. If you want, however, you can vary the interval (step 3). Alternatively, see the REMEMBER tip to insert single tabs.

Setting tab stops – the Infobox route

First, select the paragraph(s) in which you need to set tab stops. Pull down the Text menu and click Text Properties. Follow steps 1–3 below:

Re step 2 – if you don't want to enter a series of tabs, choose 'From left edge' (to enter a tab relative to the left margin) or 'From right edge' (to enter one relative to the right margin). Alternatively, click Remove Local Tabs to remove previously assigned tab settings.

Click the Misc tab

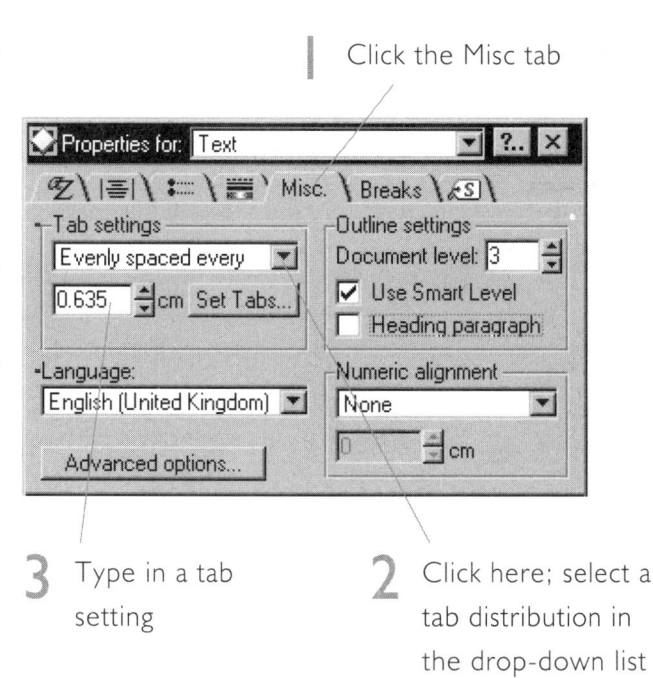

3 Type in a tab setting

2 Click here; select a tab distribution in the drop-down list

4 Text Formatting

...cont'd

Setting tab stops – the Ruler route

A quicker and more convenient method to set tabs is to use the on-screen Ruler:

> **HANDY TIP**
> **If the Ruler isn't currently visible,** pull down the View menu and click Show/Hide, Ruler.

A tab marker   The Ruler

> **HANDY TIP**
> **Normally, the symbols Word Pro inserts within documents to denote tab stops do not display.**
> **If you want to make them visible, as here, follow the procedures on page 57.**

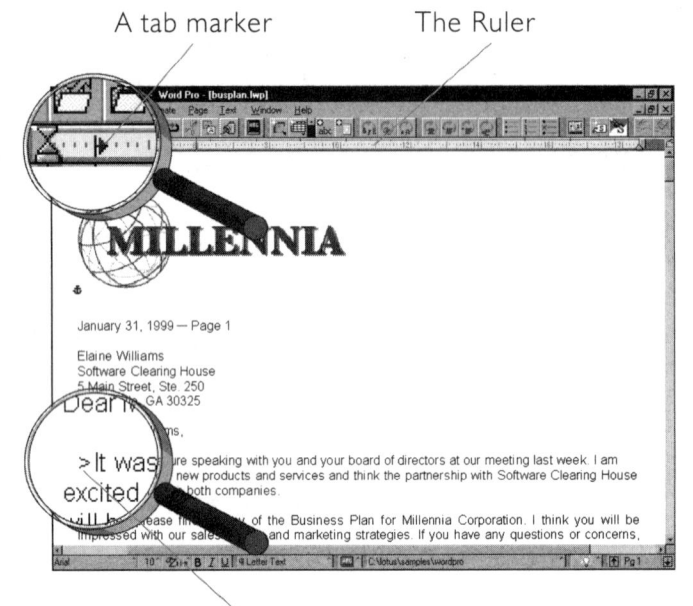

An inserted tab stop

You can use the Ruler in the following ways:

- To add a new tab – simply click the Ruler where you want it to appear.

- To remove a tab, left-click it. Hold down the mouse button and drag it off the Ruler. When you release the button, it disappears.

- To move an existing tab to a new position, left-click its marker in the Ruler. Hold down the mouse button and drag it to a new location. Release the button to confirm the move.

Viewing tab stops

Normally, Word Pro does not display tab stops within documents. However, you can view these if you want. You can also view paragraph returns.

Viewing tab marks or paragraph returns
Pull down the View menu and click Set View Preferences. Now carry out the following steps:

HANDY TIP — **To hide tab stops or paragraph returns again, follow steps 1–2. In step 3, deselect the appropriate entries. Finally, perform step 4.**

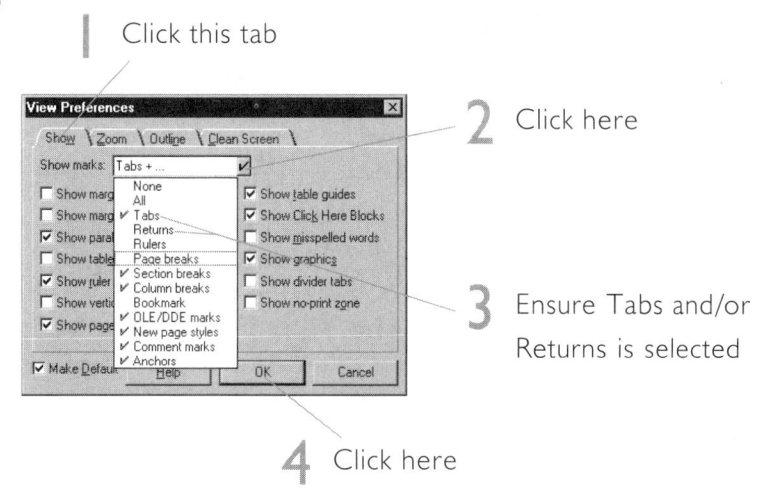

1 Click this tab

2 Click here

3 Ensure Tabs and/or Returns is selected

4 Click here

REMEMBER — **See the figure on page 56 for an illustration of what tab stops look like when viewed.**

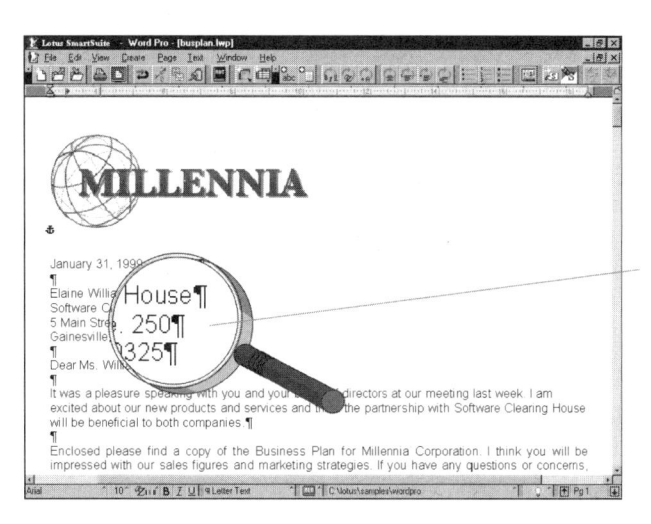

The result of viewing paragraph returns

4 Text Formatting **57**

Aligning paragraphs

The following are the principal types of alignment:

Left
Text is flush with the left page margin.

Center
Text is aligned equidistantly between the left and right page margins.

Right
Text is flush with the right page margin.

Justified
Text is flush with the left *and* right page margins

You can align text from within the Text Properties Infobox, or by using a 'Cycle' SmartIcon.

Using the Text Properties Infobox
Select the relevant paragraph(s). Pull down the Text menu and click Text Properties. Now do the following:

HANDY TIP

The Infobox alignment buttons are:

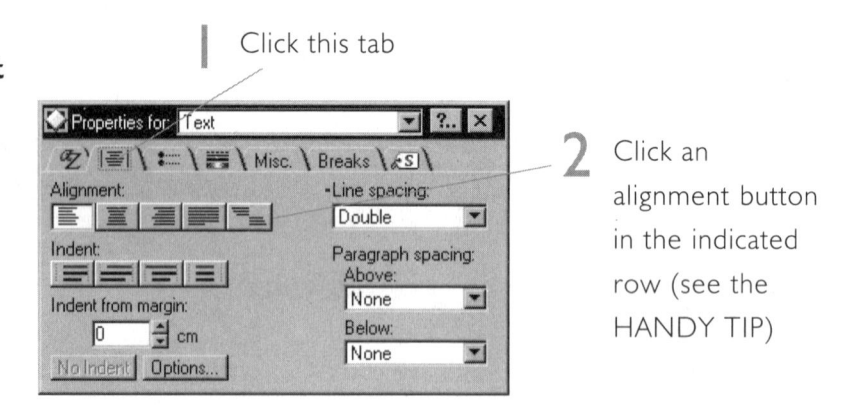

- Left
- Center
- Right
- Justified

1 Click this tab

2 Click an alignment button in the indicated row (see the HANDY TIP)

Using cycling
Select the relevant paragraph(s). Then do the following:

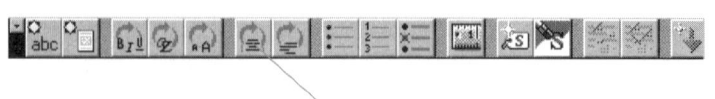

Click here repeatedly to step up through alignment types

Specifying paragraph spacing

You can customise the vertical space before and/or after specific text paragraphs. This is a useful device for increasing text legibility.

BEWARE As a general rule, set low paragraph spacing settings: a little goes a long way.

You can only adjust paragraph spacing from within the Text Properties Infobox.

By default, SmartSuite defines paragraph spacing in terms of preset line measurements (e.g. 1½ or 2 lines). However, if none of these are suitable you can specify your own number of lines, or enter measurements in different units (picas, inches, centimetres or points).

REMEMBER 72 points are roughly equivalent to one inch (points are used in typography to measure type size).

Picas are an alternative measure (1 pica is almost equivalent to one-sixth of an inch) and are often used to define line length.

Applying paragraph spacing

First, select the paragraph(s) whose spacing you want to adjust. Pull down the Text menu and click Text Properties. Then carry out steps 1–2 below.

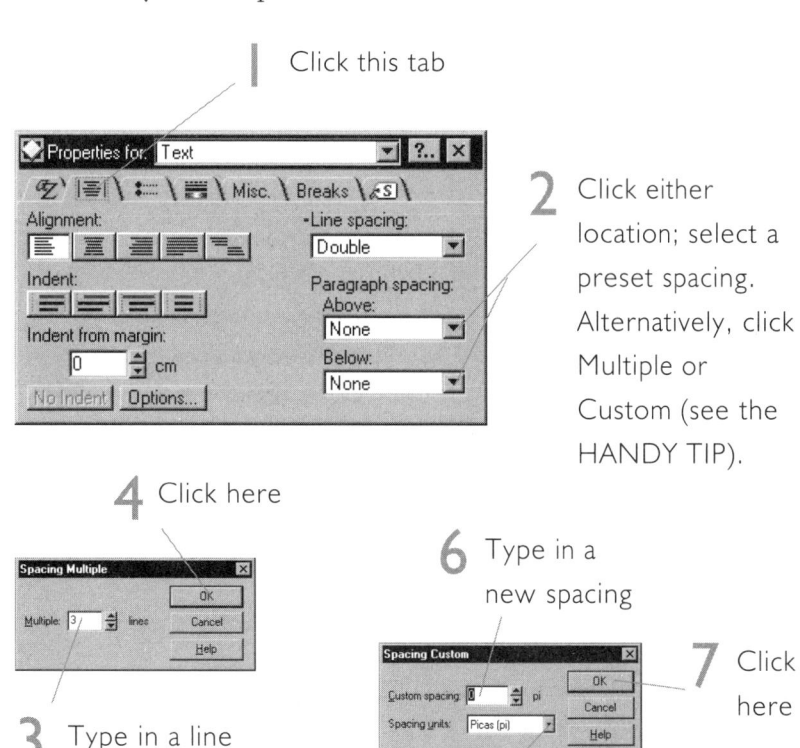

1 Click this tab

2 Click either location; select a preset spacing. Alternatively, click Multiple or Custom (see the HANDY TIP).

HANDY TIP Re step 2 – click Multiple to set your own line multiple (and then follow steps 3–4); or click Custom to set your own spacing using a different unit (and then follow steps 5–7).

3 Type in a line multiple

4 Click here

5 Click here; select a new unit

6 Type in a new spacing

7 Click here

4 Text Formatting **59**

Line spacing – an overview

It's often necessary to amend line spacing. This is the vertical distance between individual lines of text, or more accurately between the baseline (the imaginary line on which text appears to sit) of one line and the baseline of the previous.

REMEMBER**: **Line spacing is also known as leading (pronounced 'ledding').

Word Pro lets you apply preset line spacings – Single, ½, 1½ and Double.

Alternatively, you can:

- specify your own line multiples (e.g. 4 – four lines);

- specify a number followed by a measurement in inches, centimetres, picas or points (e.g. 2 points, 0.167 picas), or;

- specify a leading addition (where the spacing you choose is *added to* the type size). In other words, if you specify a leading adjustment of 4 points on text which is set at 13 points, the resultant spacing is 17 points.

This paragraph is in single line spacing. Newspapers frequently use this. —— Single line spacing

This paragraph is in 1½ line spacing. Probably no one uses this, but it serves as a useful illustration. —— 1½ line spacing

This paragraph is in double line spacing; writers use this when preparing manuscripts —— Double line spacing

Adjusting line spacing

First, select the relevant paragraph(s). Then pull down the Text menu and click Text Properties. Carry out steps 1–2, then refer to the REMEMBER tip:

HANDY TIP — **If you've just created a new document, you can set the line spacing before you begin to enter text. Simply leave the insertion point at the start of the document, and then follow the procedures outlined here.**

1 Click the Alignment tab

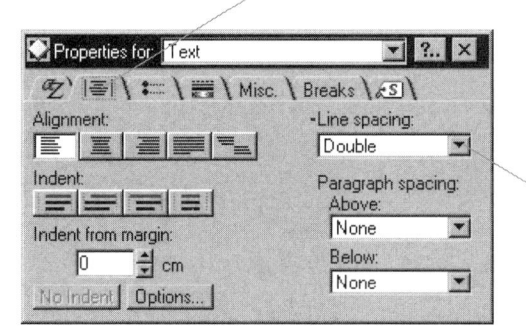

2 Click here; select a preset line spacing. Alternatively, click Multiple, Custom or Leading (see the REMEMBER TIP).

REMEMBER — **Re step 2 – click Multiple to set your own line multiple (and then follow steps 3–4). Or click Custom to set your own spacing using a different unit (and then follow steps 5–7).**
Alternatively, click Leading to set a leading addition (and then follow steps 8–10).

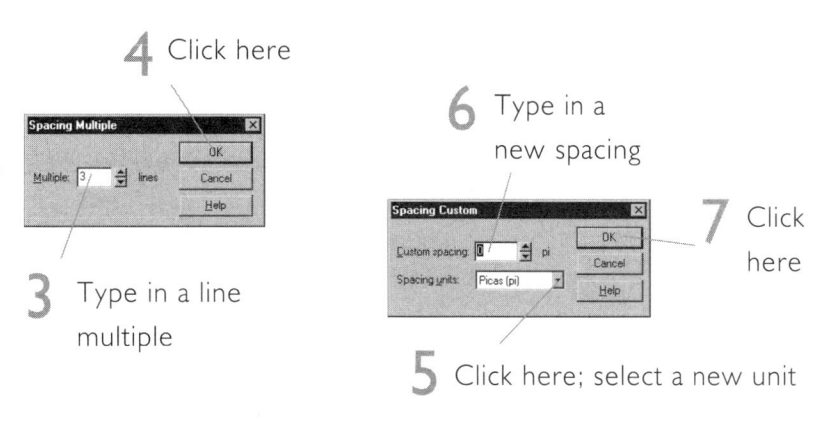

4 Click here

3 Type in a line multiple

6 Type in a new spacing

7 Click here

5 Click here; select a new unit

9 Type in a leading addition

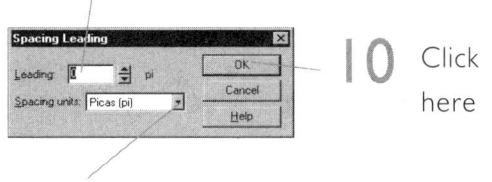

10 Click here

8 Click here; select a new unit

4 Text Formatting   **61**

Paragraph borders

By default, Word Pro does not border paragraph text. However, you can apply a wide selection of borders if you want. You can specify:

- the border type and thickness;
- how many sides the border should have;
- the border colour;
- whether the bordered text should have a drop shadow, and;
- the distance between the border and the enclosed text.

Applying a border

First, select the paragraph(s) you want to border. Then pull down the Text menu and click Text Properties. Follow steps 1–6, as appropriate (if you carry out step 6, also follow 7).

HANDY TIP

Re step 2 – click the final icon on the right:

if you want to border all four sides of the selected paragraph(s) AND apply a drop shadow.

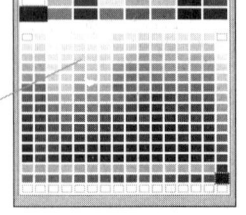

HANDY TIP

If you want the border to stretch from the left to right margins, click in the 'Line length' field; select To margins.

1 Click this tab

2 Select the extent of the border

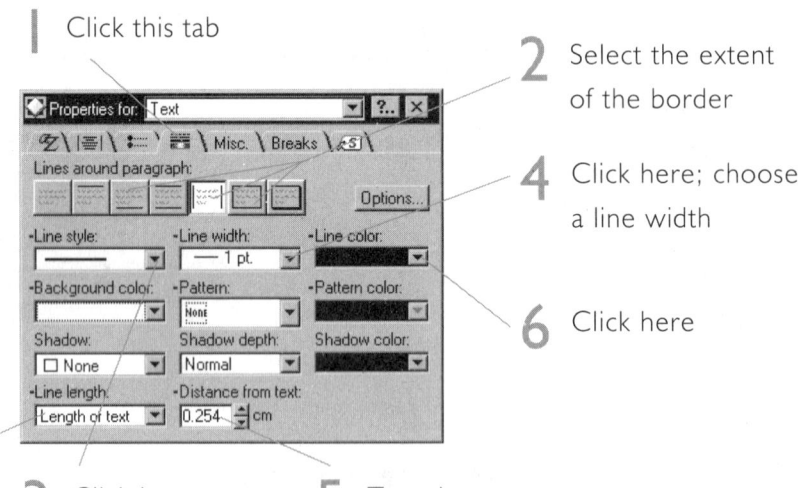

4 Click here; choose a line width

6 Click here

3 Click here; choose a line style

5 Type in a separation distance

7 Choose a colour

Fast Format

Word Pro has a feature which makes applying the formatting enhancements we've already discussed even easier. Fast Format lets you copy the following from text:

- typeface information;
- type size information;
- font attributes (Bold, Italic etc.);
- text colours, and;
- text backgrounds;

and apply them automatically to selected text.

You can also copy text style information (for more information on text styles, see chapter 6).

Using Fast Format

First, place the insertion point in the text whose format you want to copy. Then pull down the Text menu and do the following:

Click here

...cont'd

REMEMBER

Re step 2 – choose one of the following options:

- *'the look of the text at the insertion point'* – copies character formatting only

- *'the paragraph's named style only (advanced)'* – copies the relevant text style

REMEMBER

When you've finished using Fast Format, press Esc to deactivate the feature.

3 Click here

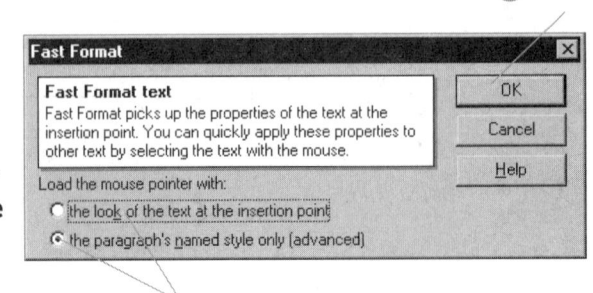

2 Click a formatting option

Now do the following:

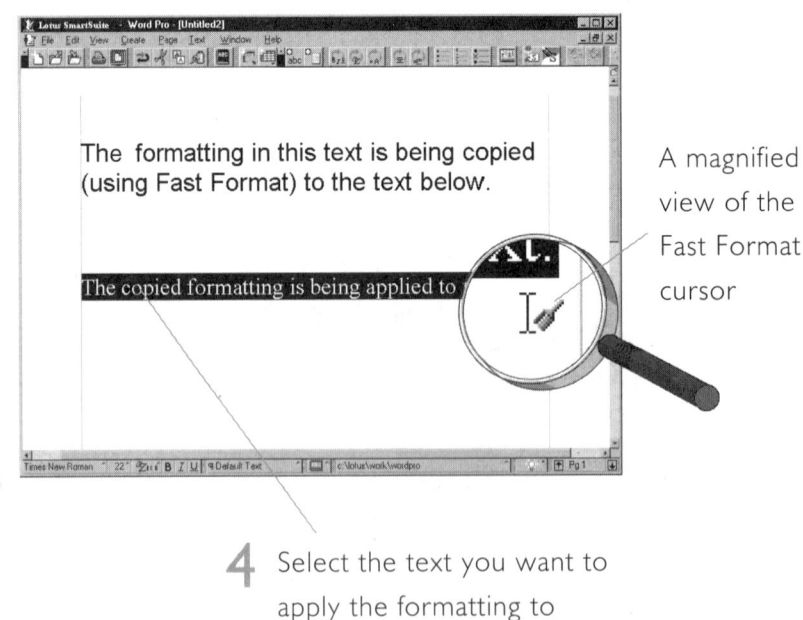

A magnified view of the Fast Format cursor

4 Select the text you want to apply the formatting to

After step 4, release the mouse button; Fast Format applies the formatting characteristics picked up in the original text to the new text.

Adding drop caps

Typography uses drop caps – an enlargement of the first character in a paragraph – to make text more visually effective. You can easily insert drop caps in Word Pro.

Features you can customise include:

- the drop cap height, and;
- the drop cap position (above, below or on a level with the first line of the paragraph).

Applying a drop cap

First, place the insertion point in the paragraph in which you want to insert the drop cap. Then pull down the Create menu and do the following:

Click here

...cont'd

3 Select a placement option   **4** Click here

HANDY TIP — **Re step 3 – the option selected in the dialog:** 'Below first line (dropped)' **is the standard.**

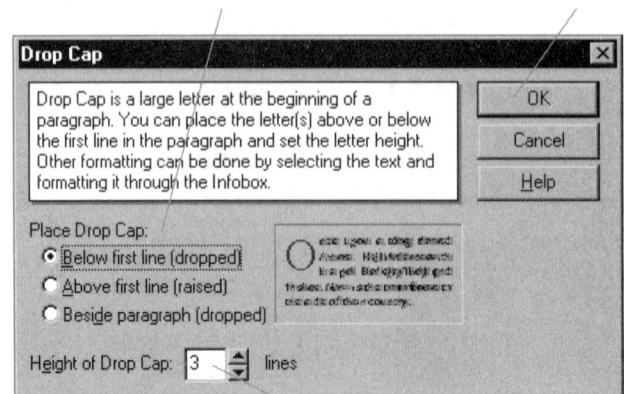

2 Specify the amount of the drop (in lines)

The illustration below shows the result:

REMEMBER — **Drop caps in Word Pro are frames;** you can manipulate these in the normal way.
   (See chapter 8 for more information on frames.)

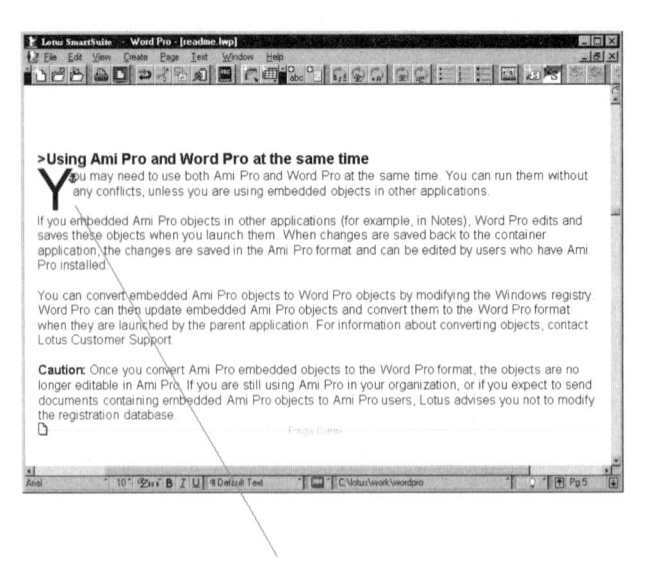

Inserted drop cap

Bulleting and Numbering paragraphs

You can have Word Pro apply bullets or numbers to selected text paragraphs, either from within the Text Properties Infobox, or by using a 'Cycle' SmartIcon.

Using the Text Properties Infobox

First, select the paragraph(s) you want to bullet or number. Pull down the Text menu and click Text Properties. Now do the following:

1 Click this tab

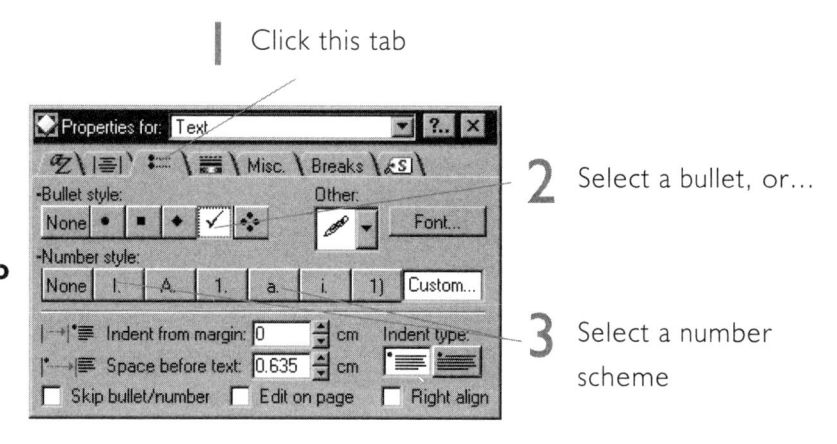

2 Select a bullet, or...

3 Select a number scheme

REMEMBER If you're not sure you're pointing to the correct SmartIcon, leave the mouse pointer over it for several seconds until its explanatory HELP bubble appears.

Using cycling

First, select the relevant paragraph(s). Then refer to the Text SmartIcon bar and do the following:

Click here repeatedly to step up through number schemes, one by one

Click here repeatedly to step up through bullet types, one by one

BEWARE The SmartIcons flagged here are not normally present in the Text SmartIcon bar.
To add them, follow the relevant procedures on page 14.

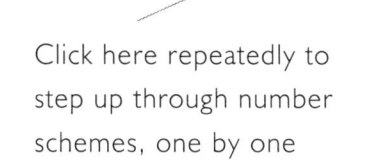

4 Text Formatting   **67**

...cont'd

Before and after...

How to get started using Word Pro for the World Wide Web

There are a few ways to get started using Word Pro to create HTML documents. HTML documents are widely used on the Web, and can be viewed by Internet browsers, such as Netscape and Internet Explorer.

Use the Internet SmartMasters
From the File menu, choose New Document.
Click the Create from any SmartMaster tab.
Select the desired Internet category under "Select a type of SmartMaster."
Select the desired SmartMaster under "Select a look."
Click OK.

Use the HTML Export Assistant to convert existing documents to HTML
Open the document to be converted to HTML.
From the File menu, choose Internet, and then choose HTML Export Assistant.
Make any desired selections on the Content, Layout, and Preview & Save panels.
Note: For more information on the HTML Export Assistant, click the desired tab and then click Help.

Two series of lists – no bullets or numbers applied

HANDY TIP **Two different bullet types and two different number schemes are shown here, for illustration purposes.**

How to get started using Word Pro for the World Wide Web

There are a few ways to get started using Word Pro to create HTML documents. HTML documents are widely used on the Web, and can be viewed by Internet browsers, such as Netscape and Internet Explorer.

Use the Internet SmartMasters
I.   From the File menu, choose New Document.
II.   Click the Create from any SmartMaster tab.
III. Select the desired Internet category under "Select a type of SmartMaster."
IV. Select the desired SmartMaster under "Select a look."
V.   Click OK.

Use the HTML Export Assistant to convert existing documents to HTML
1. Open the document to be converted to HTML.
2. From the File menu, choose Internet, and then choose HTML Export Assistant.
3. Make any desired selections on the Content, Layout, and Preview & Save panels.
4. Note: For more information on the HTML Export Assistant, click the desired tab and then click Help.

Two series of lists – with bullets

Two series of lists – with numbers

Numbering lines

You can have Word Pro number specific lines of text, disregarding text paragraphs.

Numbering individual lines

Pull down the Page menu and click Line Numbering. Now do the following:

HANDY TIP — **If you want to insert line numbers which aren't based on lines of text, omit steps 2–3. Type in a spacing interval here:**
Finally, click in the field to the right and select a unit of measurement. Then perform step 4.

1 Ensure this is selected

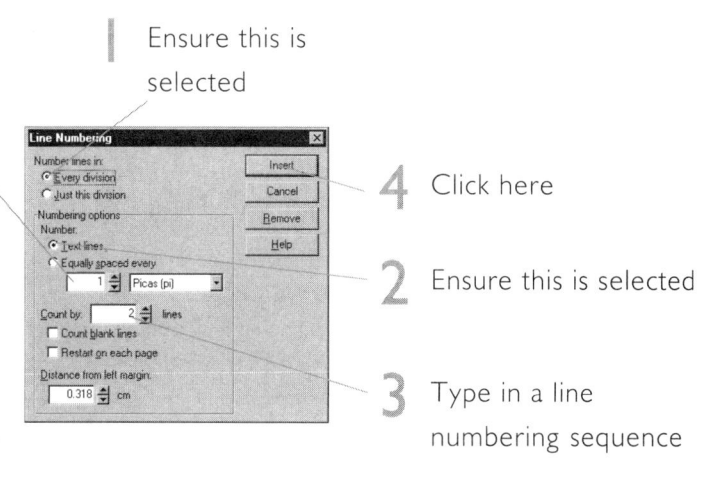

4 Click here

2 Ensure this is selected

3 Type in a line numbering sequence

REMEMBER — **To number blank lines, select Count blank lines.**

HANDY TIP — **Re step 2 – the following examples should clarify this feature. Typing:**

- '*1*' – Numbers every line
- '*3*' – Numbers lines 3, 6, 9, 12 etc.
- '*25*' – Numbers lines 25, 50, 75, etc.

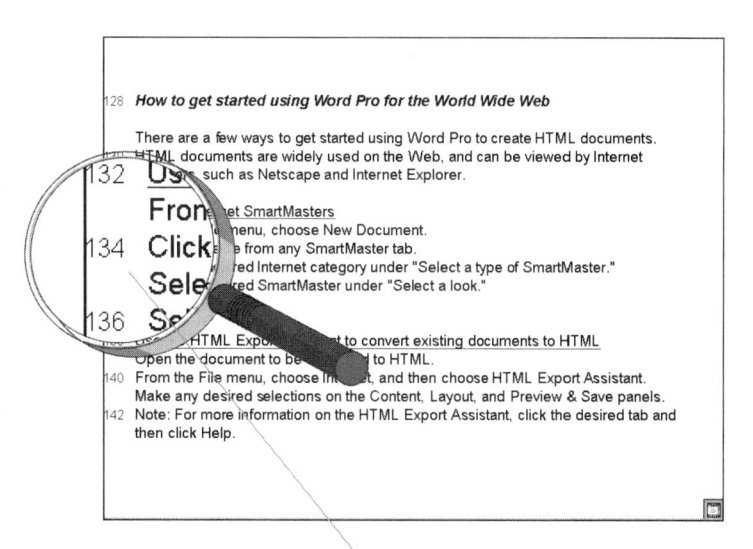

The result – in this instance, every second line (excluding blank lines) is numbered

4 Text Formatting

Text columns – an overview

Columns are a useful text feature, especially if you're undertaking Desk Top Publishing work with Word Pro (for example, if you're working with a newsletter). Word Pro recognises three column types:

Newspaper
Text in Newspaper (also known as 'snaking') columns flows down to the base of the first column, and from there to the top of the next.

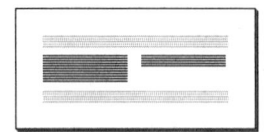

Balanced Newspaper
Balanced Newspaper columns are identical to Newspaper columns, with one exception: the columns are of equal length.

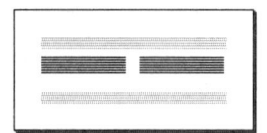

Parallel
Parallel columns are adjacent to each other and look, superficially at least, similar to Newspaper columns. The difference is that each Parallel column is a separate entity; when text reaches the bottom of a Parallel column, instead of continuing onto the next to the right, it continues onto the next page.

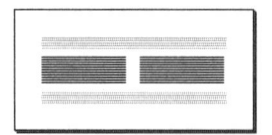

Applying newspaper columns

First, position the insertion point at the location within the open document where you want the columns to start. Right-click once and do the following:

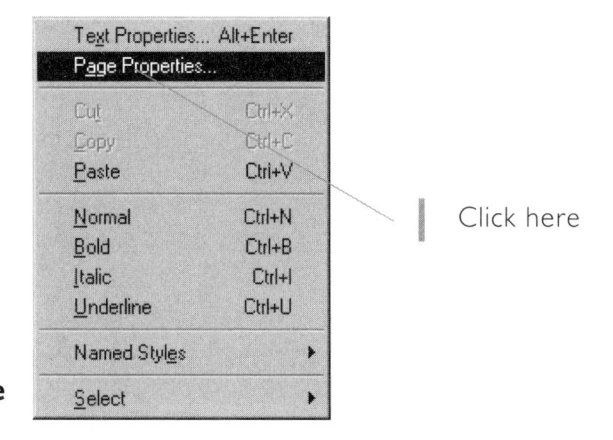

1 Click here

HANDY TIP

To balance the columns, click this field:

☑ Column balance

2 Click this tab

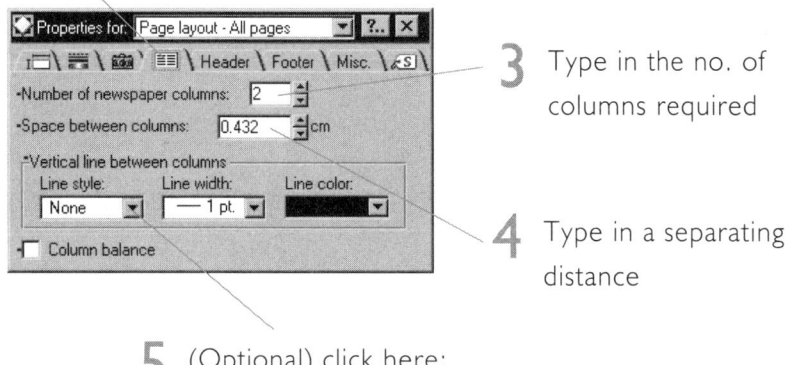

REMEMBER

Re step 5 – if you've selected a dividing line, you can also:

- specify a line width (by clicking in the 'Line width:' field and selecting a width from the list), and;
- allocate a line colour (by clicking in the 'Line color:' field and then selecting a colour in the Color drop-down list).

3 Type in the no. of columns required

4 Type in a separating distance

5 (Optional) click here; select a dividing line

4 Text Formatting

Applying parallel columns

First, position the insertion point at the location within the open document where you want the columns to start. Right-click once and do the following:

HANDY TIP

To adjust the size of a parallel column, right-click it. **In the shortcut menu, click Column Block Properties. Click this tab in the resulting Infobox:**

Type in a new width in the Column width field.

Click here

REMEMBER

Re step 3 – Quick layouts let you apply a preset parallel column layout.

HANDY TIP

To move around in parallel columns, **press Ctrl+Enter to jump to the next column (or, if you've reached the last column, to begin a new row on the left).**

Alternatively, simply click in the relevant column.

2 Type in the no. of columns

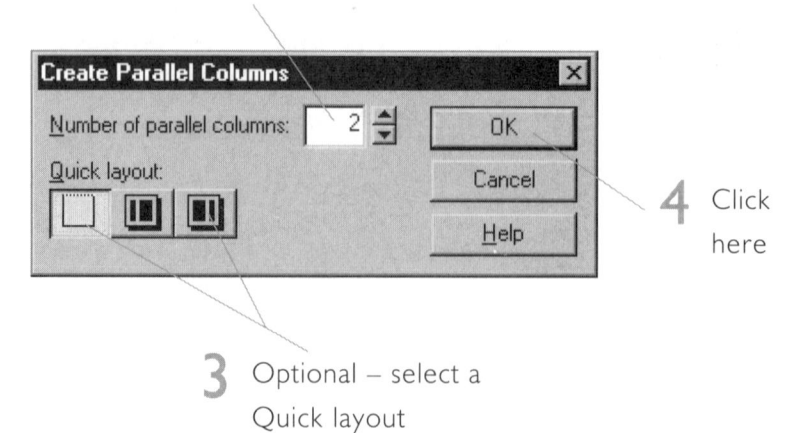

3 Optional – select a Quick layout

4 Click here

Page Formatting

This chapter shows you how to define and format headers and footers. You'll go on to insert page numbers, hyperlinks and bookmarks, then specify page and header/footer margins. You'll also apply specific page sizes, then create your own. Finally, you'll learn to apply formatting enhancements to pages; insert new pages; create and apply page styles; and insert new page layouts.

Covers

Page formatting/layout | 74

Working with headers | 76

Working with footers | 81

Inserting page numbers | 86

Inserting and activating hyperlinks | 89

Inserting and jumping to bookmarks | 90

Specifying margins | 91

Page sizes | 92

Formatting pages | 94

Inserting new pages | 99

Page styles | 100

Page layouts | 108

Chapter Five

Page formatting/layout

You can control the following aspects of page layout in Word Pro:

- the top, bottom, left and/or right page margins;

- the distance above the header (between the top page edge and the top edge of the header), and;

- the distance below the footer (between the bottom page edge and the bottom edge of the footer).

The illustration below shows the principal components:

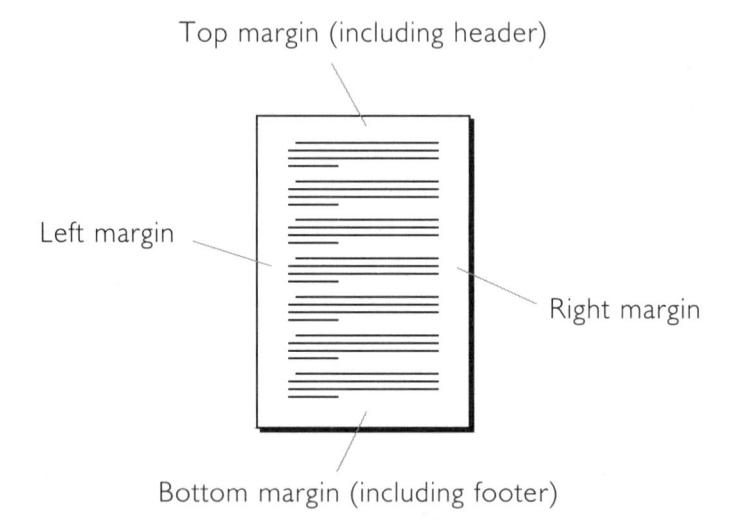

Top margin (including header)

Left margin

Right margin

Bottom margin (including footer)

You can also specify:

- the overall page size (inclusive of margins and headers/footers), and;

- the page orientation ('landscape' or 'portrait').

If none of the supplied page sizes is suitable, you can even create your own customised page size.

...cont'd

With regard to page formatting/layout, you can also perform the following actions:

- apply a border to pages;
- apply a drop shadow to pages;
- apply a background to pages;
- apply a plain or coloured pattern to pages;
- apply a watermark to pages;
- insert new pages;
- insert and activate hyperlinks;
- insert and activate bookmarks;
- group associated page formatting characteristics into page 'styles' and then apply these with just a few mouse clicks;
- amend existing page styles and have Word Pro apply the changes automatically;
- perform housekeeping on page styles (i.e. copy, rename or delete them), and;
- assign function keys to page styles (so they can be applied by simply pressing the associated key).

The majority of page formatting enhancements apply to the whole of the active document. However, Word Pro also lets you restrict the application of page formatting to parts of documents by inserting new page layouts.

Working with headers

You can have Word Pro display and print text at the top of each page within a document; the area of the page where repeated text appears is called the 'header'. In the same way, you can have text printed at the base of each page; in this case, the relevant page area is called the 'footer'. Headers and footers are printed within the top and bottom page margins, respectively.

Headers and footers are commonly used to display document titles, origination details and page numbers.

Inserting a header

In Layout view (headers and footers are not visible in Draft view), move to the top of the first page, then click in the Header area. Now do the following:

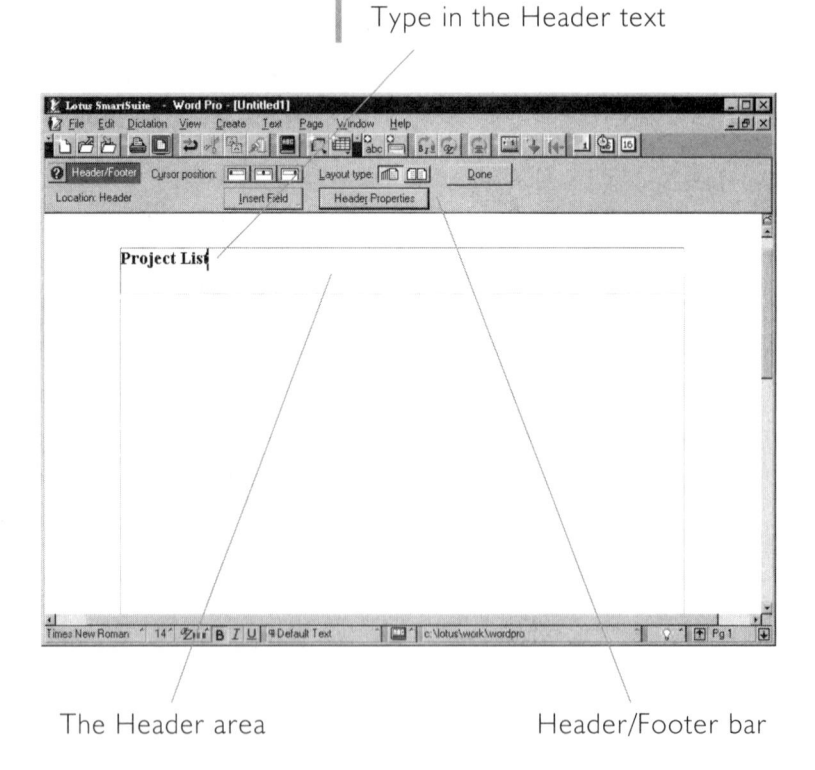

Type in the Header text

The Header area

Header/Footer bar

...cont'd

Editing existing headers
In Layout view, move to the top of the first page, then click in the Header area. Now do the following:

Amend the Header text

REMEMBER

Header text can be formatted in the usual way – for how to format text, see chapter 4.

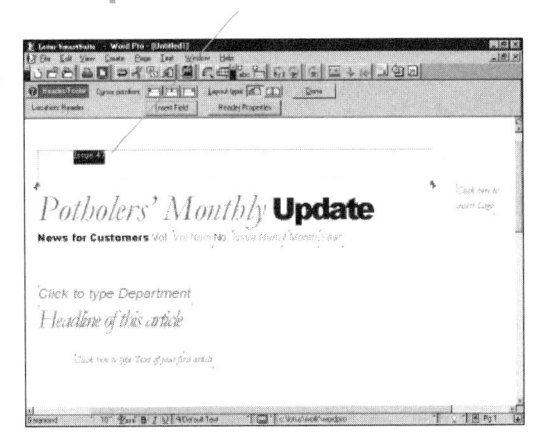

Amending header margins
To specify precise header dimensions, click this button in the Header/Footer bar:

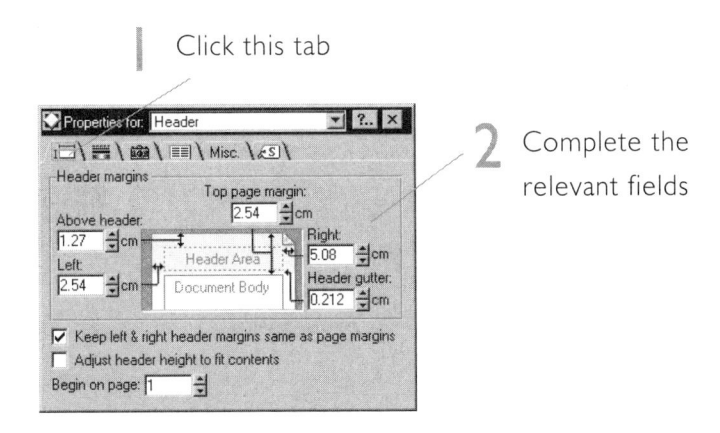

Header Properties

Do the following:

Click this tab

2 Complete the relevant fields

5 Page Formatting **77**

...cont'd

Bordering/colouring headers

Click this button in the Header/Footer bar:

[Header Properties]

**Re step 2 –
click either
of these
icons:**

HANDY TIP

if you want to
border all four sides
of the header AND
apply a drop
shadow.

Follow steps 1–6 below, as appropriate (if you carry out step 6, also follow 7):

1 Click this tab

2 Select a border style

4 Click here; choose a line width

6 Click here

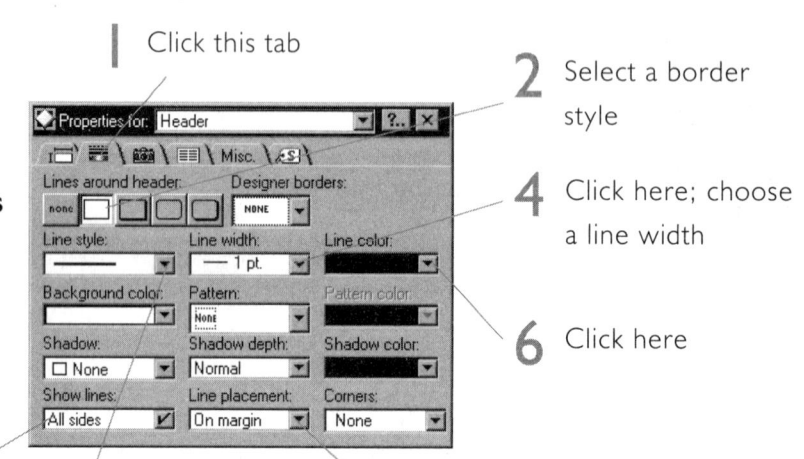

HANDY TIP

**If you
want the
border to
display on
all sides of the
header, click in the
'Show lines:' field;
select All sides.**

Alternatively,
select one of these:
- Left;
- Right;
- Top, or;
- Bottom.

3 Click here; choose a line style

5 Click here; select a placement option

7 Choose a colour

...cont'd

REMEMBER A watermark is a graphic displayed as a faint greyscale image; use watermarks to visually enhance your header.

Adding watermarks to headers

Click this button in the Header/Footer bar:

Header Properties

Follow steps 1–4, as appropriate:

1 Click this tab

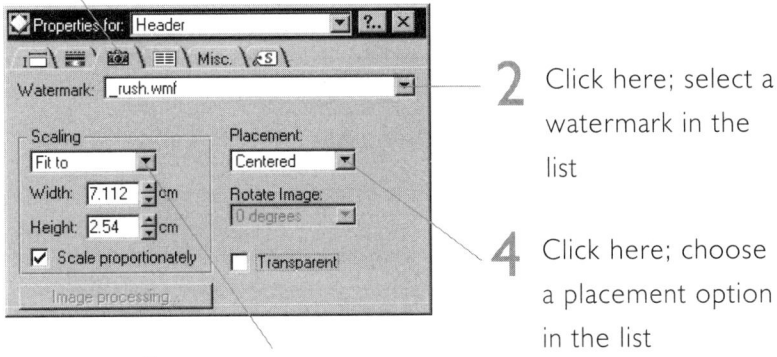

2 Click here; select a watermark in the list

3 Click here; select a scaling option in the list

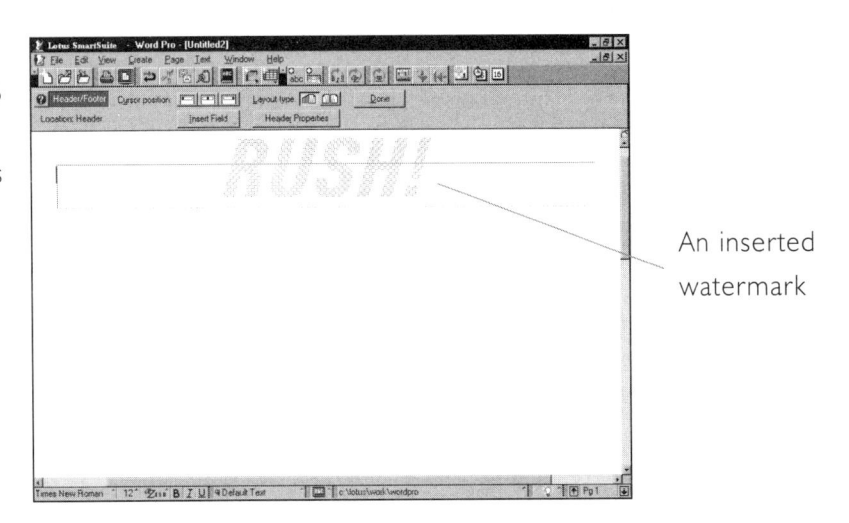

4 Click here; choose a placement option in the list

REMEMBER Re step 3 – you can choose from the following options:

- *'Original size'* – the graphic has its original dimensions
- *'Fit to'* – the graphic conforms to the header
- *'Percentage'* – A box displays – specify a %
- *'Custom'* – specify your own dimensions in the Width and Height fields

An inserted watermark

5 Page Formatting

...cont'd

Adding columns to headers

Click this button in the Header/Footer bar:

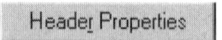

> Header Properties

Follow steps 1–4, as appropriate:

1 Click this tab

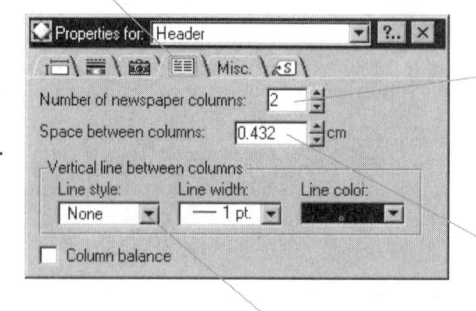

2 Type in the no. of columns required

3 Type in a separating distance

4 (Optional) click here; select a dividing line

REMEMBER

Re step 4 – if you've selected a dividing line, you can also:

- specify a line width (by clicking in the 'Line width:' field and selecting a width from the list), and;
- allocate a line colour (by clicking in the 'Line color:' field and then selecting a colour in the Color drop-down list).

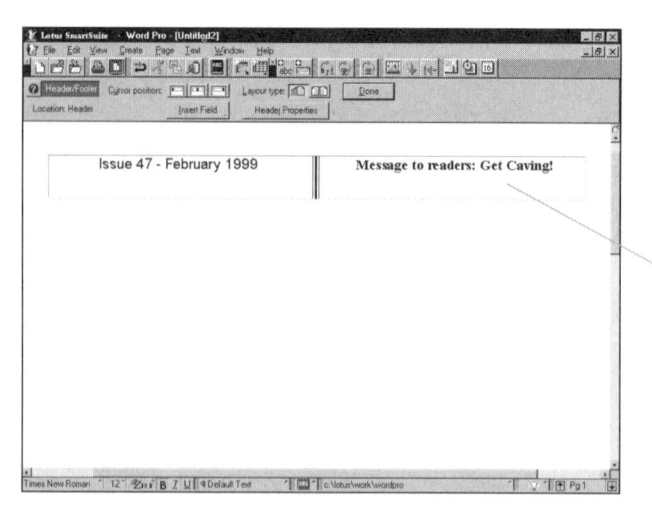

This header has been split into 2 columns with a dividing line

80   Word Pro in easy steps

Working with footers

You can have Word Pro automatically display and print text at the bottom of each page within a document. The area of the page where this repeated text appears is called the 'footer'.

Footers are often used to display an abbreviated version of the document's title and/or the page number.

Inserting a footer

In Layout view, move to the bottom of the first page then click in the Footer area. Do the following:

Type in the Footer text

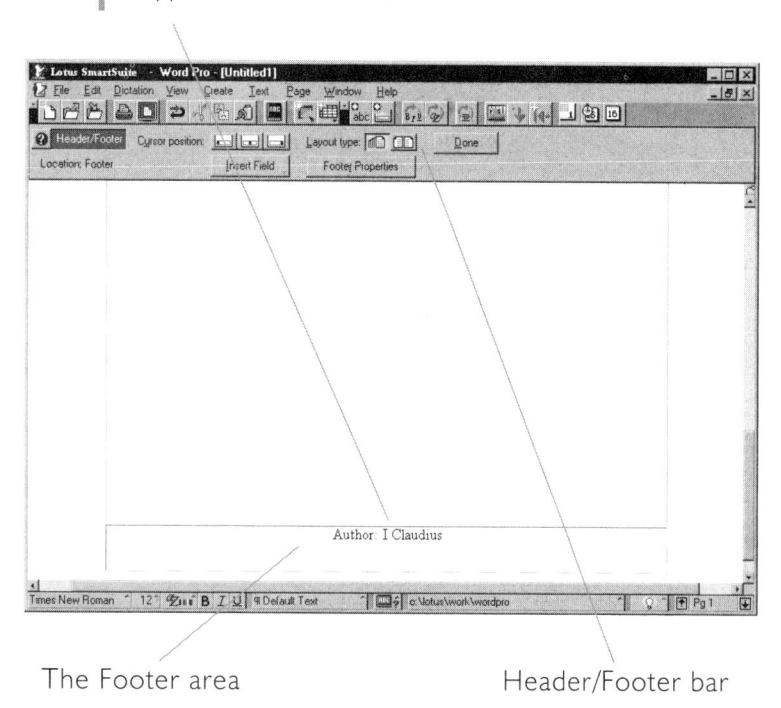

The Footer area — Header/Footer bar

5 Page Formatting

...cont'd

Editing existing footers
In Layout view, move to the bottom of the first page, then click in the Footer area. Now do the following:

REMEMBER Footer text can be formatted in the usual way – for how to format text, see chapter 4.

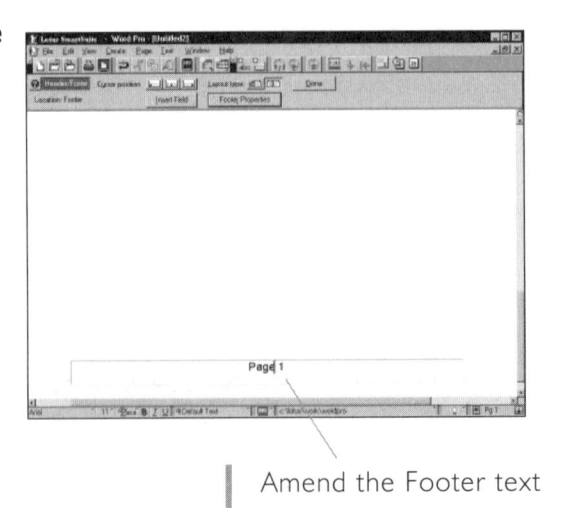

| Amend the Footer text

Amending footer margins
To specify precise footer dimensions, click this button in the Header/Footer bar:

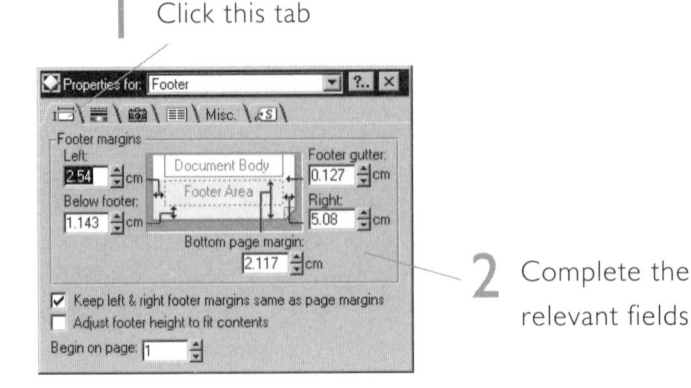

Footer Properties

Do the following:

| Click this tab

2 Complete the relevant fields

...cont'd

Bordering/colouring footers

Click this button in the Header/Footer bar:

Footer Properties

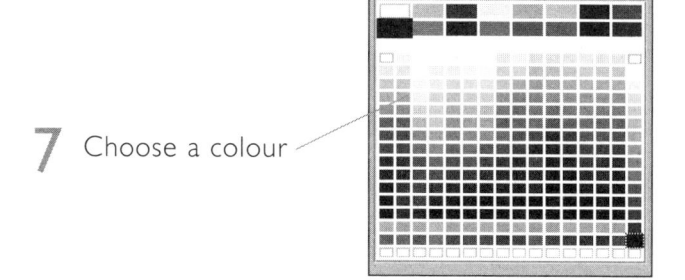

HANDY TIP — **Re step 2 – click either of these icons:**

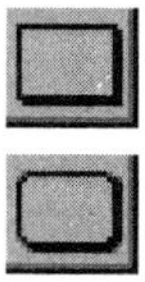

if you want to border all four sides of the footer AND apply a drop shadow.

Follow steps 1–6, as appropriate (if you carry out step 6, also follow 7):

1 Click this tab

2 Select a border style

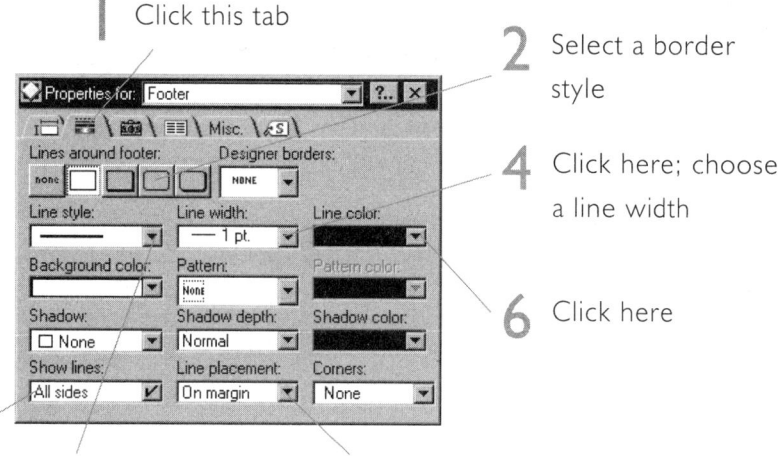

4 Click here; choose a line width

6 Click here

3 Click here; choose a line style

5 Click here; select a placement option

7 Choose a colour

HANDY TIP — **If you want the border to display on all sides of the footer, click in the 'Show lines:' field; select All sides.**

Alternatively, select one of these:
- Left;
- Right;
- Top, or;
- Bottom.

5 Page Formatting **83**

...cont'd

REMEMBER

A watermark is a faint graphic displayed as a greyscale image; use watermarks to visually enhance your footer.

Adding watermarks to footers

Click this button in the Header/Footer bar:

Footer Properties

Follow steps 1–4, as appropriate:

1 Click this tab

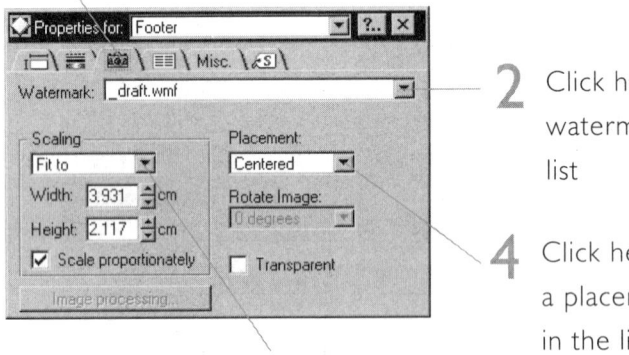

2 Click here; select a watermark in the list

3 Click here; select a scaling option in the list

4 Click here; choose a placement option in the list

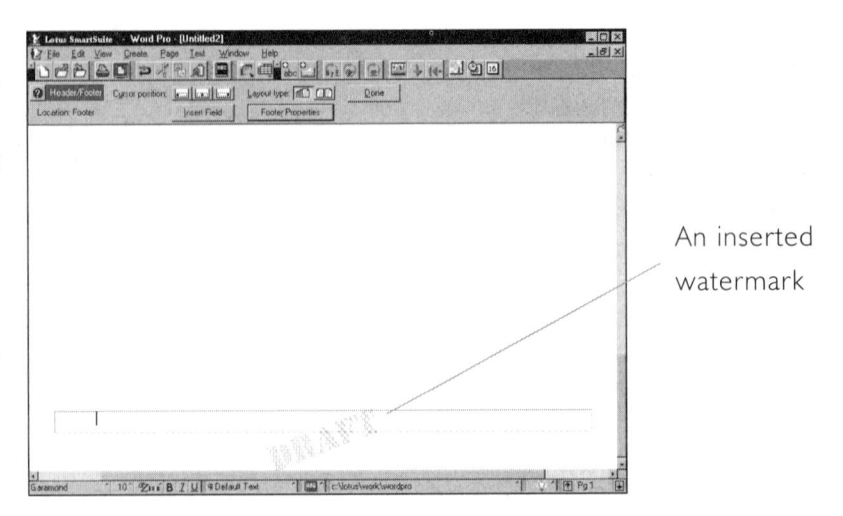

REMEMBER

Re step 3 – you can choose from the following options:

- *'Original size'* – the graphic has its original dimensions

- *'Fit to'* – the graphic conforms to the footer

- *'Percentage'* – A box displays – specify a %

- *'Custom'* – specify your own dimensions in the Width and Height fields

An inserted watermark

...cont'd

Adding columns to footers

Click this button in the Header/Footer bar:

> Footer Properties

Follow steps 1-4, as appropriate:

1 Click this tab

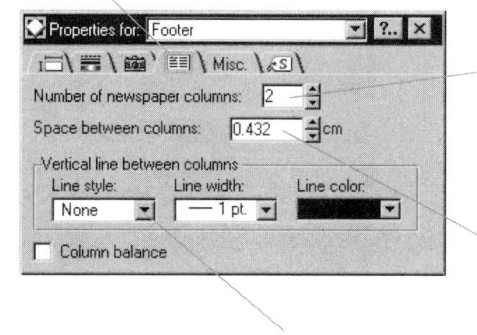

2 Type in the no. of columns required

3 Type in a separating distance

4 (Optional) click here; select a dividing line

REMEMBER

Re step 4 – if you've selected a dividing line, you can also:

- specify a line width (by clicking in the 'Line width:' field and selecting a width from the list), and;
- allocate a line colour (by clicking the 'Line color:' field and then selecting a colour in the Color drop-down list).

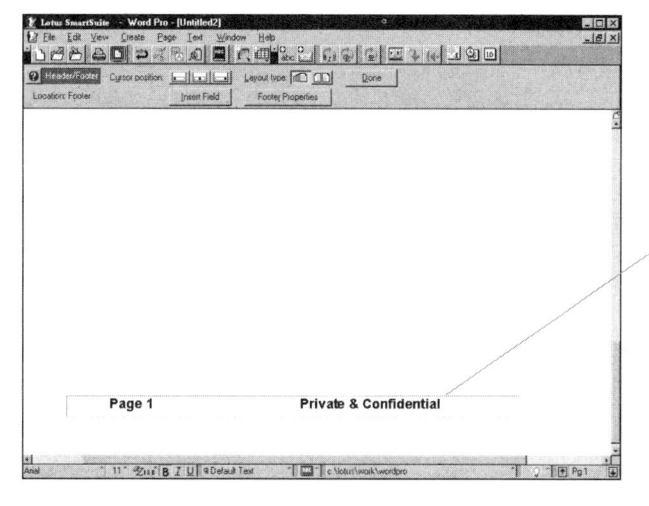

This footer has been split into 2 columns without a dividing line

Page Formatting

Inserting page numbers

REMEMBER

What is actually inserted is a hidden code which tells Word Pro to display the current page number.

You can have Word Pro insert page numbers in the following ways:

- into the body of a document, or;

- into headers and footers.

Numbering the body of a document

Word Pro lets you insert automatic page numbers anywhere in the main body of a document. You can also specify:

- the number format – e.g. 'I', 'A', 'a' or 'i';

- the start number, and;

- text (e.g. 'Page') to appear before and/or after the inserted page number.

The illustration below shows a numbered document.

A page number inserted at the top of a document (but not in the header)

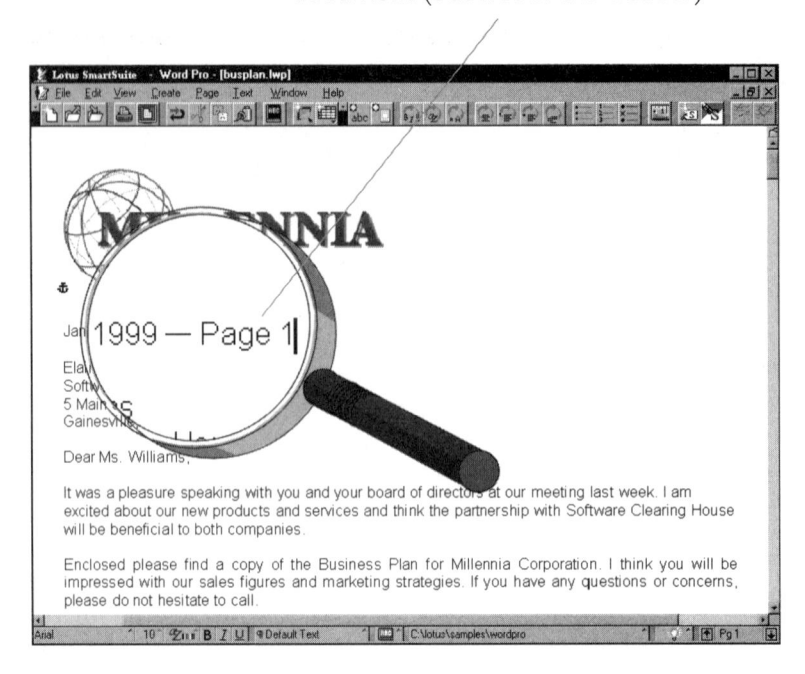

...cont'd

To insert a page number into the body of a document, first place the insertion point at the relevant location within it. Pull down the Page menu and click Insert Page Number. Now carry out the following steps:

1 Click here; in the list, select a number format

HANDY TIP

To have text precede or follow the page number, type in text in the 'Text before:' or 'Text after:' fields respectively.

REMEMBER

If you insert before and/or after text, don't forget to type in the relevant spaces.

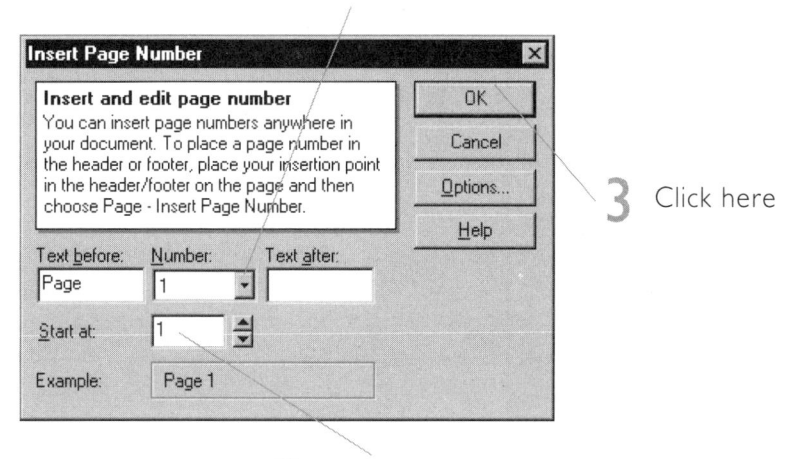

3 Click here

2 Type in a start number

Further options

You can also specify which page the numbering starts on. This is very useful because many documents (for instance, newsletters and magazines) do not have a number on the first page.

To specify a start page other than 1, click this button:

Options...

in the above dialog. In the 'Begin numbering on page:' field in the Page Number Options dialog, type in the start page number. Click OK.

Finally, carry out step 3 above.

5 Page Formatting **87**

...cont'd

Numbering headers and footers

In Layout view, click in the relevant header or footer. Now carry out the following steps:

1 Click here

2 Click here

> **HANDY TIP**
>
> **Re step 2 – choose** 'Page Numbering...' **instead to launch the Insert Page Number dialog (see page 87 for how to complete it).**

> **BEWARE**
>
> **The form of this command varies according to which page you're currently viewing.** For instance, if you're on page 6 of a 9-page document, it appears as: 'Page 6 of 9'.

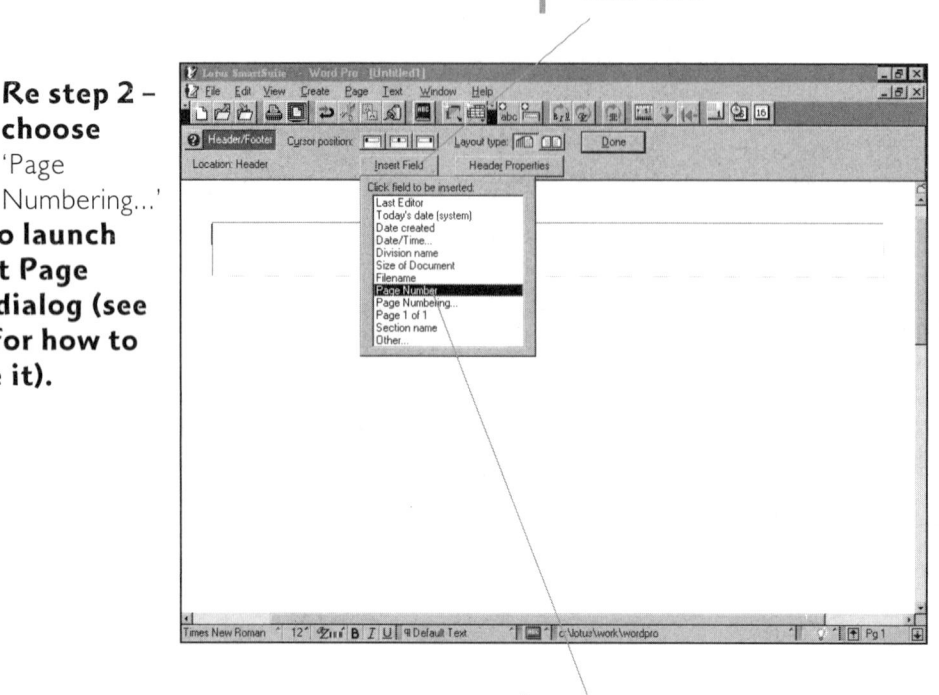

Further options

You can also insert the following type of page numbering into headers/footers:

page x of y

where x is the current page number, and y the total number of pages in the document.

To do this, click 'Page 1 of 1' in step 2.

Inserting and activating hyperlinks

REMEMBER **To amend a hyperlink, place the insertion point within it.** Pull down the Edit menu and click **Edit Hyperlink**. Complete the Edit Hyperlink dialog. Click OK.

You can insert hyperlinks into Word Pro documents. Hyperlinks are text or graphics which are linked to:

- another location in the same document, or a different document on your local hard-drive (see page 90), or;
- a document on the World Wide Web or local Intranet (see also pages 44–45).

Creating a hyperlink

Select the text or graphic you want to be the source of the link. Pull down the Create menu and do the following:

REMEMBER **To delete a hyperlink, place the insertion point within it.** Pull down the Edit menu and click **Remove Hyperlink**.

1 Click here

2 Click here; select a link type

3 Type in a Web document or bookmark address

4 Click here

REMEMBER **To activate a hyperlink to a World Wide Web document, first ensure your Internet connection is live.** For more on this, see chapter 3.

To activate the hyperlink, and so jump to a linked Web document, or a bookmark in the active (or another) document, double-click here.

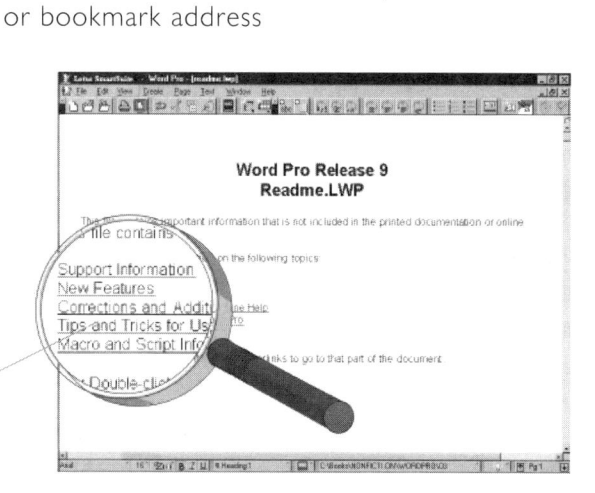

REMEMBER **Note that inserted hyperlinks are:**

- underlined, and;
- coloured blue.

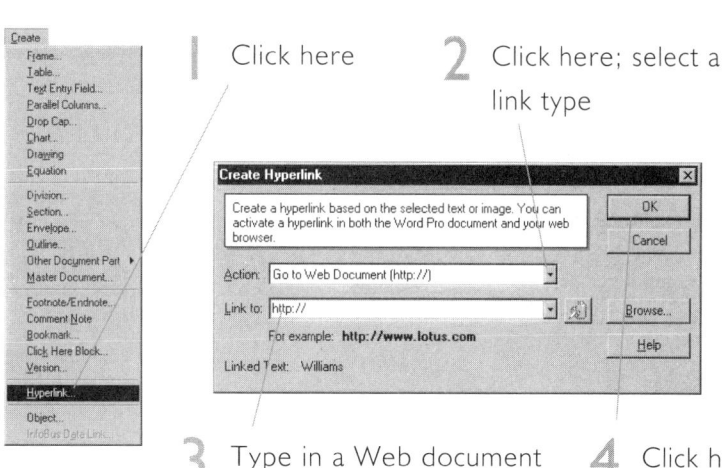

5 Page Formatting **89**

Inserting and jumping to bookmarks

In computer terms, a bookmark is a marker inserted to enable you to find a given location in a document easily and quickly.

Creating a bookmark

Place the insertion point where you want the bookmark to be inserted. Pull down the Create menu and then follow steps 1 to 3:

REMEMBER **Re step 2 – bookmarks can consist of any characters (plus spaces, if required).**

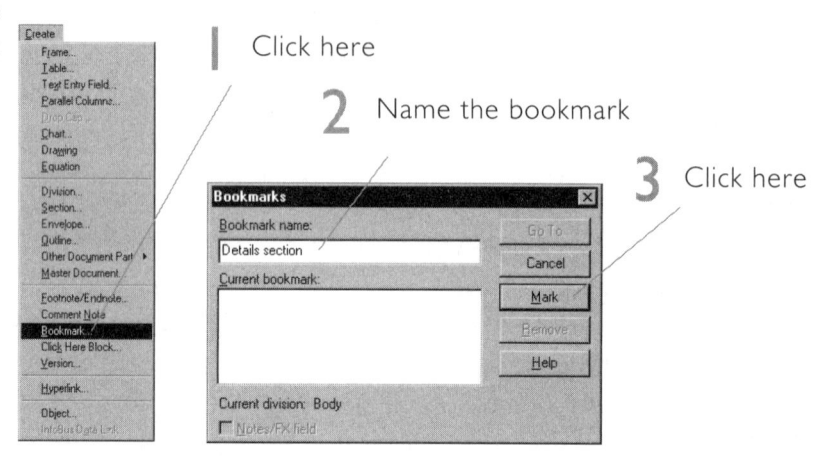

1 Click here

2 Name the bookmark

3 Click here

REMEMBER **To delete a bookmark, carry out steps 1–2. Now click this button:**

[Remove]

To go to a bookmark you've created earlier, repeat step 1 above, and then follow steps 4 and 5

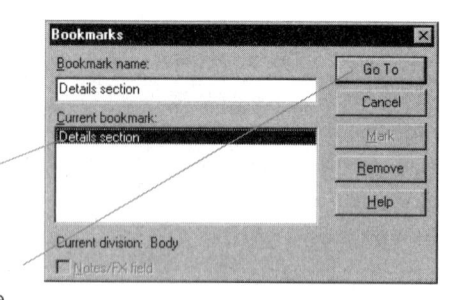

HANDY TIP **To link to a different document on your local hard-drive, first open the document you want to link to (wherever this may be), create a bookmark in it and then link to this bookmark.**

4 Select a bookmark

5 Click here

To link to another document on your local hard-drive, first ensure both documents are open. Follow step 1 on page 89. In step 2 (page 89), choose 'Go to a bookmarked location'. Ignore step 3. Click the Browse button, and in the 'Open document to link to:' field in the Open Documents and Bookmarks dialog, select the file you want to link to. In the 'Bookmarks:' field, select the bookmark. Click OK. Back in the Create Hyperlink dialog, follow step 4 (page 89).

Specifying margins

REMEMBER

Margin settings are the framework on which indents and tabs are based.

All documents have margins because they need a certain amount of 'white space' (the unprinted portion of the page) to balance the areas which contain text and graphics. Margins make documents more visually effective.

Customising document margins

Pull down the Page menu and click Page Properties. Now do the following:

1 Click here

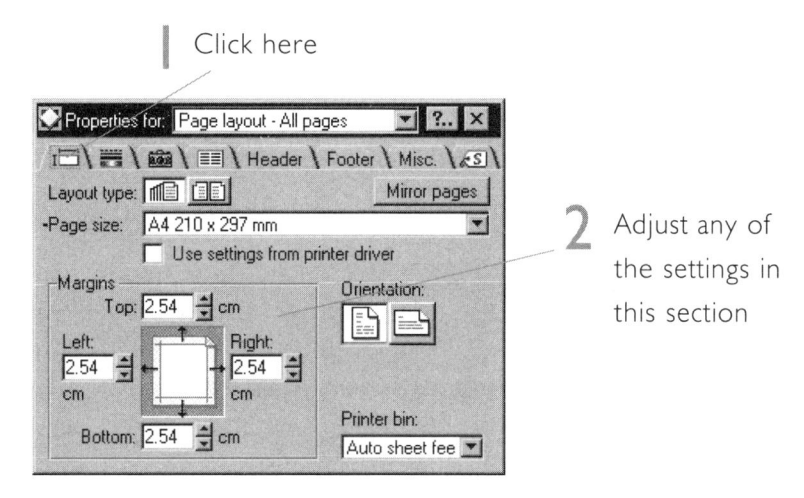

2 Adjust any of the settings in this section

HANDY TIP

To amend footer margins, launch the Page Layout Infobox, as here. Click the Footer tab. Now adjust the Below footer field.

Customising header/footer margins

To adjust header margins, pull down the Page menu and click Page Properties. Now do the following:

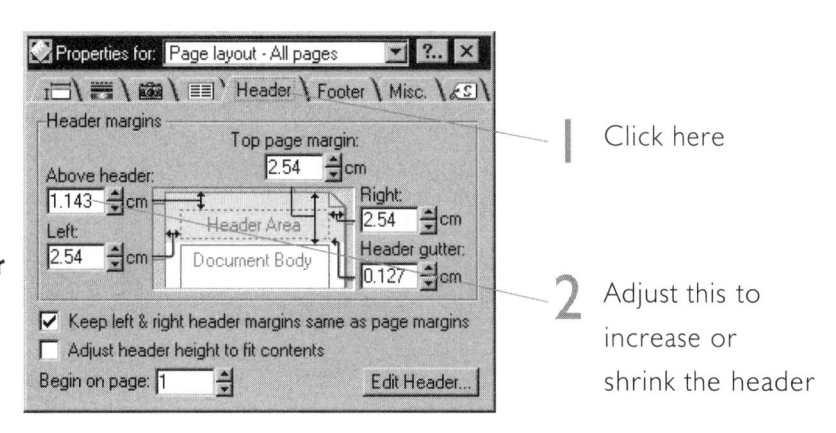

1 Click here

2 Adjust this to increase or shrink the header

HANDY TIP

Adjust the entries in the Left: or Right: fields to adjust left and right header margins.

5 Page Formatting   91

Specifying page sizes

Word Pro comes with several preset page sizes. These are suitable for most purposes. However, if you need to, you can also set up your own page definition.

There are two aspects to every page size:

- a vertical measurement, and;
- a horizontal measurement.

There are two possible orientations:

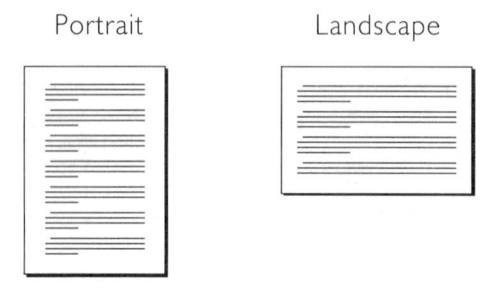

Portrait

Landscape

Setting the page size

Pull down the Page menu and click Page Properties. Perform step 1 below, then 2 and/or 3:

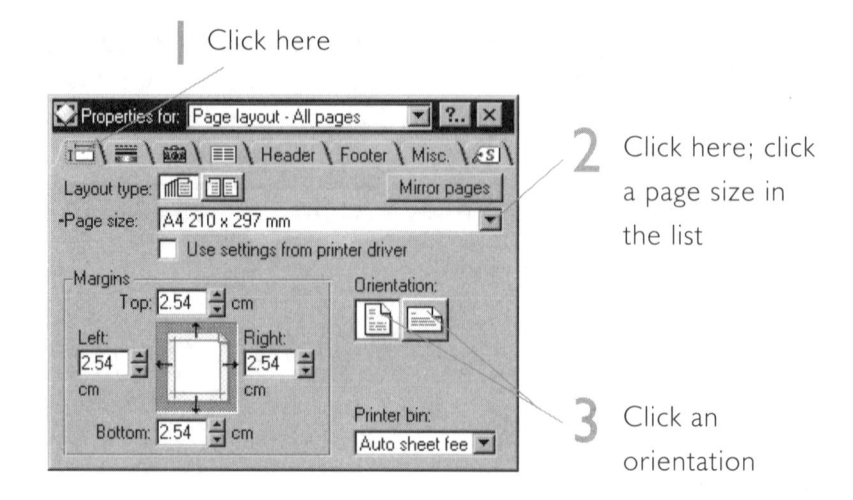

1 Click here

2 Click here; click a page size in the list

3 Click an orientation

Customising page sizes

Given the wide range of preset page sizes Word Pro provides, you *may* never need to define your own. However, there are times when you may want to do so. For example, you might decide to create business cards. In this case, you could create a suitable page size and then output the result on disk to a copy-shop for subsequent printing . . .

Setting your own page size

Pull down the Page menu and click Page Properties. Perform step 1 below, then 2–4:

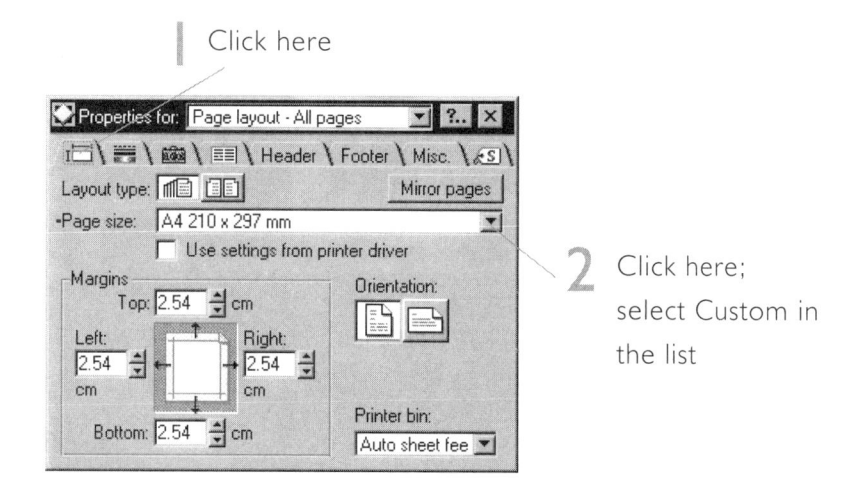

1 Click here

2 Click here; select Custom in the list

4 Click here

3 Type in height and width measurements

5 Page Formatting   **93**

Bordering pages

You can apply borders to pages.

Right-click once on any page and click Page Properties in the shortcut menu. Do the following:

HANDY TIP

Re step 2 – click either of these icons:

if you want to border all four sides of the page AND apply a drop shadow. (But see page 95 for how to customise the shadow.)

1 Click this tab

2 Select a border style

4 Click here; choose a line width

6 Click here

REMEMBER

If you want the border to display on all sides of the page, click in the 'Show lines:' field; select All sides.

Alternatively, select one of these:

- Left;
- Right;
- Top, or;
- Bottom.

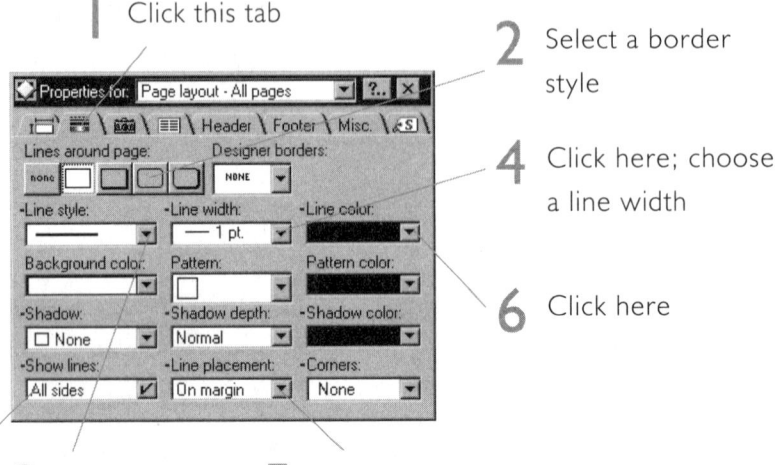

3 Click here; choose a line style

5 Click here; select a placement option

7 Choose a colour

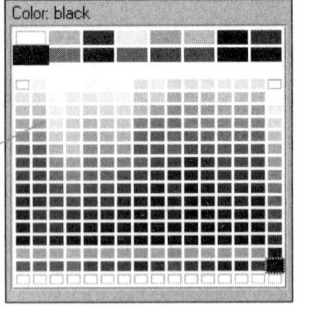

94 Word Pro in easy steps

Shadowing pages

If you:

- followed step 2 on page 94

and

- carried out the procedures discussed in the HANDY TIP on page 94,

Word Pro automatically applies a drop shadow to all the pages in the active document. You can now customise the shadow, if you want.

In the Page layout Infobox, carry out step 1 to apply a new shadow style; step 2 to specify a depth; and steps 3–4 to colour it:

REMEMBER **Re step 2 – you can choose from the following:**

- Shallow;
- Normal, or;
- Deep.

REMEMBER **Re step 2 – if you want to specify your own depth, choose Other...**
Do the following:

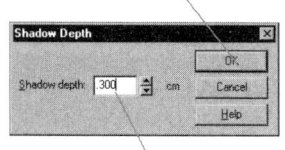

B Click here

A Type in a depth (in cm)

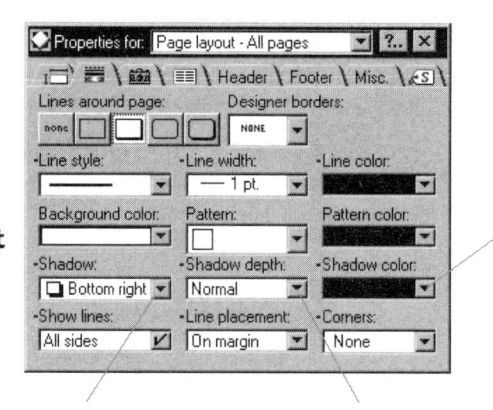

1 Click here; choose a shadow style

2 Click here; select a shadow depth

3 Click here

4 Choose a colour

5 Page Formatting

Applying backgrounds to pages

You can apply coloured backgrounds to pages.

Right-click once on any page and click Page Properties in the shortcut menu. Do the following:

1 Click here

REMEMBER

Experiment with combining background colours with plain or coloured patterns.

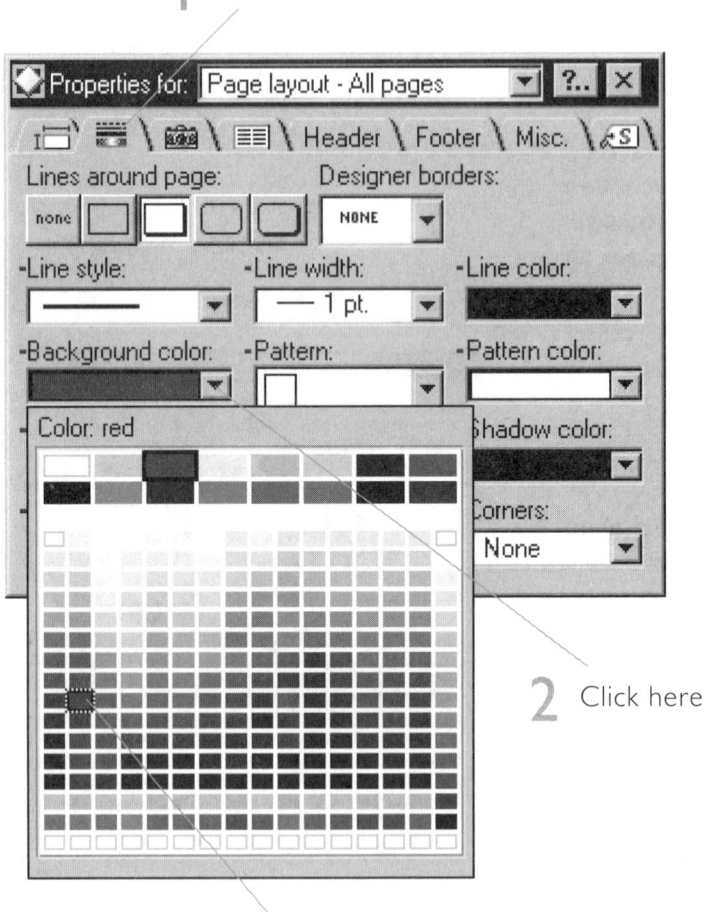

2 Click here

3 Click a background colour

96 Word Pro in easy steps

Applying patterns to pages

You can apply plain or coloured patterns to pages.

Right-click once on any page and click Page Properties in the shortcut menu. Perform step 1. Then carry out steps 2–3 to apply a pattern and (optionally) steps 4–5 to colour it:

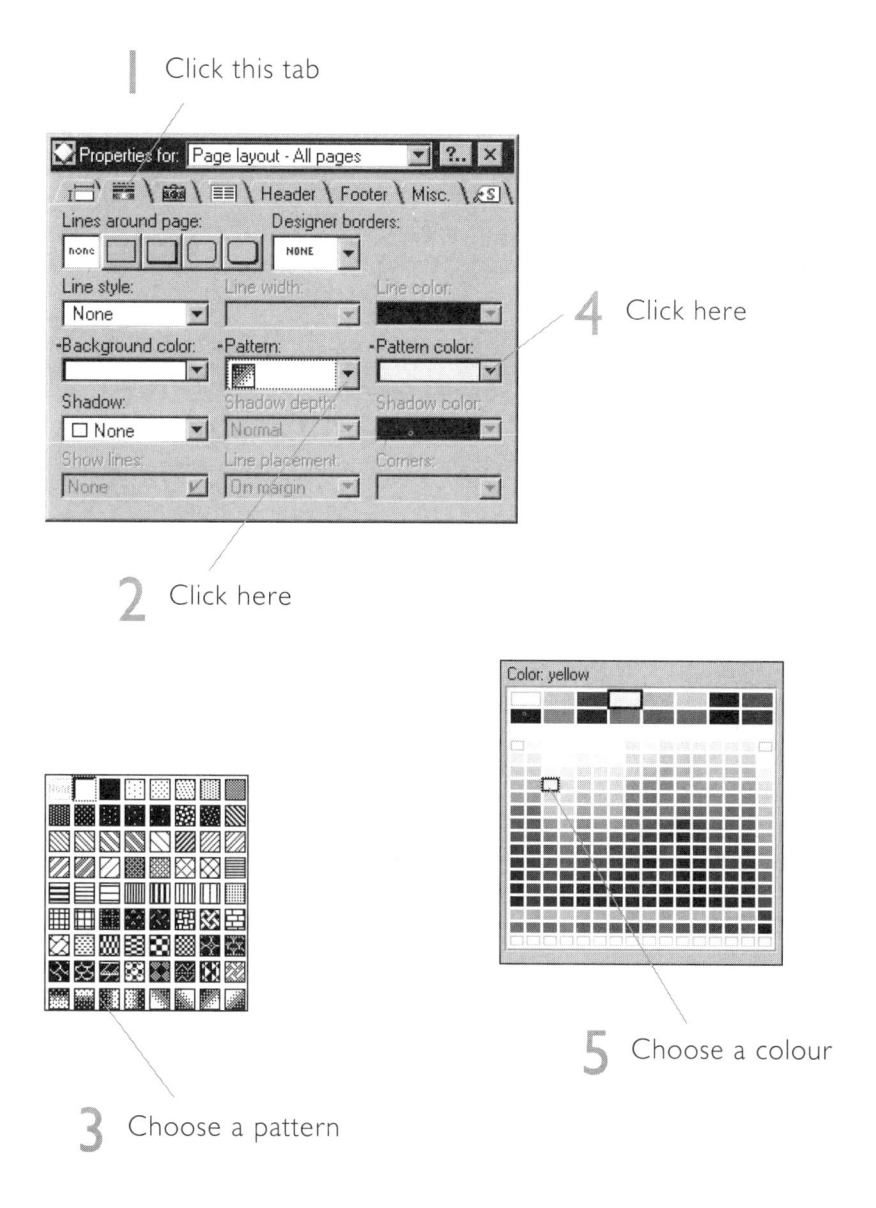

1 Click this tab

4 Click here

2 Click here

3 Choose a pattern

5 Choose a colour

5 Page Formatting

Applying watermarks to pages

REMEMBER

A watermark is a faint graphic displayed as a greyscale image; use watermarks to visually enhance pages.

You can apply watermarks to pages.

Right-click once on any page and click Page Properties in the shortcut menu. Do the following:

1 Click this tab

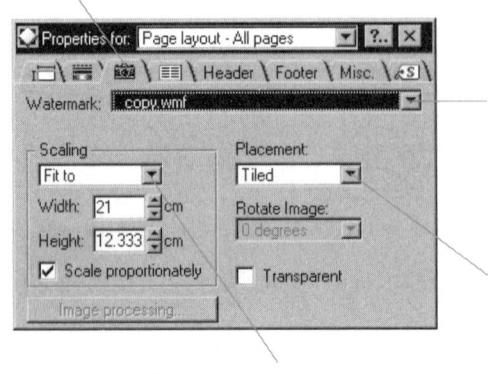

2 Click here; select a watermark in the list

3 Click here; select a scaling option in the list

4 Click here; choose a placement option in the list

REMEMBER

Re step 3 – you can choose from the following options:

- *'Original size'* – the graphic has its original dimensions
- *'Fit to'* – the graphic conforms to the footer
- *'Percentage'* – A box displays – specify a %
- *'Custom'* – specify your own dimensions in the Width and Height fields

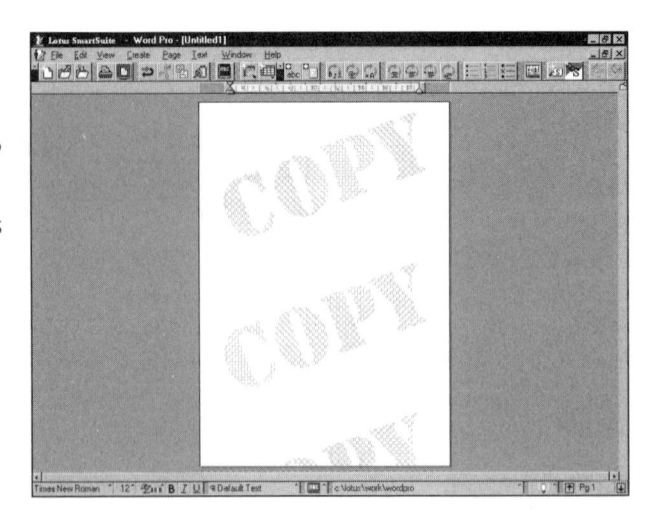

A tiled watermark – to achieve this effect, choose 'Tiled' in step 4

Inserting new pages

You can create new pages in two ways in Word Pro:

The menu route
Position the insertion point at the location following which you want the new page to be inserted. Then pull down the Page menu and do the following:

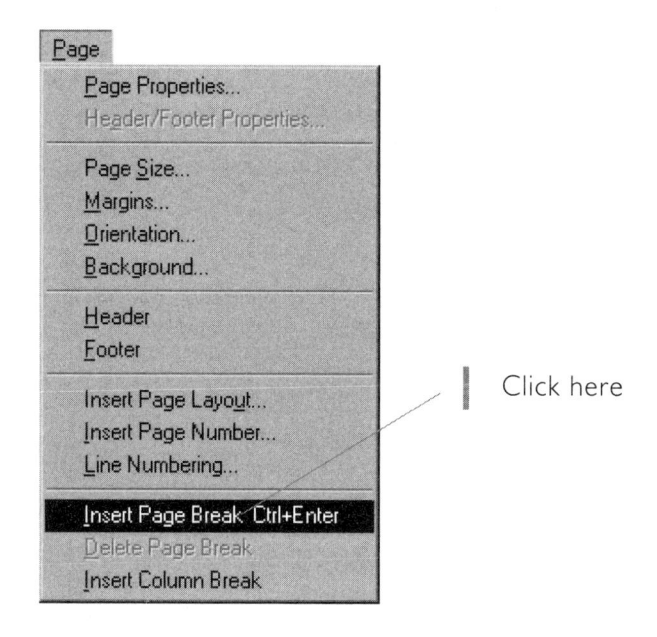

| Click here

The keyboard route
Position the insertion point at the location following which you want the new page to be inserted. Then simply press:

Ctrl+Return

or

Ctrl+Enter

Page styles – an overview

Styles are named collections of associated formatting commands. Word Pro makes extensive use of styles in all areas, but particularly when it comes to text and page formatting.

> **HANDY TIP**
>
> See chapter 6 for how to use text-based styles.

The advantage of using styles is that you can apply more than one formatting enhancement in one go. In terms of page formatting, you can apply any or all of the formatting changes we've discussed in earlier topics in the space of a few mouse clicks.

Once a page style is in place, you can easily change one or more elements of it; Word Pro implements the changes automatically.

You can have Word Pro apply page styles:

- throughout the whole of the active document, or;

- (if you insert a new page layout – see pages 108–110) from the point of insertion onwards.

Both methods result in an enormous saving in time and effort.

New (blank) documents you create in Word Pro contain only one pre-defined page style:

Default Page — applies default page formatting (e.g. the paper size/orientation is A4 Portrait and left, right, top and bottom margins of 2.54cm apply)

The same applies to documents created with the help of SmartMasters, except that different formatting may apply. For example, one of Word Pro's Newsletter SmartMasters applies A4 Portrait but varies the margin settings appropriately...

You can easily create (and apply) your own page styles.

Creating a page style

Creating a page style is a simple, three-stage process of:

A. applying the appropriate page formatting enhancements;

B. clicking in any page, and then;

C. telling Word Pro to save this formatting as a page style.

First, carry out A–B above. Then pull down the Page menu and click Page Properties. Now do the following:

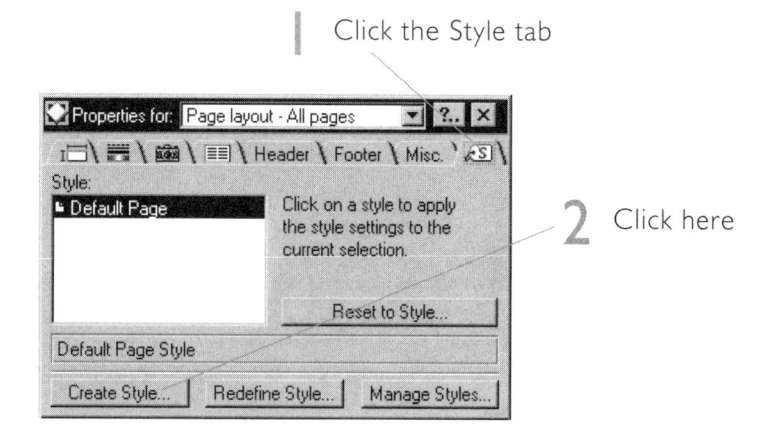

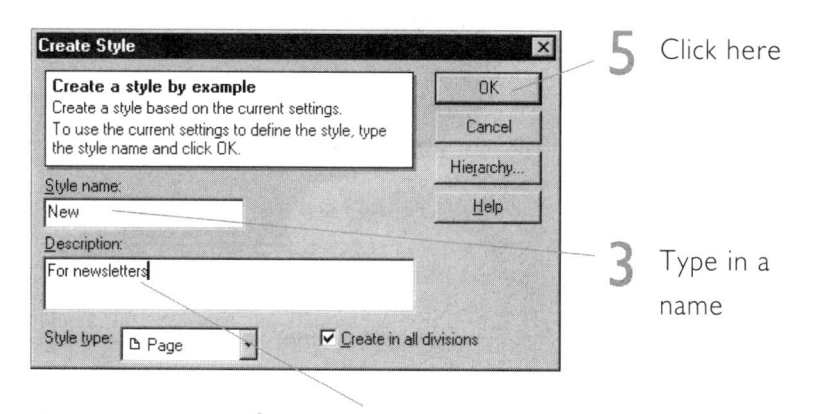

1 Click the Style tab

2 Click here

5 Click here

3 Type in a name

4 (Optional) Type in a description

See 'Applying a page style' on the following page for how to use your new style.

Applying a page style

Word Pro makes applying page styles easy.

REMEMBER

If you want to restrict the effect of applying a style to part of the active document, see page 110.

To apply the style to the whole of the active document, first pull down the Page menu and do the following:

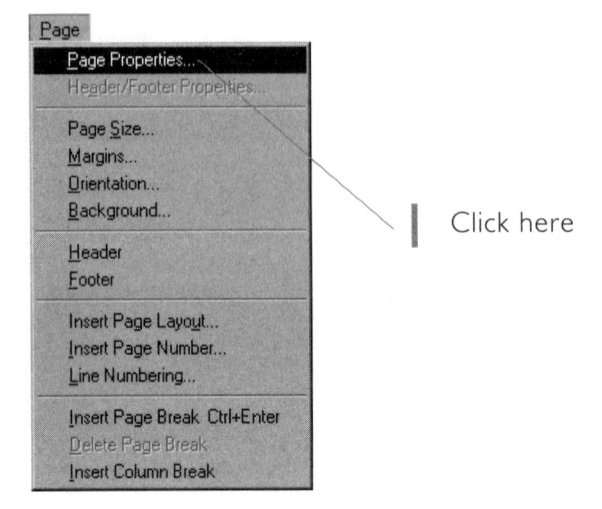

1 Click here

2 Click the Style tab

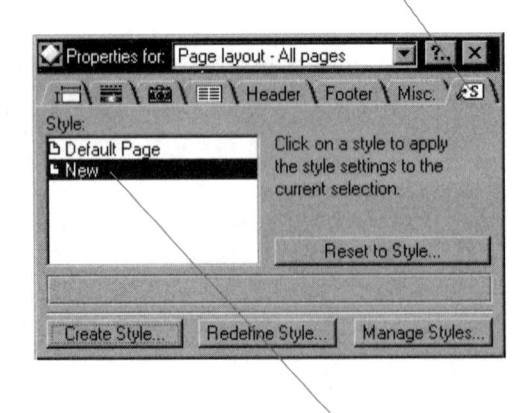

3 Click a style to apply it

Amending a page style

The easiest way to modify an existing page style is to:

A. right-click a page to which the style you want to amend has been applied;

B. choose Page Properties in the shortcut menu;

C. use the Page Properties Infobox to apply the appropriate formatting enhancements (see earlier topics for how to do this), and then;

D. tell Word Pro to redefine the associated style based on your amendments.

First, carry out A–C above. Then do the following:

> **HANDY TIP**
>
> **When you redefine a style, all other instances of the style in the open document are automatically updated accordingly.**

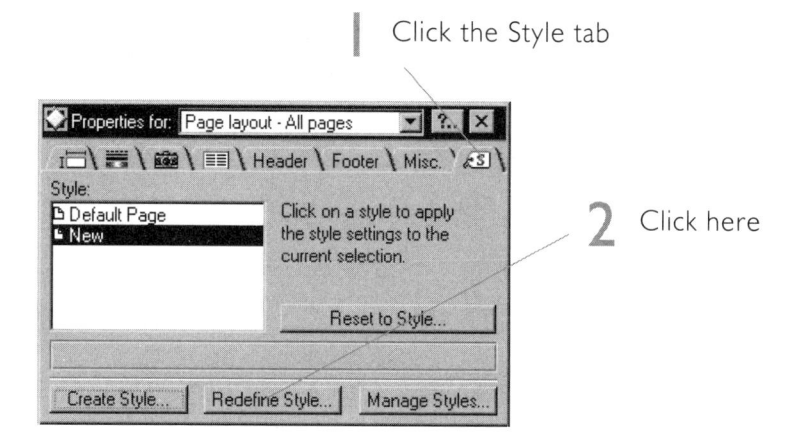

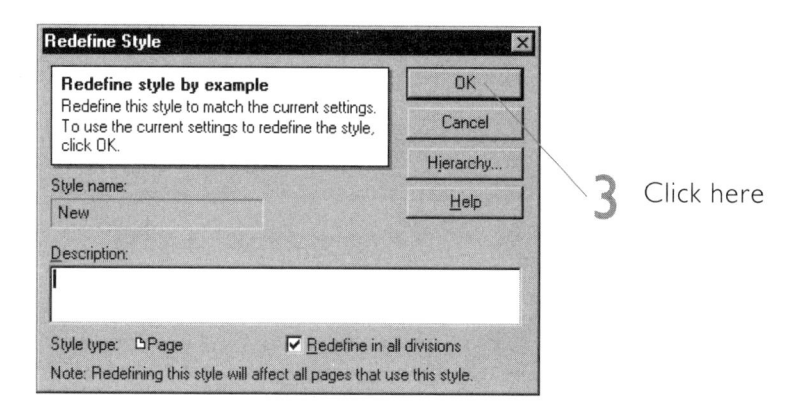

1 Click the Style tab

2 Click here

3 Click here

5 Page Formatting **103**

Page style management

Good housekeeping means that you will sometimes need to remove unwanted page styles. Word Pro lets you do this very easily. You can also copy page styles from document to document, or rename them.

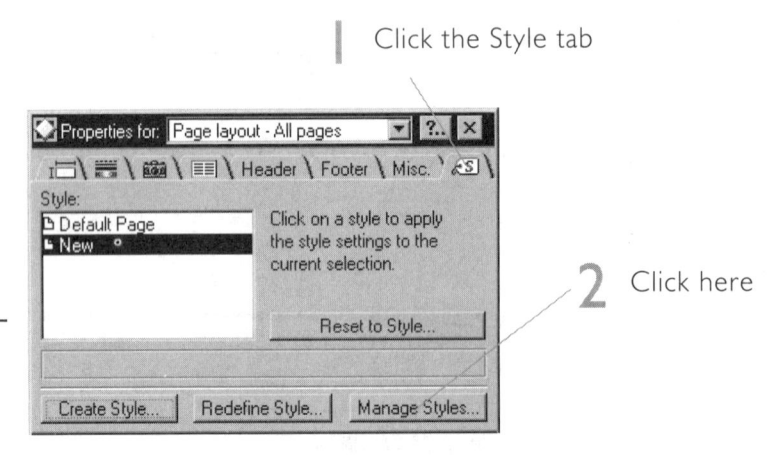

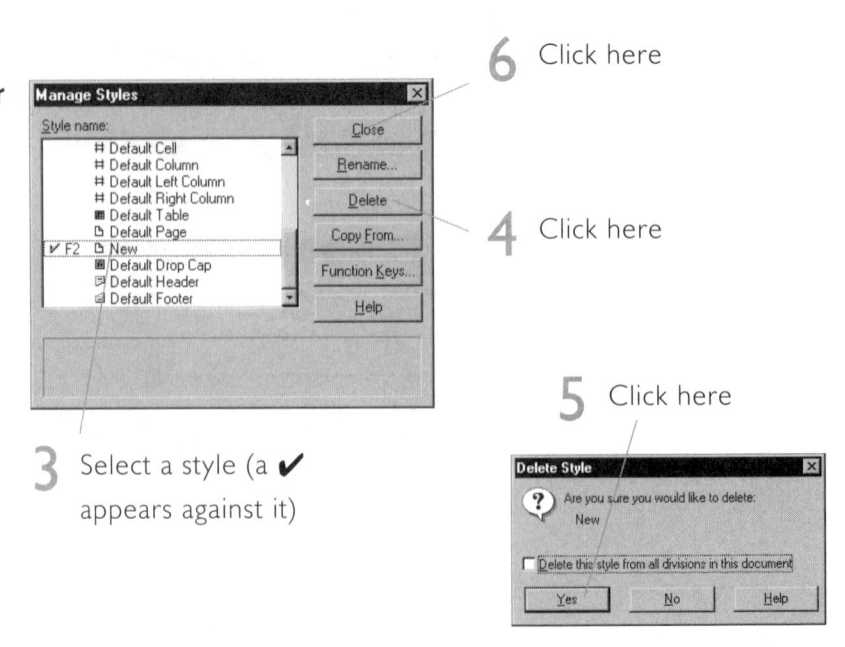

Deleting page styles

Pull down the Page menu and click Page Properties. Now do the following:

HANDY TIP — **You can delete more than one style at a time. Simply repeat step 3 as often as required, then follow steps 4–6 as normal.**

1 Click the Style tab

2 Click here

REMEMBER — **You can tell page styles from other style types: they're preceded by this icon:**

6 Click here

4 Click here

3 Select a style (a ✔ appears against it)

5 Click here

104 Word Pro in easy steps

Copying page styles

You can copy page styles from a SmartMaster or another Word Pro document into the current document.

Pull down the Page menu and click Page Properties. Now carry out the following steps:

REMEMBER

To rename a page style, follow steps 1–2. In the 'Style name:' field in the Manage Styles dialog, select the relevant page style. Click this button:

Rename...

Complete the Rename Style dialog. Finally, click OK and follow step 8.

1 Click the Style tab

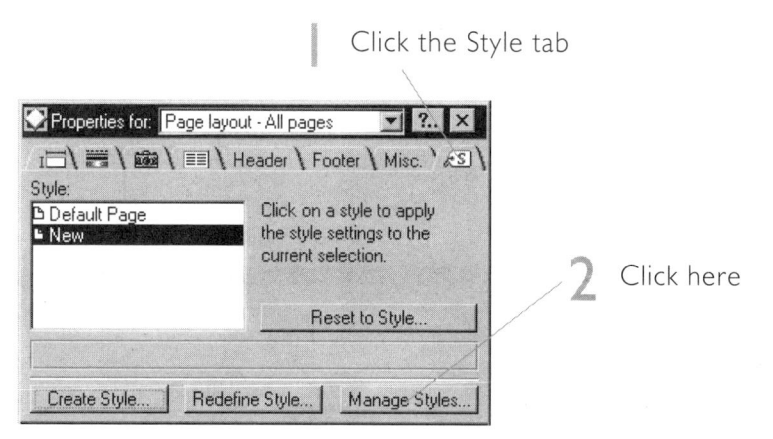

2 Click here

8 Click here

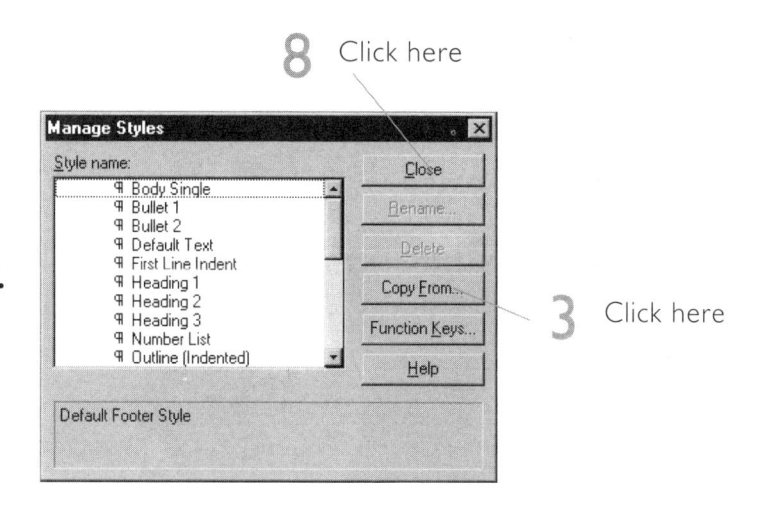

REMEMBER

See page 106 for steps 4–7.

3 Click here

5 Page Formatting **105**

...cont'd

4 Click here

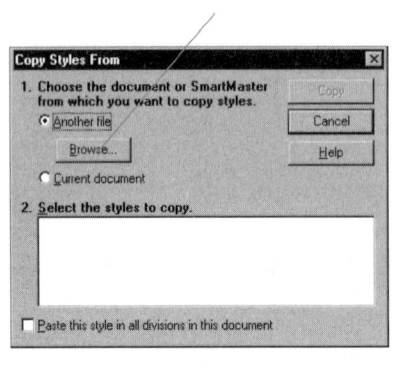

Re step 7 – if the page style you're copying has the same name as a page style which already exists in the document you're copying it into, Word Pro launches a special message. Do one of the following:

5 Double-click a SmartMaster or another Word Pro document

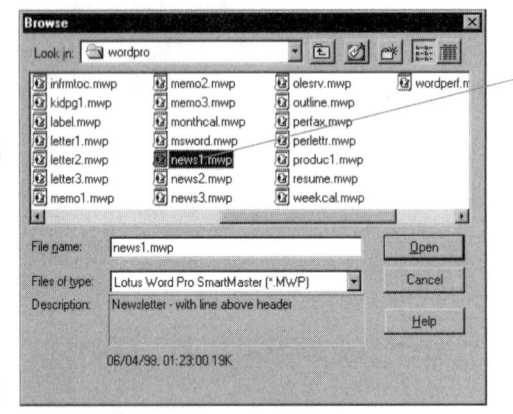

A Click here (and complete the dialog which launches) to apply a new name to the copied style

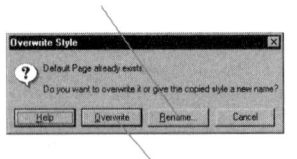

7 Click here

B Click here to overwrite the original page style

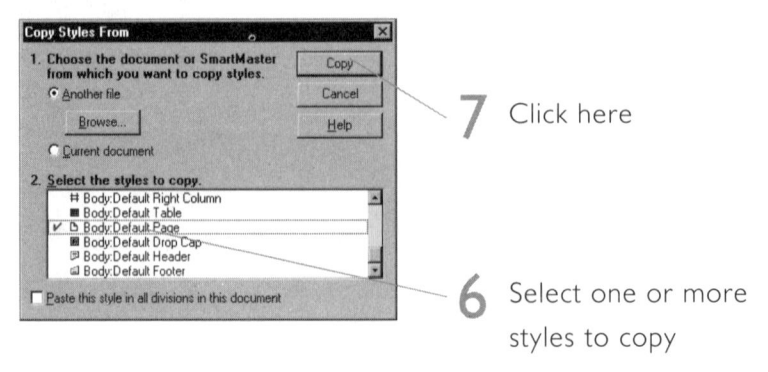

6 Select one or more styles to copy

Now carry out step 8 on page 105.

Using function keys with page styles

You can assign function keys to page styles, so that they can be applied with just a single keystroke.

Assigning a function key to a page style

Pull down the Page menu and click Page Properties. Now carry out the following steps:

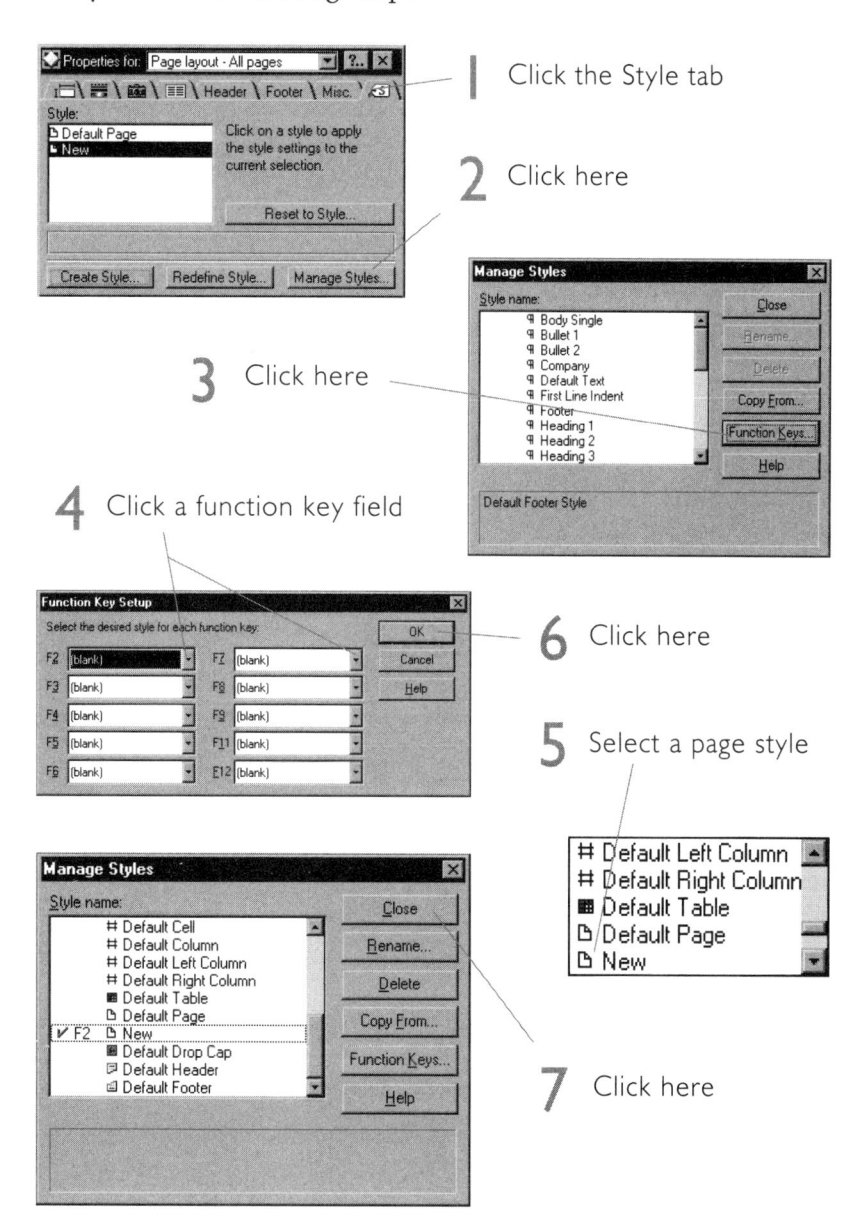

1 Click the Style tab

2 Click here

3 Click here

4 Click a function key field

6 Click here

5 Select a page style

7 Click here

REMEMBER **Repeat steps 4–5 for as many function keys as you want allocated to page styles.** Then carry out steps 6–7.

REMEMBER **In the example shown here, the** F2 **function key is being assigned to the** New **page style.**

5 Page Formatting **107**

Page layouts – an overview

The page layout/formatting changes described in earlier topics in this chapter apply to the whole of the active Word Pro document. If, however, you only want the changes to apply to the current and subsequent pages, you need to insert a new page layout.

When you insert a new page layout, the following happens:

1. Word Pro uses the original default page layout settings until it encounters the new page layout you've inserted.

2. When it encounters the new page layout, Word Pro inserts a manual page break and applies the new settings from that point onwards.

3. If and when Word Pro encounters another inserted page layout, *these* new settings apply.

And so on.

When you insert a new page layout, you can do one of two things. You can:

- opt to edit the page layout after insertion, using the techniques discussed in earlier topics and principally using the Page Properties Infobox (see page 109), or;

- apply a page style you've created with the techniques discussed on page 101 (see page 110).

Inserting a new page layout

The insert-and-edit route

To insert a new page layout and edit it immediately, first position the insertion point at the location from which you want the new page formatting to apply. Pull down the Page menu and carry out these steps:

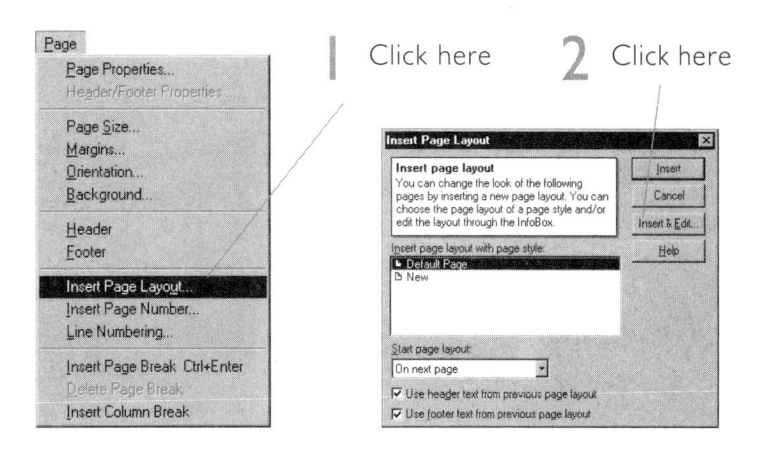

1 Click here

2 Click here

Word Pro now creates a new page and launches the Page Layout Infobox:

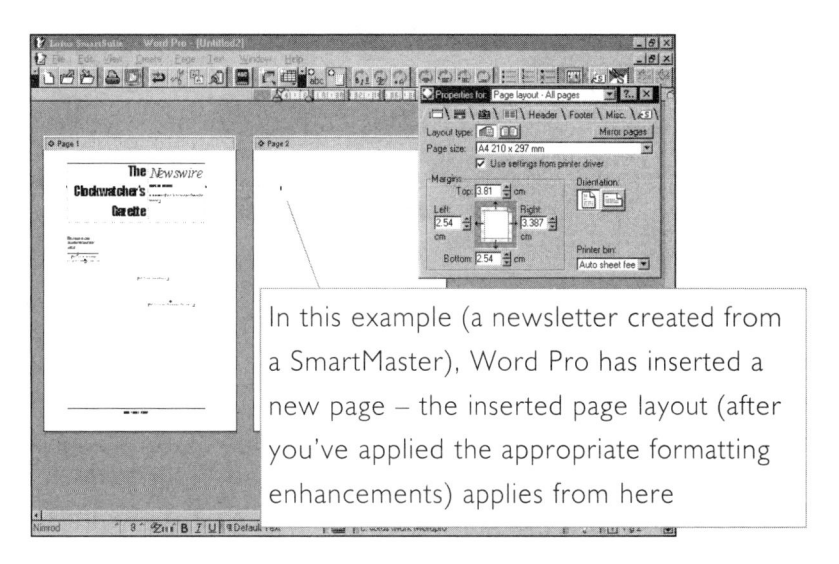

In this example (a newsletter created from a SmartMaster), Word Pro has inserted a new page – the inserted page layout (after you've applied the appropriate formatting enhancements) applies from here

Use the Infobox to amend the page formatting in the usual way (utilising the techniques discussed in earlier topics).

...cont'd

The insert-and-apply-a-new-style route

To insert a new page layout and apply a page style to it, do the following.

First, position the insertion point at the location from which you want the new page formatting to apply. Pull down the Page menu and carry out these steps:

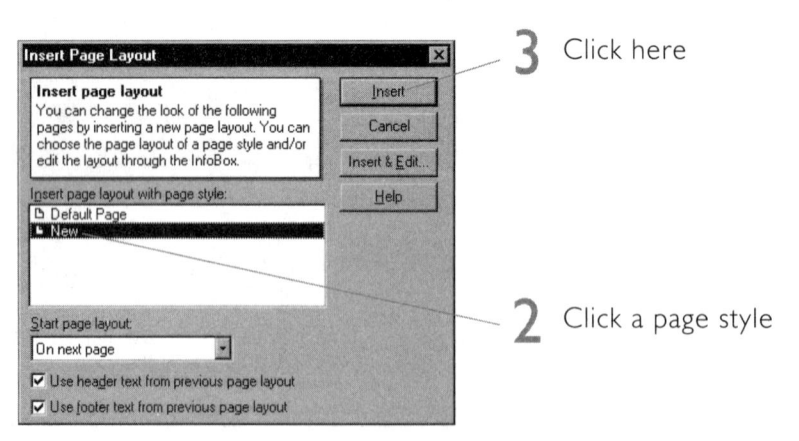

1 Click here

3 Click here

2 Click a page style

Word Pro now creates a new page and applies the new page style to it (and to subsequent pages).

Text Styles

Chapter Six

This chapter shows you how to save a lot of time and effort by working with text styles (collections of associated formatting). You'll create your own text styles, then apply them to text. Then you'll reverse the process by altering text formatting and using the changes to redefine existing styles. Finally, you'll learn to copy, delete and rename text styles, and assign function keys to them so they can be launched even more easily.

Covers

Text styles – an overview | 112

Creating text styles | 114

Applying text styles | 115

Amending text styles | 118

Text style management | 119

Copying text styles | 120

Renaming text styles | 122

Using function keys with text styles | 123

Text styles – an overview

See chapter 5 for how to use page-based styles.

Styles are named collections of associated formatting commands. Word Pro makes extensive use of styles in all areas, but particularly when it comes to text and page formatting.

The advantage of using styles is that you can apply more than one formatting enhancement in one go. In terms of text formatting, you can apply any or all of the formatting changes we discussed in chapter 4 in the space of a few mouse clicks.

Once a text style is in place, you can easily change one or more elements of it; Word Pro implements the changes automatically.

Styles in action

As an admittedly simple example, you might have a large document which uses several quite distinct typefaces. The overall heading might use a display font such as Helvetica, while the main bulk of the text (the 'body text') might well be in a variant of Times. Subheadings could well have yet another font, or one of the existing fonts in a different type size. All the typefaces used would have their own type size...

This is the overall heading

This is a sub-heading
This is body text. Notice the difference in typefaces and type sizes. Each of these components:

- The overall heading - title HEADING 1
- The sub-heading - title HEADING 2
- The body text - title DEFAULT TEXT

is a separate text style, with its own individual formatting.

A very simple document with 3 styles

...cont'd

Another aspect of text styles is the split into Paragraph and Character styles.

As a general rule, use paragraph styles to apply block formatting to headings, subheadings and/or body text. Then, if you want to apply localised changes to specific text, consider applying a character style instead of simply altering the formatting in the normal way.

In terms of content, paragraph styles can contain (in addition to information about text appearance):

- alignment, tab and indent information;
- bullets, and;
- border information.

Document text styles

Below is a list of the principal text styles found in new (blank) documents:

Body Single	–	used for text which forms the body of a document
Default Text	–	ditto
Bullet 1 and *Bullet 2*	–	creates bulleted lists
Heading 1	–	used for headings
Heading 2	–	ditto (but smaller)
Heading 3	–	ditto (even smaller)
Title	–	a bold heading
Number List	–	creates automatically numbered lists
First Line Indent	–	automatically applies a preset paragraph indent

Other SmartMasters/templates have many more preset styles. (Some are context-dependent, e.g. the Newsletter SmartMasters have a text style which formats illustration captions.)

You can easily create (and apply) your own styles.

Creating text styles

Creating a text style is a simple, three-stage process of:

A. applying the appropriate formatting enhancements to specific text;

B. clicking in the text (or selecting it), and then;

C. telling Word Pro to save this formatting as a text style.

First, carry out A–B above. Then pull down the Text menu and click Text Properties. Now do the following:

1 Click the Style tab

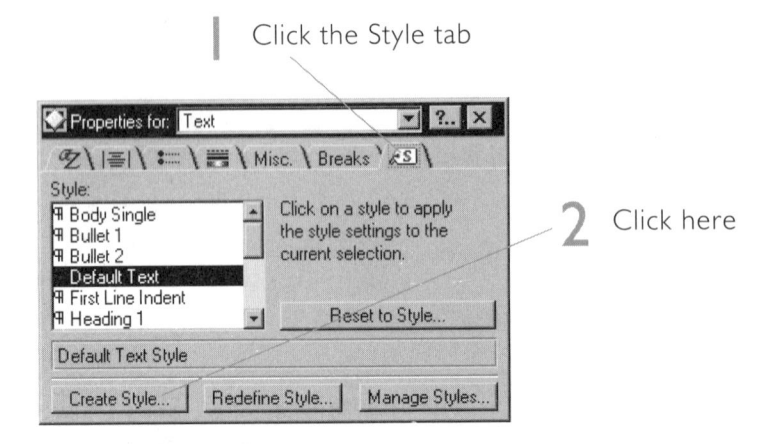

2 Click here

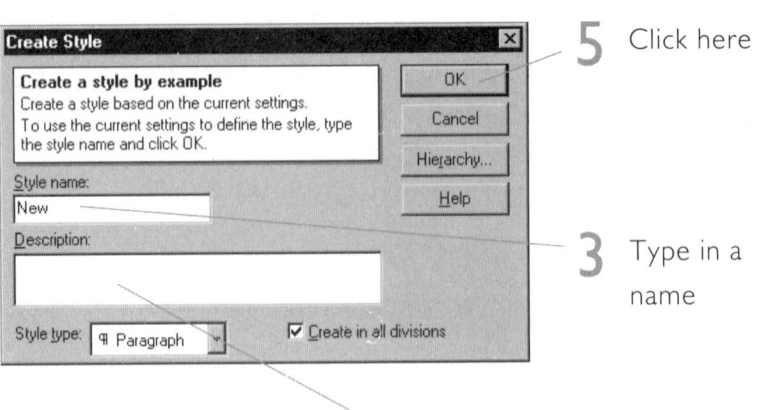

3 Type in a name

4 (Optional) Type in a description

5 Click here

HANDY TIP **If you want to create a character (as opposed to a paragraph) style, click the arrow to the right of the 'Style type' field; select Character in the drop-down list.**

See 'Applying a text style' on the following page for how to use your new style.

Applying text styles

Word Pro makes applying text styles easy. You can use the following methods:

- the Text Properties Infobox;
- the Style button on the Status bar, or;
- 'cycling'.

The Infobox route

First, select the text you want to apply the style to. Or, if you only want to apply it to a single paragraph, place the insertion point inside it. Pull down the Text menu and do the following:

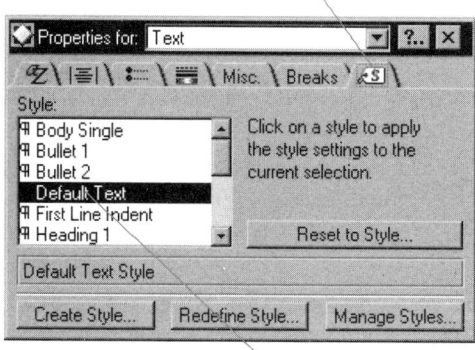

1 Click here

2 Click the Style tab

3 Click a style to apply it

Text Styles

...cont'd

The Style button route

First, select the text you want to apply the style to. Or, if you only want to apply it to a single paragraph, place the insertion point inside it. Refer to the Style button in the Status bar at the base of the Word Pro screen and carry out the following steps:

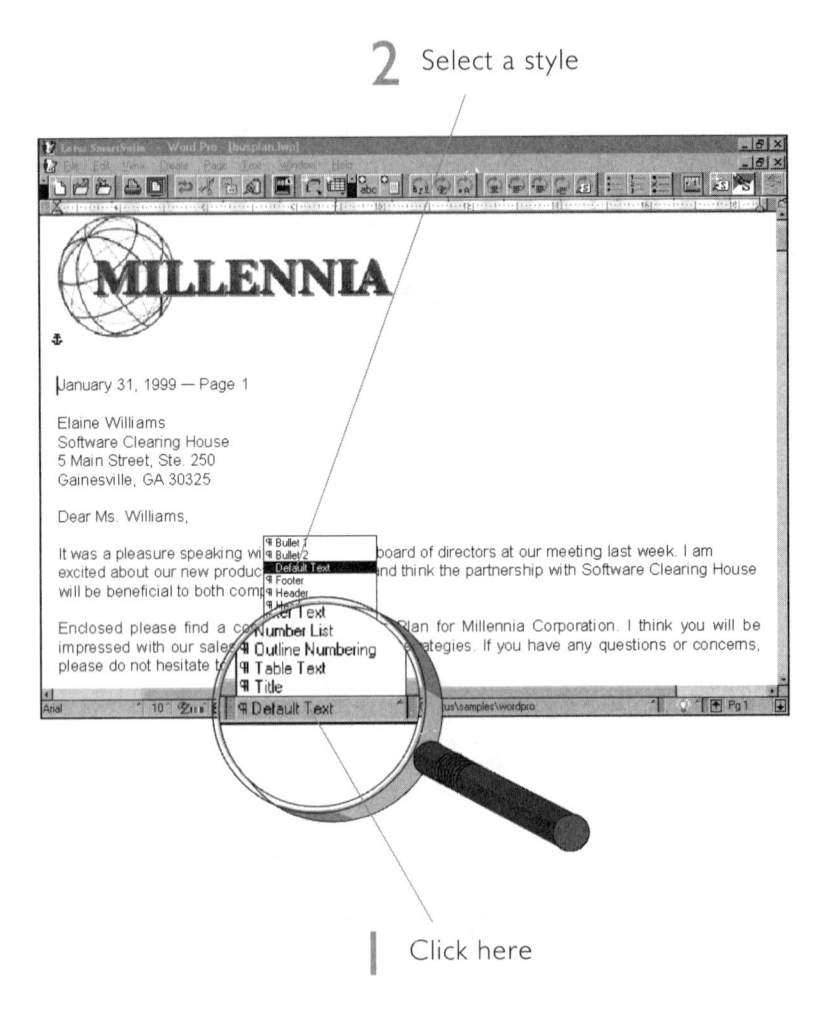

2 Select a style

1 Click here

...cont'd

BEWARE — **The SmartIcon flagged here is not normally present in the Text SmartIcon bar.**

To add it, follow the relevant procedures on page 14.

REMEMBER — **In this example, both the Universal and Text SmartIcon bars are on-screen.**

This may not be the case on your system.

The SmartIcon route

First, select the text you want to apply the style to. Or, if you only want to apply it to a single paragraph, place the insertion point inside it. Refer to the Text SmartIcon bar and do the following:

Click here repeatedly to step up through available text styles, one by one

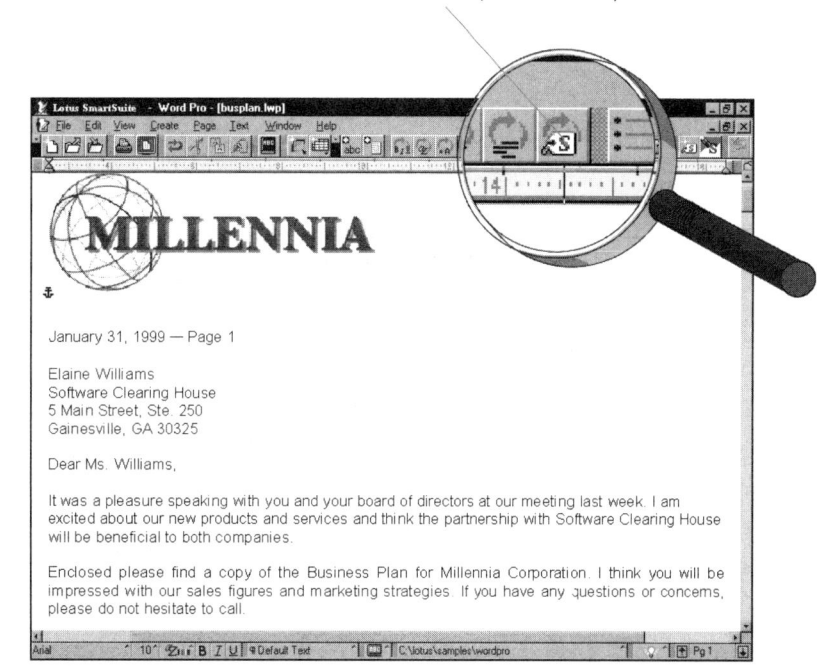

6 Text Styles 117

Amending text styles

The easiest way to modify an existing text style is to:

HANDY TIP

When you redefine a text style, all other instances of the style in the open document are automatically updated accordingly.

A. right-click text which has the style you want to amend;

B. choose Text Properties in the shortcut menu;

C. use the Text Properties Infobox to apply the appropriate formatting enhancements (see chapter 4 for how to do this), and then;

D. tell Word Pro to redefine the associated text style based on your amendments.

First, carry out A–C above. Then do the following:

1 Click the Style tab

2 Click here

3 Click here

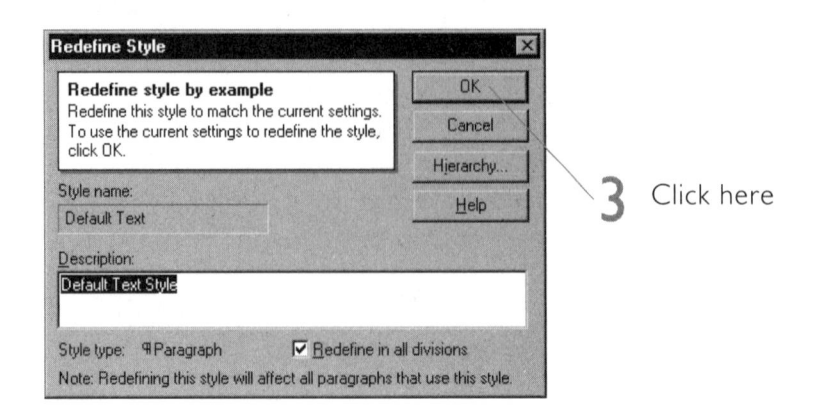

118 Word Pro in easy steps

Text style management

Good housekeeping means you will sometimes need to remove unwanted text styles. Word Pro lets you do this very easily. You can also copy text styles from document to document, and rename text styles.

Deleting text styles

Pull down the Text menu and click Text Properties. Now do the following:

1 Click the Style tab

HANDY TIP **You can delete more than one style at a time.** Simply repeat step 3 as often as required, then follow steps 4–6 as normal.

2 Click here

REMEMBER **You can tell text styles from other style types: they're preceded by either of these icons:**

- Character style
- Paragraph style

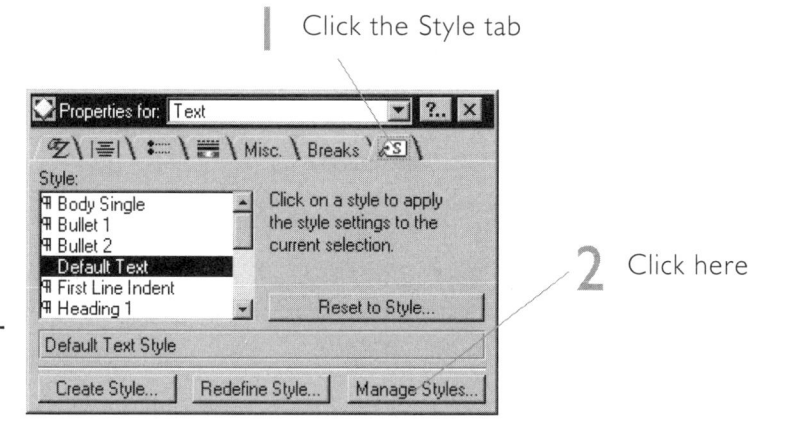

6 Click here

4 Click here

3 Select a style (a ✔ appears against it)

5 Click here

6 Text Styles **119**

Copying text styles

You can copy text styles from a SmartMaster or another Word Pro document into the current document.

Pull down the Text menu and click Text Properties. Now carry out the following steps:

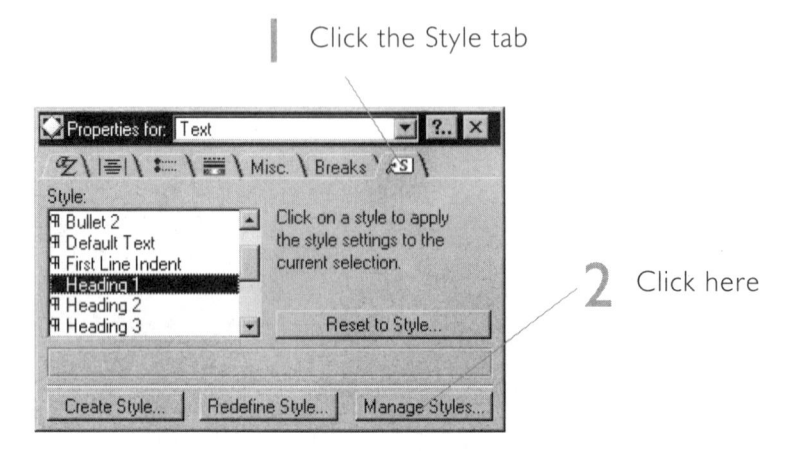

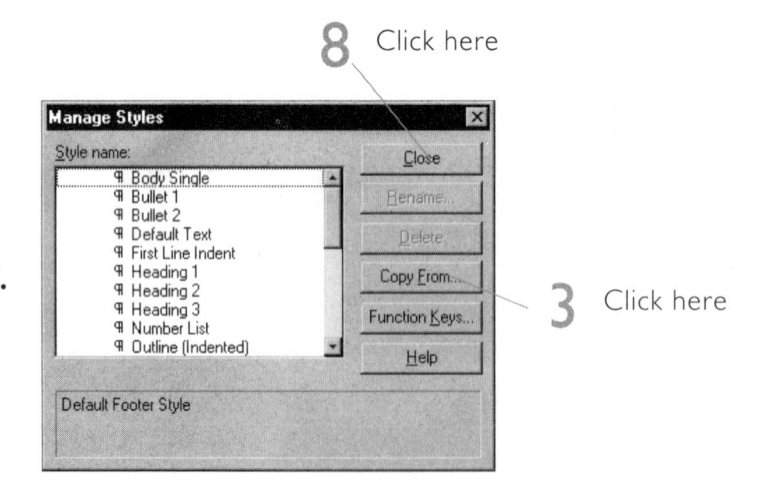

1 Click the Style tab

2 Click here

8 Click here

3 Click here

REMEMBER

See page 121 for steps 4-7.

...cont'd

HANDY TIP

Re step 5 – if you want to target a Word Pro document, select All Files (*.*) in the 'Files of type:' field. Then use the Browse dialog to locate it.

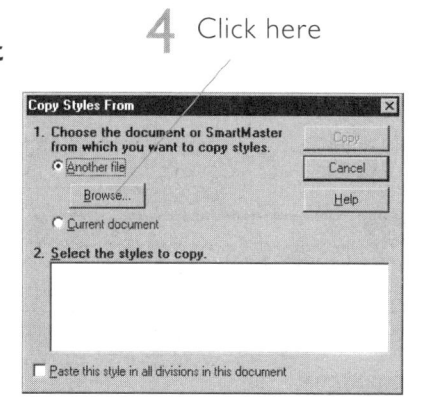

4 Click here

REMEMBER

Re step 7 – if the copied text style has the same name as a style in the document you're copying it into, Word Pro launches a special message. Do one of these:

A Click here (and complete the dialog which launches) to apply a new name to the copied style

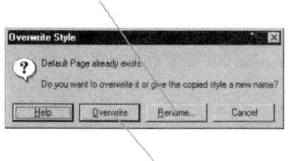

B Click here to overwrite the original text style

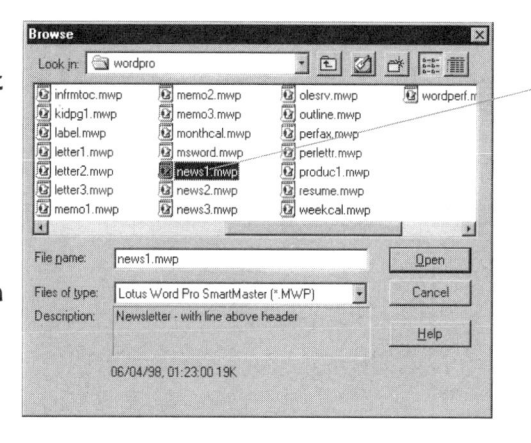

5 Double-click a SmartMaster or another Word Pro document

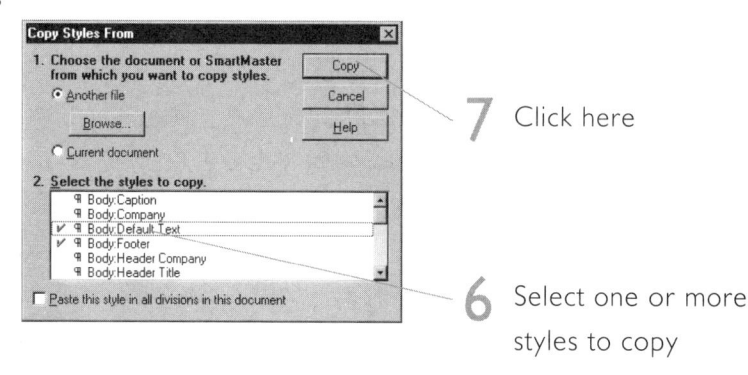

7 Click here

6 Select one or more styles to copy

Now carry out step 8 on page 120.

6 Text Styles

Renaming text styles

Pull down the Text menu and click Text Properties. Now carry out the following steps:

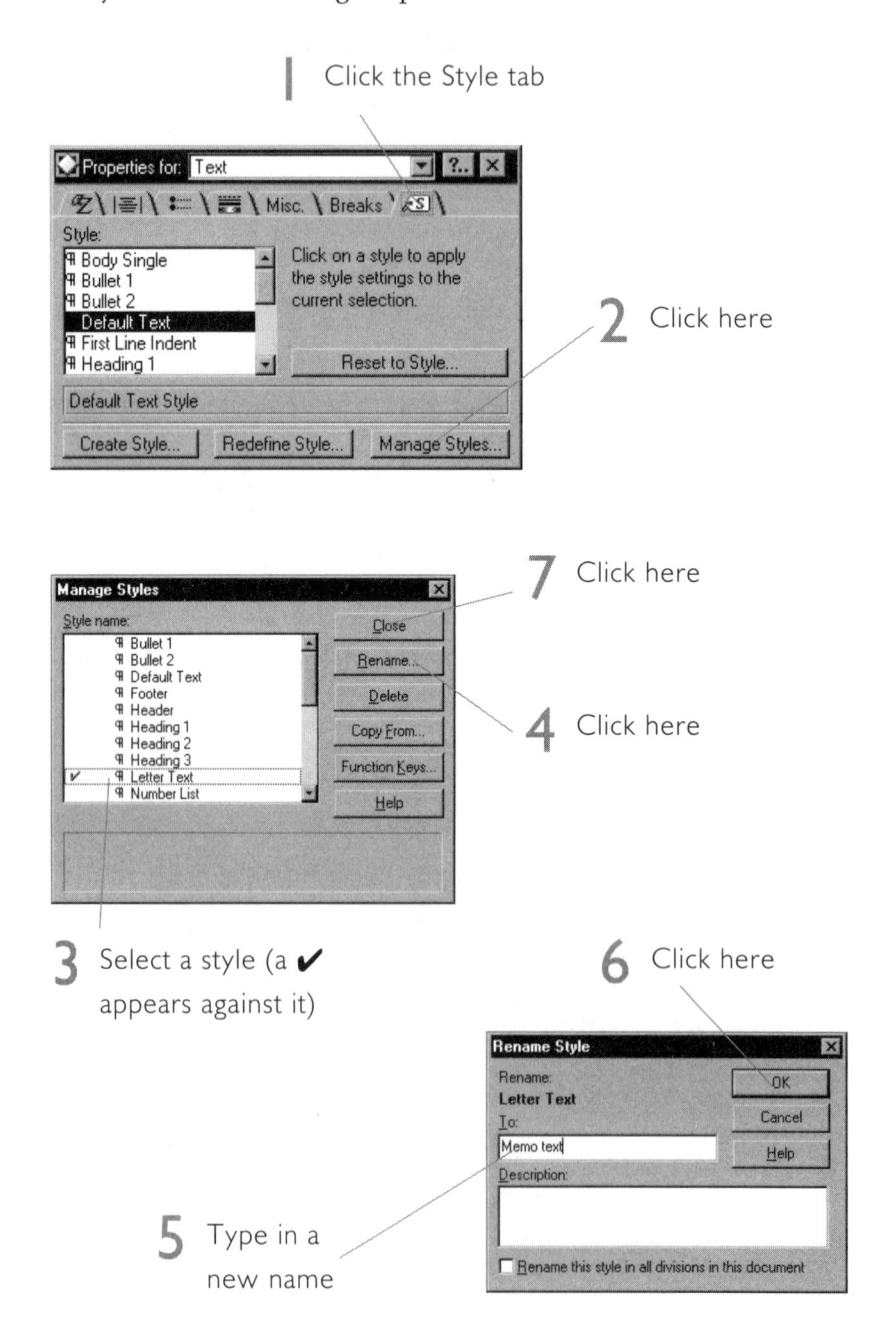

1 Click the Style tab

2 Click here

7 Click here

4 Click here

3 Select a style (a ✔ appears against it)

6 Click here

5 Type in a new name

Using function keys with text styles

You can assign function keys to text styles, so that they can be applied with just a single keystroke.

Assigning a function key to a text style

Pull down the Text menu and click Text Properties. Now carry out the following steps:

1 Click the Style tab

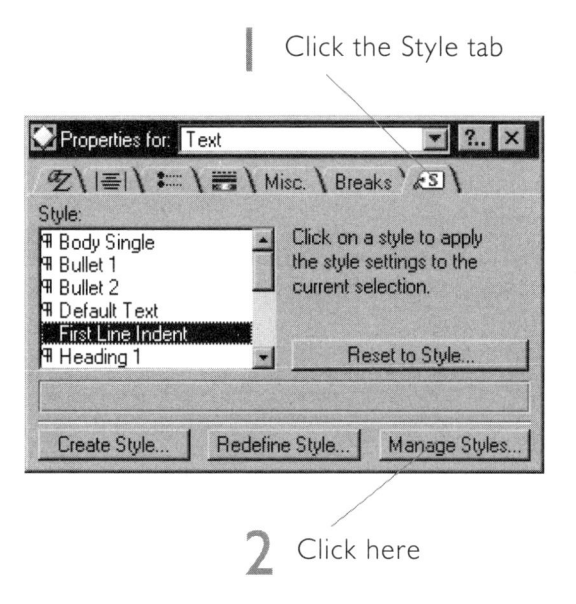

2 Click here

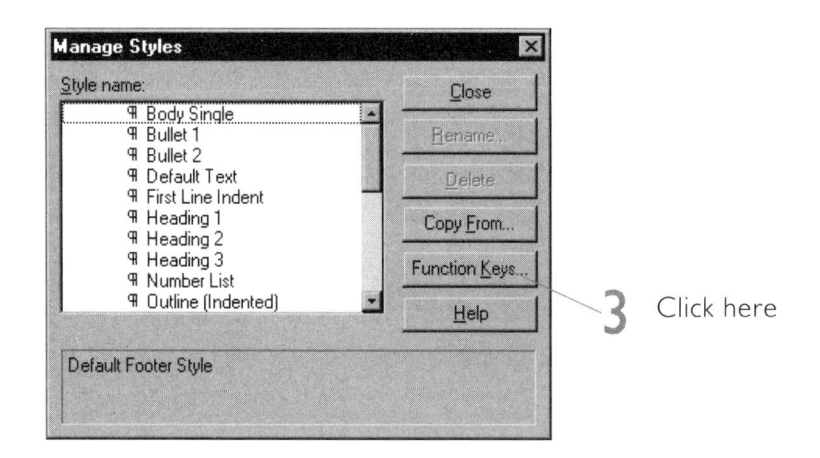

3 Click here

...cont'd

4 Click a function key field

Repeat steps 4-5 for as many function keys as you want allocated to text styles.

Then carry out steps 6-7.

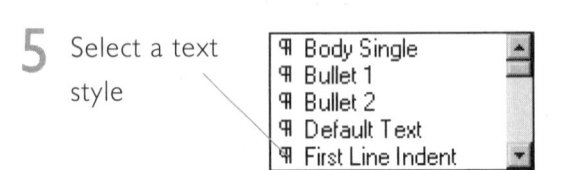

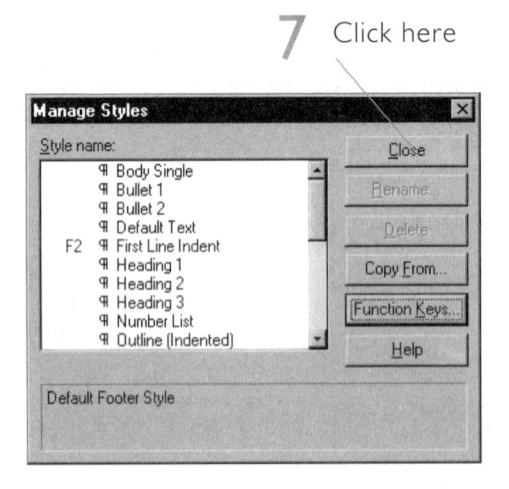

6 Click here

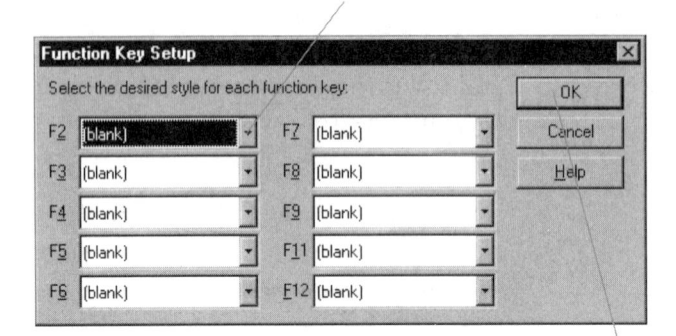

5 Select a text style

7 Click here

Proofing Tools

Chapter Seven

This chapter shows you how to verify documents you've created. You'll carry out spell- and grammar-checks (with the options you choose), and look up synonyms in Word Pro's Thesaurus. You'll use Check Format and SmartCorrect to correct common errors automatically. Finally, you'll mark up and review editing revisions, and work with multiple versions of files.

Covers

Proofing – an overview | 126

Spell-checking | 127

Customising spell-checks | 134

Using the Thesaurus | 139

Using the Grammar Checker | 141

Customising grammar-checks | 145

Using SmartCorrect | 147

Customising SmartCorrect | 150

Using Check Format | 152

Customising Check Format | 154

Tracking revisions | 155

Document versions | 157

Proofing – an overview

Word Pro lets you verify document text in the following ways:

- You can spell-check it on-the-fly (as you edit it), subsequently (after editing is complete) or both at the same time. Spell-check operations detect misspelled words, duplicated words (e.g. 'the the') and irregular capitalisations (e.g. 'hEllo').

- With the use of the inbuilt Thesaurus, you can have Word Pro suggest synonyms for a selected word. When you've chosen one, you can have it replace the original in your document.

- You can have Word Pro check the active document's grammar. You can specify:

    — the formality level;

    — which grammatical rules are used, and;

    — other features (e.g. whether split infinitives are flagged).

- You can use SmartCorrect to have Word Pro automatically correct previously defined errors as you work. For instance, if you consistently mistype words (e.g. 'ws' for 'was', or 'teh' for 'the') you can have SmartCorrect correct the errors automatically (when you press the Space Bar or Return/Enter key *immediately after* the incorrect word).

- You can inspect editing changes to your documents (Word Pro calls these mark-ups) and decide whether to accept or reject them.

- You can have Word Pro save previous versions of documents within the original file – the result is fewer files and more free hard disk space.

REMEMBER

Word Pro's spell- and grammar-check operations are highly customisable.

Spell-checking – an overview

You can use two principal methods to spell-check a document:

- background checking (or checking on-the-fly), or;
- independent checking after editing is complete.

Whichever method you use, Word Pro uses the same basic methodology. Words in the document can be referred to the following:

- Any appropriate user dictionaries. User dictionaries have the suffix: .UDC. The default user dictionary is LTSUSER1.UDC.
- A large dictionary called LOTUSEN3.DIC (or something similar).

You can create and use as many user dictionaries as you need. Generally, of course, you won't need many, but you might like to create them for:

- specific documents, or;
- specific work areas (for instance, if you're involved with legal documentation you could create a user dictionary containing legal terms).

When a spell-check operation (of either sort) highlights a word which is correct but currently unrecognised as such, you tell Word Pro to add it to the current user dictionary. In this way, whenever the words are encountered again, in whatever documents, they're automatically recognised. The large dictionary, on the other hand, is inviolate: it contains most of the words against which documents are checked, but can't be edited under any circumstances.

Alternatively, you can simply 'skip' flagged words, so that they're ignored now but not in future editing sessions.

Spell-checking on-the-fly

Spell-checking text as you go, rather than in one all-inclusive operation when editing is complete, is a very useful feature in Word Pro.

When on-the-fly spell-checking is in force, Word Pro does two things:

- It flags words it doesn't recognise (i.e. which aren't in its various dictionaries). It does this by highlighting them.

- The Spell-Check button in the Status bar displays a question mark.

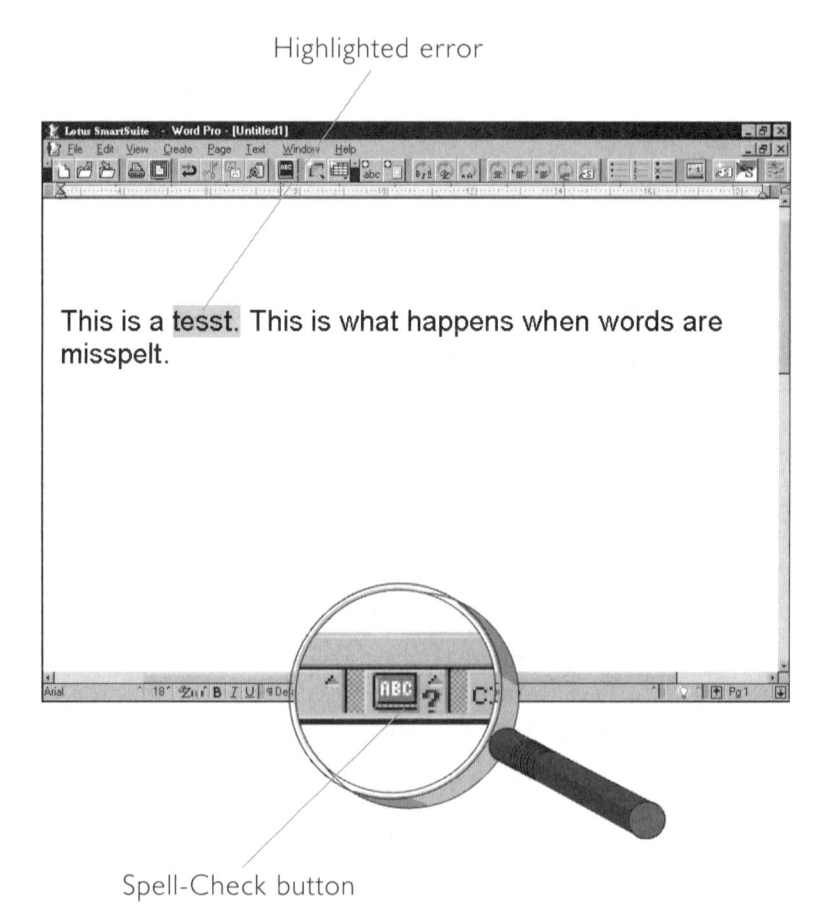

Highlighted error

This is a tesst. This is what happens when words are misspelt.

Spell-Check button

128 Word Pro in easy steps

...cont'd

Enabling background spell-checking

Pull down the File menu and do the following:

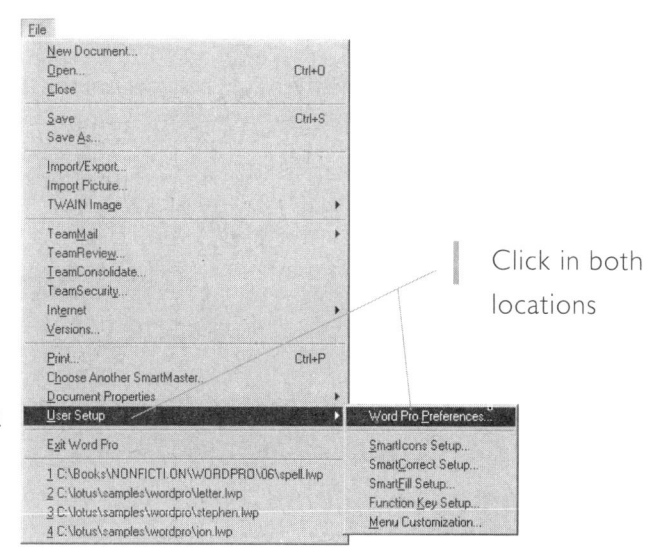

REMEMBER To ensure on-the-fly checking works properly, you may also have to carry out another procedure.

Pull down the View menu and click Set View Preferences. In the View Preferences dialog, ensure the Show tab is active. Make sure 'Show misspelled words' is ticked. Click OK.

1 Click in both locations

2 Click here

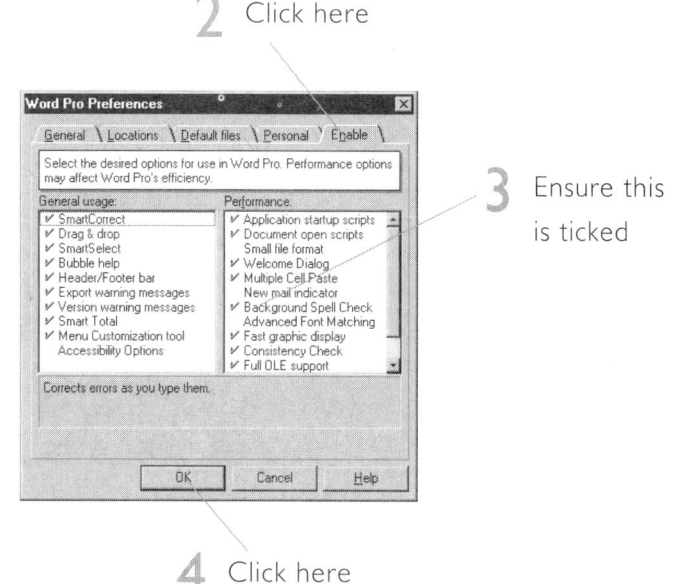

3 Ensure this is ticked

HANDY TIP Repeat steps 1–4 to turn off on-the-fly checking (but ensure – in step 3 – that the tick disappears).

4 Click here

7 Proofing Tools **129**

...cont'd

REMEMBER **See page 128 for the location of the Spell-Check button.**

Using background spell-checking

With on-the-fly spell-checking in operation, Word Pro flags suspect words just after you've typed them. At any point in your editing of the active document, do the following.

Click the Spell-Check button in the Status bar. Now carry out step 1 OR 2 below (additionally, see the HANDY TIP):

2 If the flagged word is correct, click Add to Dictionary to store it in the relevant User dictionary

HANDY TIP **You can also click back in your document and amend errors manually.**

HANDY TIP **Re steps 1 and 2 – there are two further choices you can make:**

- *'Skip'* – ignores the current instance only of the flagged word
- *'Skip All'* – ignores all instances of the flagged word (but only in the current document)

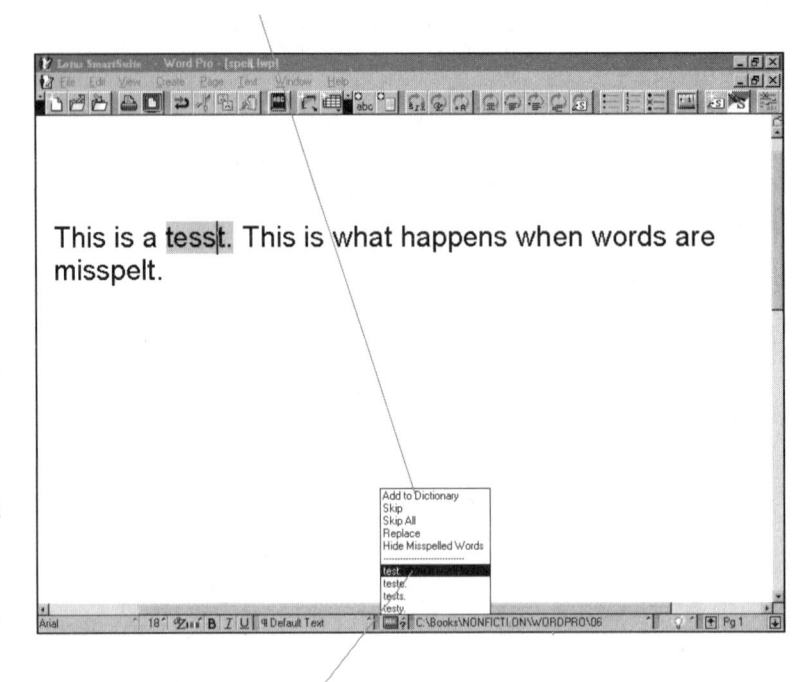

If the flagged word is incorrect and the correct word is shown here, click it; the correct version replaces the original in the document

130 Word Pro in easy steps

Spell-checking after editing

REMEMBER — **There are more available options in checking after editing, too.**

In some ways, running a complete spell-check when document editing has been finalised can be more convenient: the alternative, background checking, is sometimes rather distracting, especially in a large document.

Launching a separate spell-check

Pull down the Edit menu and do the following:

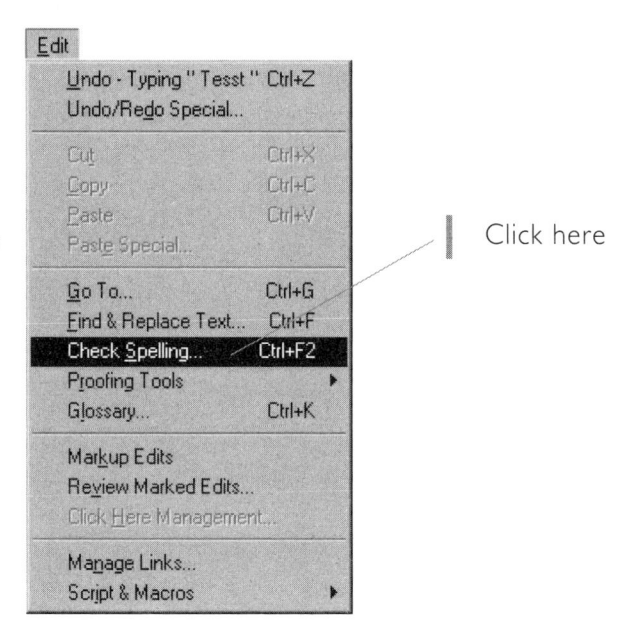

HANDY TIP — **If you only want to spell-check a part of the active document, select it before you follow step 1.**

Click here

REMEMBER — **You can even edit a document with the Spell-Check bar on-screen and active; this provides access to more spell-checking options than on-the-fly spell checking.**

Word Pro now launches its inbuilt Spell-Checker. By default, it begins checking text immediately, starting from the beginning of the document and working steadily through to the end. See page 132 for what to do next.

(Note that it's perfectly possible to have background spell-checking active AND carry out an independent spell-checking operation at the same time.)

7 Proofing Tools **131**

...cont'd

When you follow step 4, the flagged word is stored in user dictionary LTSUSER1.DOC and recognised in future checking sessions.

Re step 1 – if the flagged word isn't correct and Word Pro's suggestions are also wrong, type in the correct version in the 'Replace with' field. Then carry out step 2 or 3.

**If you want to close the Spell-Check bar before the check is complete, click the Done button.
Failing this, simply follow the on-screen instructions.**

Word Pro now launches its Spell-Check bar, highlights all words it doesn't recognise within the current document and takes you to the first (flagged with a different colour). Usually, it provides alternative suggestions; if one of these is correct, you can opt to have it replace the flagged word. You can do this singly (i.e. just this instance is replaced) or globally (where all future instances – within the current checking session – are replaced).

Alternatively, you can have Word Pro:

- ignore *this* instance of the flagged word and resume checking;

- ignore *all* future instances of the word and resume checking, or;

- add the word to your personal dictionary and resume checking.

Carry out step 1 below (if Word Pro has produced a viable suggestion), then follow step 2 or 3. Alternatively, perform any one of steps 4, 5 and 6.

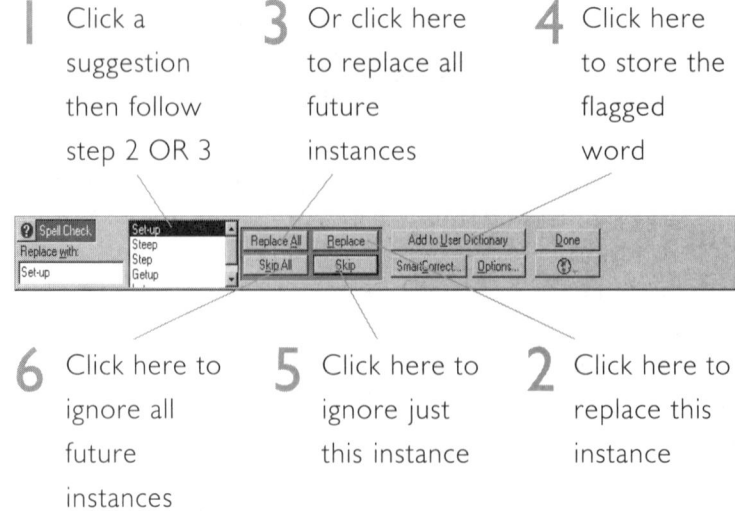

1 Click a suggestion then follow step 2 OR 3

3 Or click here to replace all future instances

4 Click here to store the flagged word

6 Click here to ignore all future instances

5 Click here to ignore just this instance

2 Click here to replace this instance

132 Word Pro in easy steps

Spell-check options – an overview

When you carry out a spell-check after editing is complete (see pages 131–132), certain defaults apply:

- The spell-check is initiated immediately; no confirmation is required from the user.

- Word Pro begins checking from the beginning of the relevant document (irrespective of where the insertion point was located when you initiated the spell-check) and works through it to the end. This does not apply if you selected text before launching the spell-check; in this case, the check is restricted to the specified text.

- Words with numbers are included in the check. For example, 'hel60' would be flagged. Normally, this is desirable, but there are occasions when it isn't. For example, the computer industry often uses combinations of names and numbers which aren't separated by spaces (FAT32, 80486DX2, i486...).

- Duplicated words (e.g. 'and and') are flagged.

- Incorrect capitalisations (for instance, words with capitals in the middle) are flagged. Also, Word Pro checks words which began with capitals.

- Word Pro may not be set up to look up flagged words in a user dictionary. You can, however, enable this feature if you want.

- If the use of a user dictionary is enabled, the default dictionary used is LTSUSER1.DOC.

Many of these defaults can be changed. For instance, you can create your own user dictionaries, if you want, and then force Word Pro to use one or more of these, or you can stop Word Pro from checking words which begin with capitals.

Customising spell-checks

Setting general spell-check options
Pull down the Edit menu and do the following:

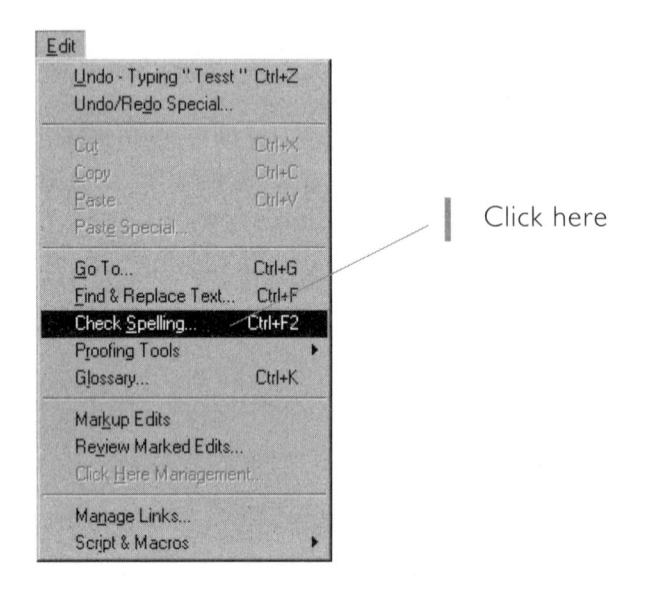

Click here

2 Click here

You can customise the way an independent spell-check works.

...cont'd

3 Select or deselect the relevant option(s)

HANDY TIP **Re step 3 – if you select 'Include user dictionary alternatives', apply the relevant dictionaries here:**

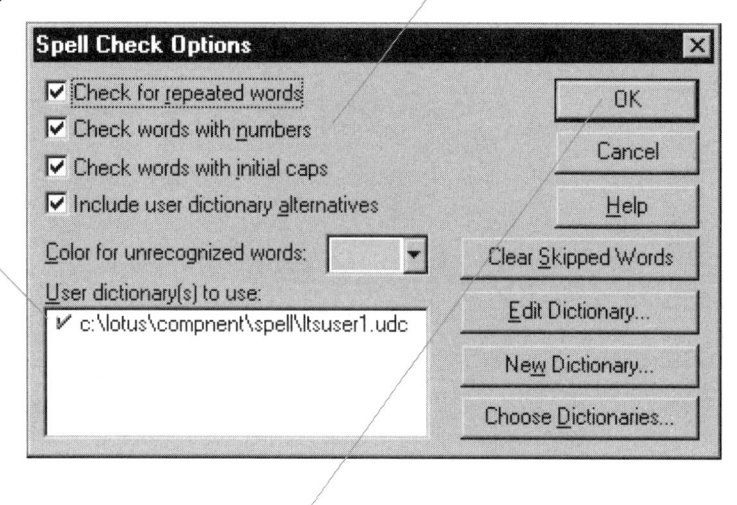

4 Click here

After you've finished setting customisation options, proceed with the spell-check as normal. Or do the following to close the Spell-Check bar:

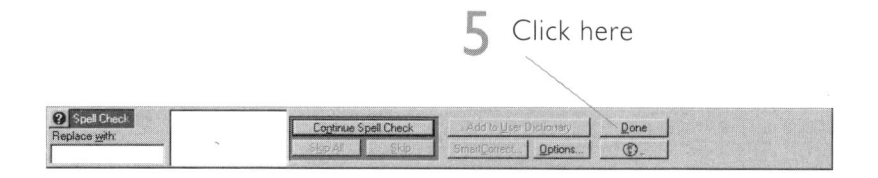

5 Click here

Proofing Tools

...cont'd

Creating a new user dictionary

Follow steps 1–2 on page 134. Then do the following:

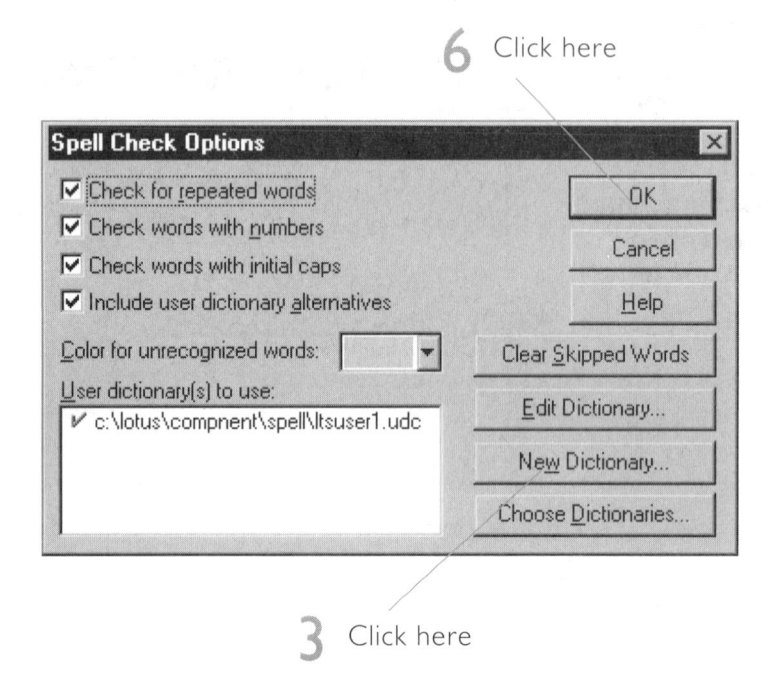

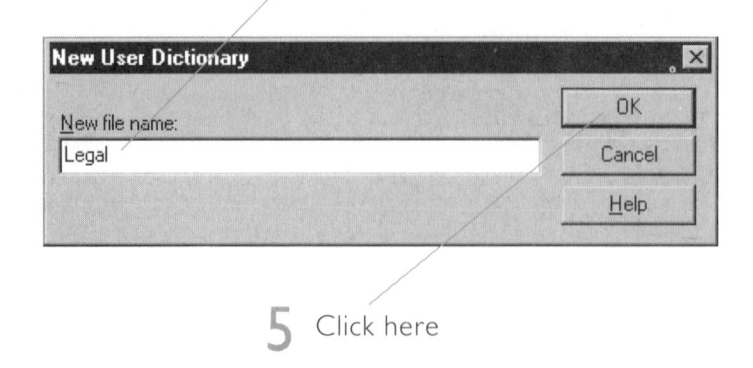

6 Click here

3 Click here

4 Name the new dictionary

5 Click here

...cont'd

Adding words to user dictionaries

To manually add words to user dictionaries, follow steps 1–2 on page 134. Then do the following:

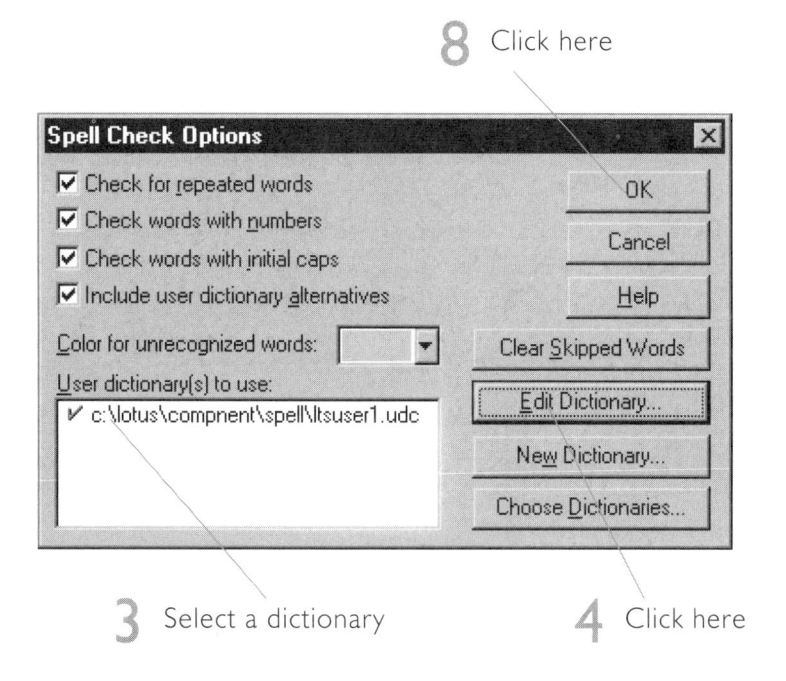

8 Click here

3 Select a dictionary

4 Click here

5 Type in the word you want to add

HANDY TIP **Repeat steps 5–6 for as many words as you want to add. Then perform steps 7 and 8.**

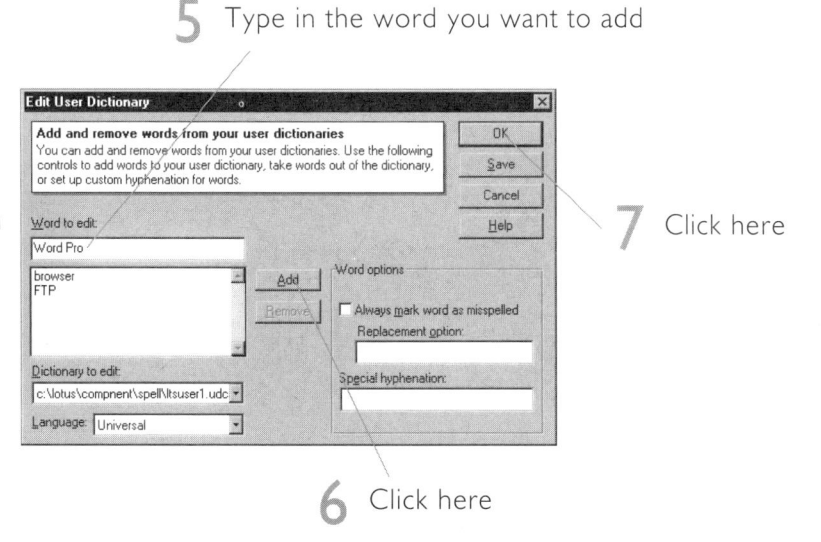

7 Click here

6 Click here

...cont'd

Specifying a highlight colour

To have Word Pro highlight misspellings with a different colour, follow steps 1–2 on page 134. Then do the following:

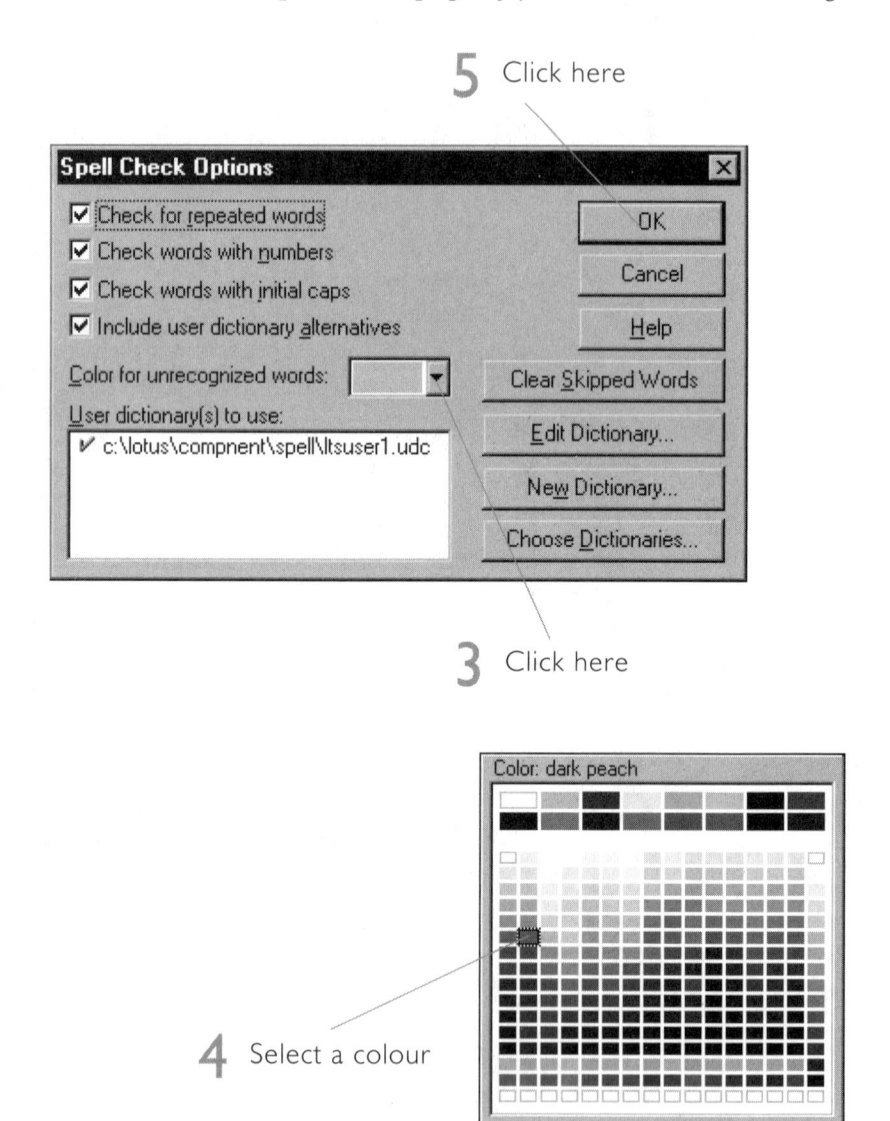

5 Click here

3 Click here

4 Select a colour

Using the Thesaurus

You can have the Thesaurus display synonyms:

- for the word in which the insertion point was located (or which was selected) *before* the Thesaurus was launched;

- for any word you type in within the Thesaurus dialog itself, or;

- for any word listed alphabetically in the dialog (see the HANDY TIP).

Looking up synonyms from within a document

First, select the word for which you require a synonym (or simply position the insertion point within it). Pull down the Edit menu and click Proofing Tools, Check Thesaurus. Now do the following:

HANDY TIP — **You can also click an entry directly in the 'Meanings for:' box to have Word Pro display synonyms in the 'Synonyms for' field.**

The selected word appears here

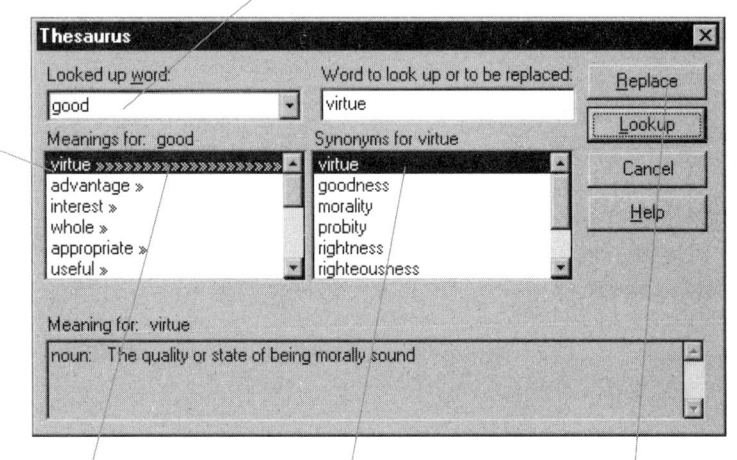

REMEMBER — **Click the Cancel button to close the Thesaurus when you've finished using it.**

1. Click the appropriate meaning

2. Click the synonym you want to replace the selected word with

3. Click here to substitute the synonym for the selected word

7 Proofing Tools **139**

...cont'd

Looking up synonyms from within the Thesaurus

With the Thesaurus on-screen, do the following:

BEWARE

You can't launch the Thesaurus unless a word has been pre-selected, or the insertion point placed within it.

1 Type in the word you want synonyms for (in this case, 'good')

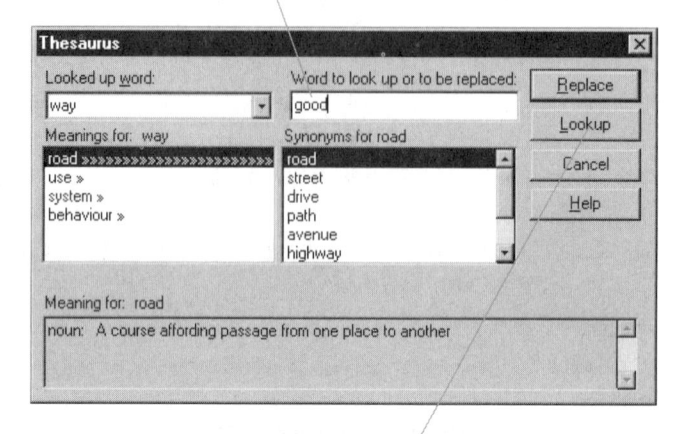

2 Click here

HANDY TIP

To insert a synonym into the underlying document, select it here:
Then click:

Replace

This is the result:

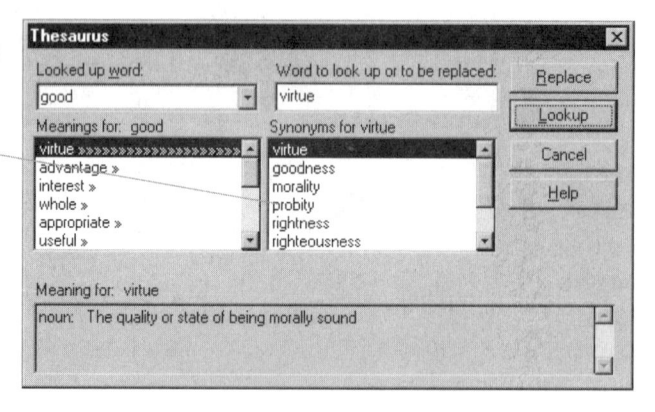

Word Pro is now displaying synonyms for 'good'

140 Word Pro in easy steps

The Grammar Checker – an overview

You can only carry out grammar-checks *after* editing, not on-the-fly.

The Grammar Checker picks up a sizable proportion of grammatical errors, but not all of them; you need to verify documents yourself, after you've completed the check.

The number of rules applied depends on the following factors:

- whether Word Pro is applying a Full Proof or a Quick Proof, and;
- the Formality level.

You can also turn individual rules on or off, manually.

You can have Word Pro check a document's grammar. You can specify:

- whether Word Pro applies a Full Proof or a Quick Proof;
- the level of formality, and;
- what grammatical rules Word Pro applies.

See the subheadings below for more information.

Full Proof v. Quick Proof

If you tell Word Pro to carry out a Full Proof, it uses all of the available rules. Quick Proof, on the other hand, uses a reduced rule set (as does selecting the Informal and Standard formality levels – see below).

Formality levels

There are three formality levels:

- Informal;
- Standard, and;
- Formal.

Consider using Informal for personal correspondence. Standard should suffice for most purposes. Formal is the most rigorous and uses all of the available rule sets (though fewer if Quick Proof is selected).

Rules

Word Pro checks grammar by applying a series of rules e.g.:

- Capitalization errors;
- Double negatives;
- Punctuation errors;
- Archaic expressions, and;
- Clichés.

7 Proofing Tools 141

Using the Grammar Checker

Launching the Grammar Checker

First, do the following:

1. open the document you want to check;

2. (optional) if you want to limit the grammar check to a specific part of the document, select it, and then;

3. pull down the Edit menu and do the following:

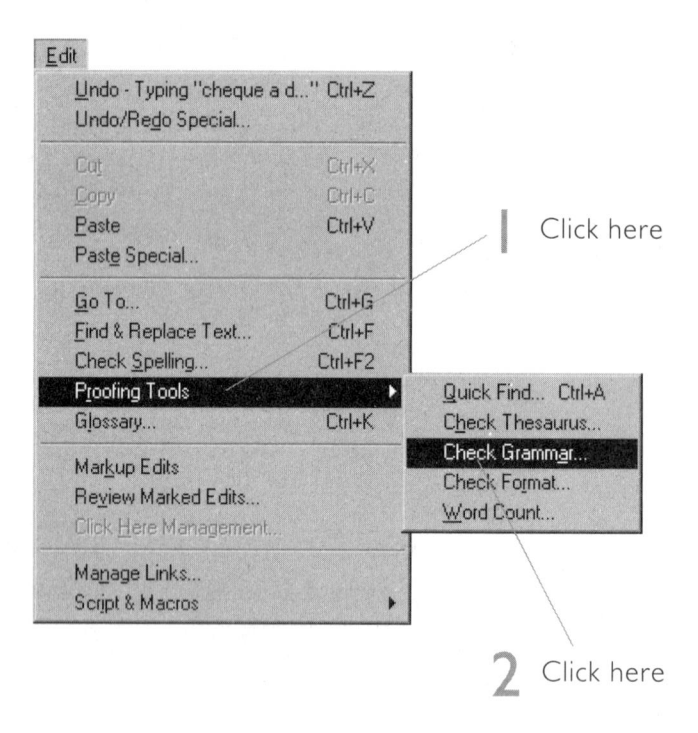

1 Click here

2 Click here

Word Pro now begins checking text immediately, starting from the beginning of the document and working steadily through to the end.

See pages 143–144 for what to do next.

...cont'd

Word Pro now launches its Grammar Check bar and highlights the first word it considers incorrect within the current document:

The Grammar Check bar

> **REMEMBER** — **When a grammar check has been completed, Word Pro launches a special message listing Document and Readability statistics:**

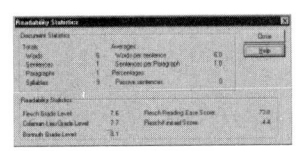

For help in interpreting these, click the Help button in the message.

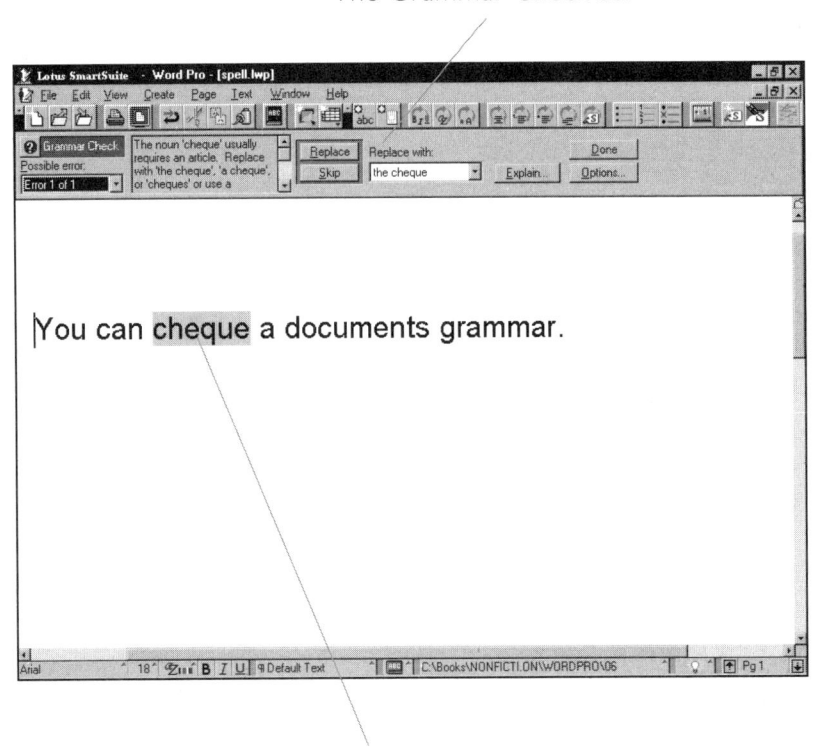

The first flagged error

> **BEWARE** — **Document and Readability statistics are inaccurate if you've edited the active document manually during a grammar check.**

See page 144 for how to proceed with the grammar check.

7 Proofing Tools   143

...cont'd

Re step 1 – Word Pro does not always produce alternative suggestions.
If it doesn't and the flagged item is wrong, click back in the document and alter it yourself. Then click:

Continue

Often, the Grammar Checker provides alternative suggestions; if one of these is correct, you can opt to have it replace the flagged item. Alternatively, you can have Word Pro:

- ignore this instance of the flagged item and resume checking, or;

- provide a more comprehensive description of the grammatical rule in force (see the HANDY TIP).

Carry out step 1 below (if Word Pro has produced a viable suggestion – see the REMEMBER tip) OR step 2 to ignore a supposed error. Make the appropriate choice for all future flagged items as the check proceeds. Carry out step 3 if you want to halt the check before it's complete.

Word Pro explains the rule currently being used:
Click Explain for a more detailed explanation:

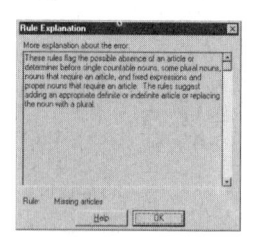

Finally, click OK.

1 Click here; choose a suggestion in the list

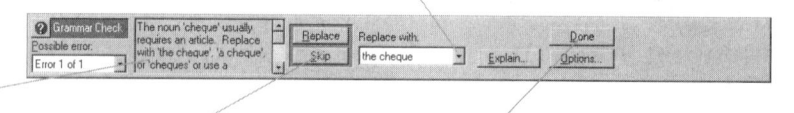

2 Click here to ignore the highlighted 'error'

3 Optional – click here to close the Grammar Check bar prematurely

If you haven't halted the check before it's complete, do the following when the whole document (or pre-selected section) has been checked:

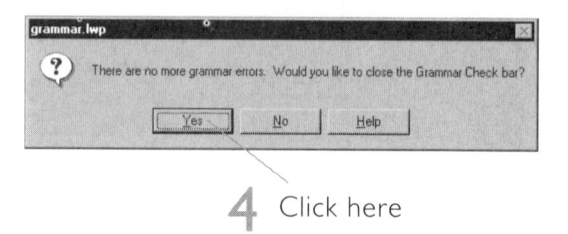

4 Click here

Customising grammar-checks

To customise how a grammar-check operates, pull down the Edit menu and do the following:

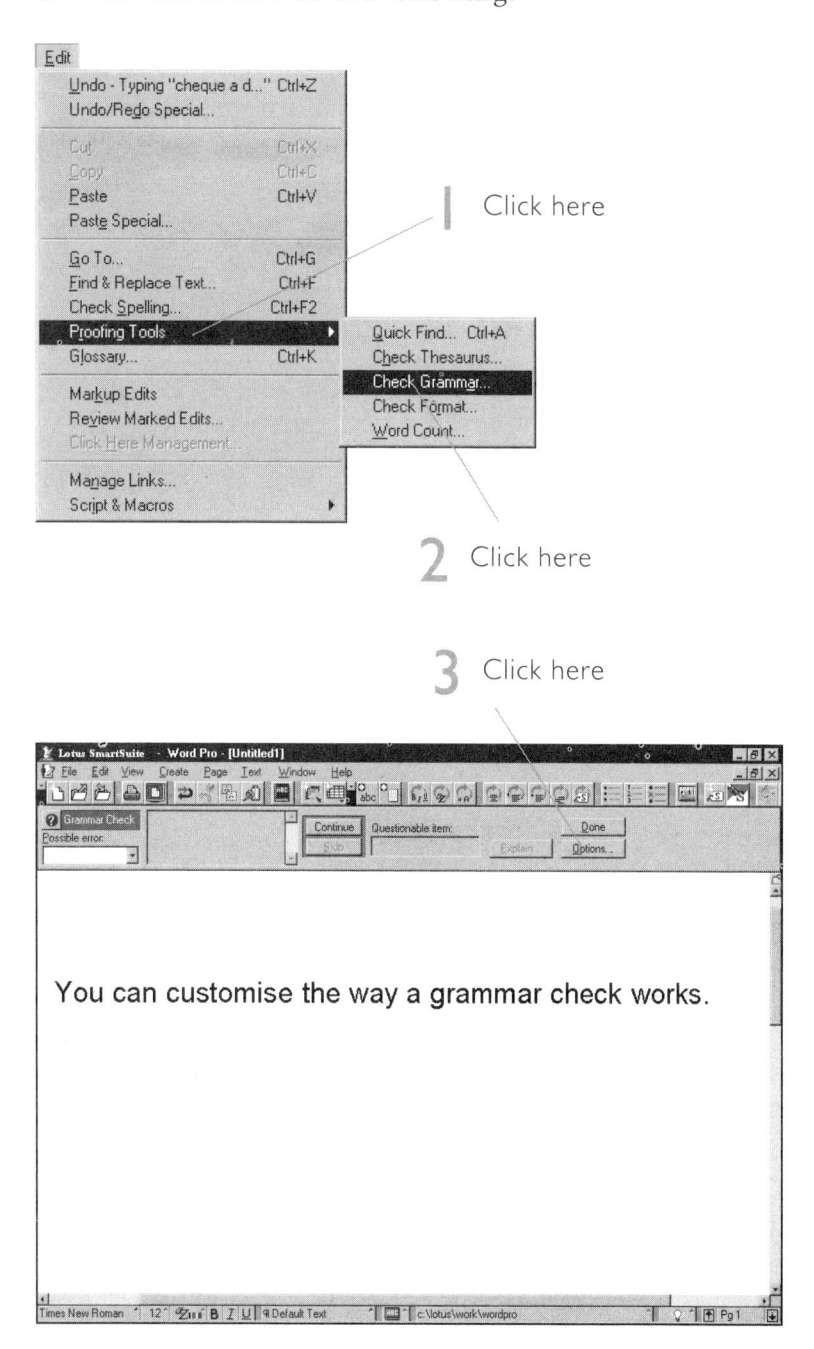

1 Click here

2 Click here

3 Click here

You can customise the way a grammar check works.

...cont'd

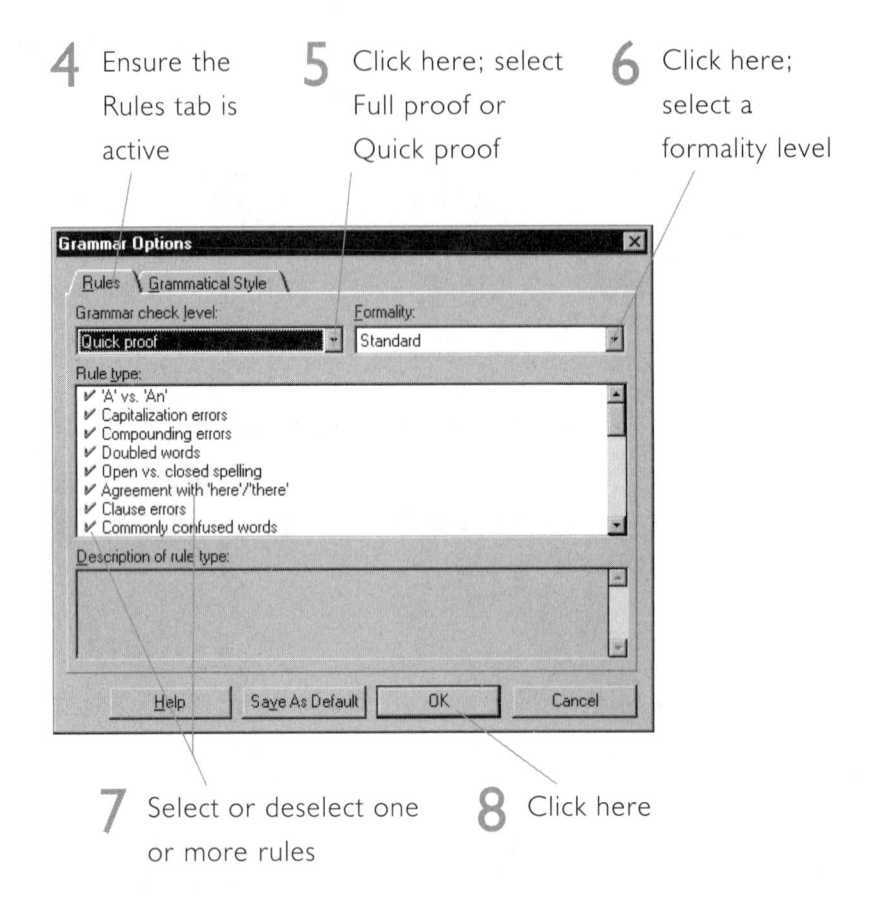

4 Ensure the Rules tab is active

5 Click here; select Full proof or Quick proof

6 Click here; select a formality level

7 Select or deselect one or more rules

8 Click here

Extra options

You can also set a number of additional options. Examples are:

- the number of spaces between sentences;
- the maximum number of words per sentence, and;
- whether Word Pro flags split infinitives.

Follow steps 1–3 on page 145. In step 4 above, activate the Grammatical Style tab instead. Complete the relevant options in the transformed diaiog, then follow step 8 above.

SmartCorrect – an overview

SmartCorrect is a very useful Word Pro feature. Its main purpose is to correct typing errors automatically. It does this by maintaining a list of inaccurate spellings and their corrected versions. When you press the Space Bar immediately after making an error, the correction is substituted for the original error.

SmartCorrect is supplied with a long list of preset corrections (e.g. allready becomes already; acomodate becomes accommodate; alot becomes a lot; don,t becomes don't; february becomes February; garantee becomes guarantee). In addition, however, you can easily define your own. If, for instance, you regularly type lthe when you mean the, you can have SmartCorrect make the correction for you.

SmartCorrect has further uses. You can have:

- the first letters of sentences capitalised;

- words which begin with two capitals corrected (e.g. 'HEllo' becomes 'Hello'), and;

- standard quote marks (' and ', " and ") converted to typographical marks, or *smart quotes* (' and ', " and ").

In addition, you can have Internet addresses automatically changed to hyperlinks. For instance, if you type:

www.computerstep.com

Word Pro will link the address to Computer Step's World Wide Web site.

> **HANDY TIP**
>
> **You can also enter shortened forms of correct words – or entire phrases – and have them expanded automatically.**
>
> **For instance, you could have SmartCorrect expand** ama **into** Amalgamated Finance Ltd...

7 Proofing Tools **147**

Using SmartCorrect

Some uses of SmartCorrect require user action. Look at the next illustration:

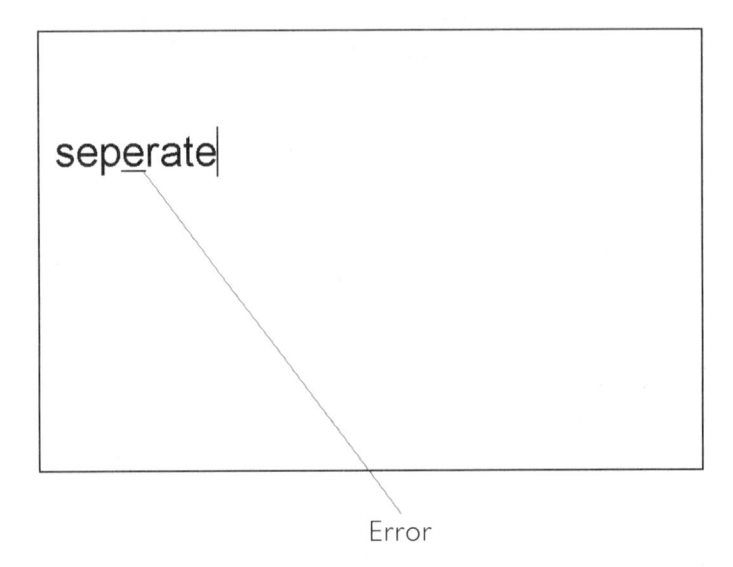

seperate

Error

Here, a common spelling mistake has been made. The insertion point is currently at the end of the word. Pressing the Space Bar (as here) or Return produces this result:

REMEMBER

Notice that the initial letter has also been capitalised automatically.

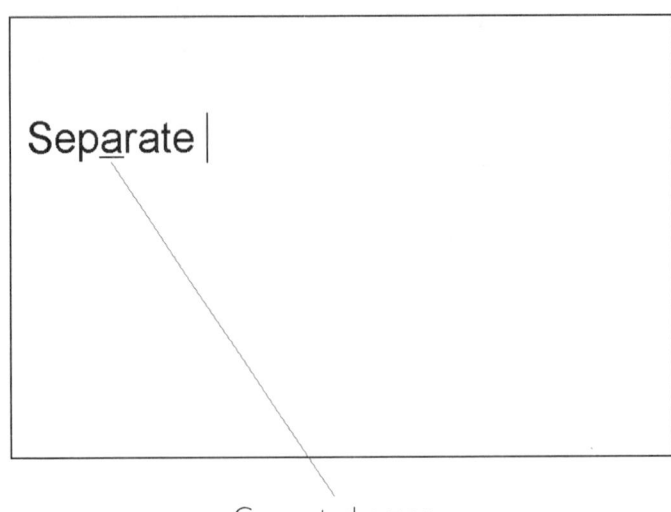

Separate

Corrected error

...cont'd

Other SmartCorrect features (when operational – see the 'Customising SmartCorrect' topic later for how to ensure they're activated) are automatic. For instance, in the following:

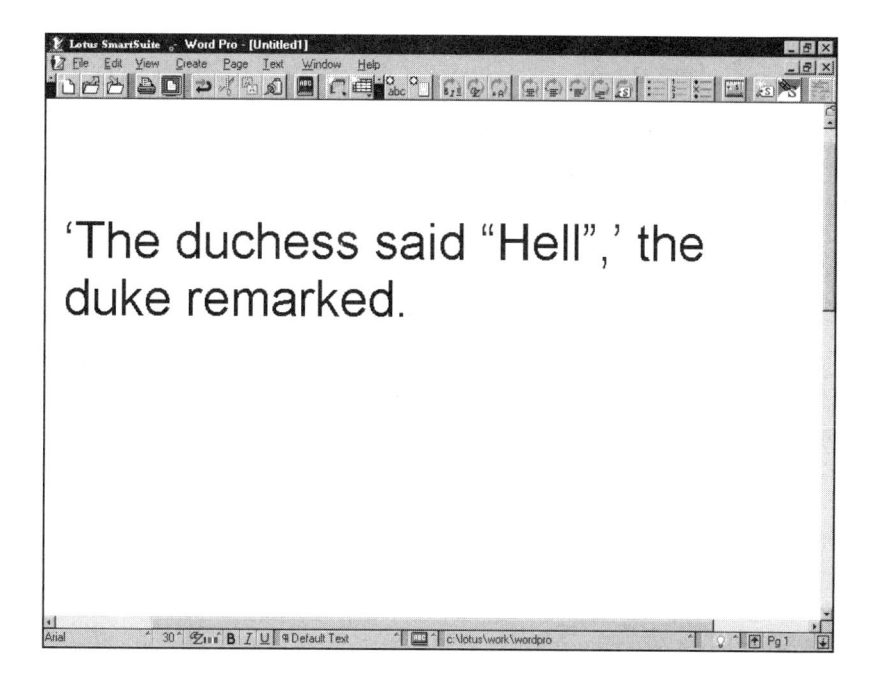

> 'The duchess said "Hell",' the duke remarked.

SmartCorrect automatically converts the speech marks to their typographical – or 'curly' – equivalents on-the-fly, without your having to press the Space Bar or Enter/Return key.

Other features which are corrected automatically are:

- correction of faulty or missing capitalisation, and;
- the conversion of Internet addresses to direct links.

Customising SmartCorrect

You can easily specify which SmartCorrect functions are active.

Adding new corrections

Pull down the File menu and click User Setup, SmartCorrect Setup. Now do the following:

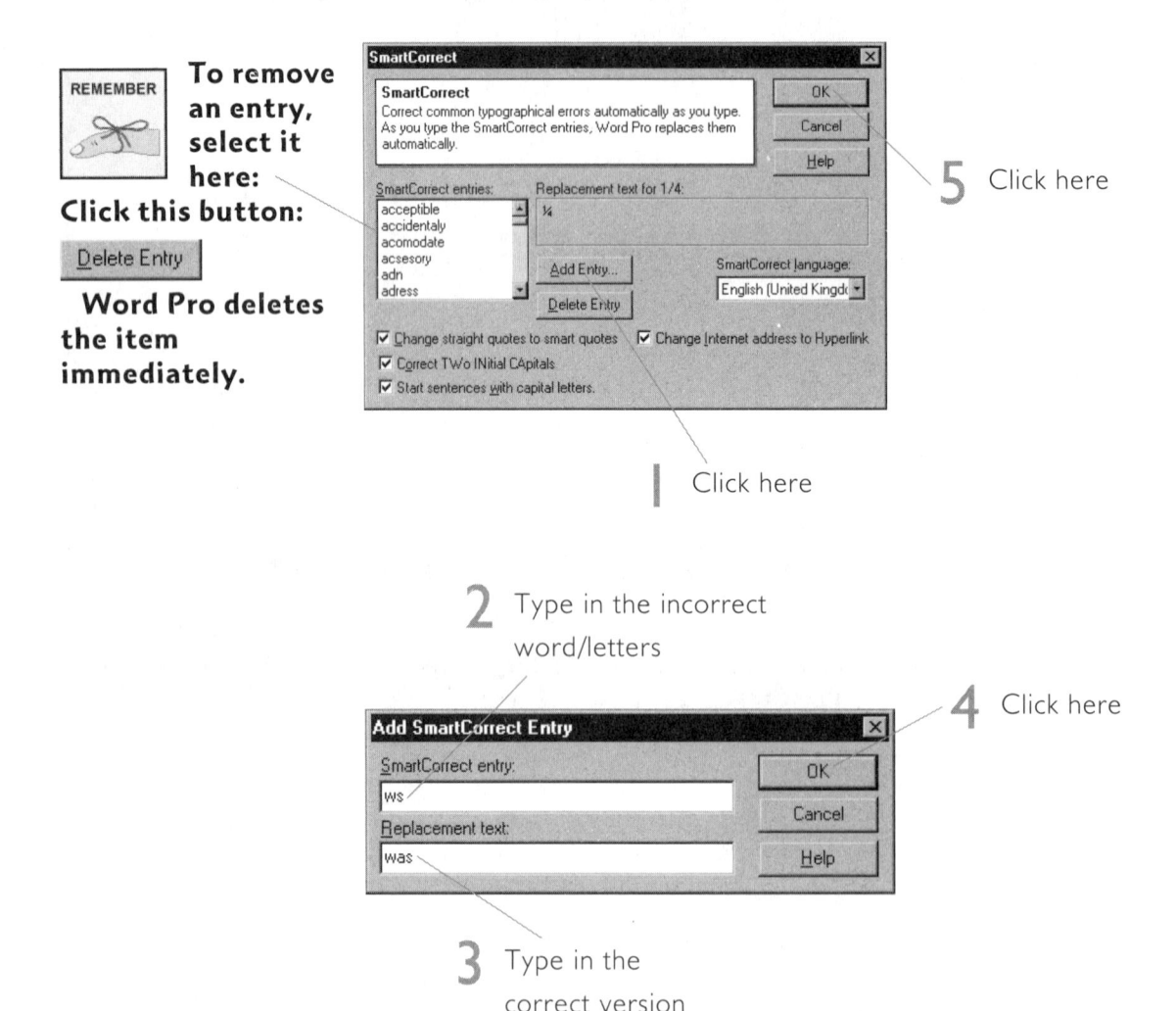

REMEMBER

To remove an entry, select it here: Click this button:

Word Pro deletes the item immediately.

5 Click here

1 Click here

2 Type in the incorrect word/letters

4 Click here

3 Type in the correct version

...cont'd

Setting other SmartCorrect options

Pull down the File menu and do the following:

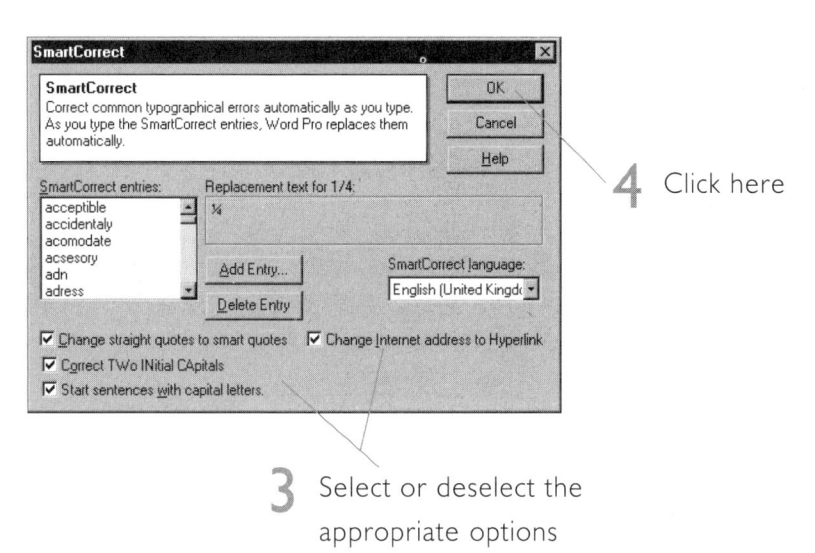

1 Click here

2 Click here

4 Click here

3 Select or deselect the appropriate options

Using Check Format

You can use another proofing tool – Check Format – to correct formatting errors. These include:

- double commas – one is deleted;

- the replacement of specific characters with the appropriate symbols – for example, Check Format replaces (c) with the copyright symbol ©;

- the format of bulleted lists is improved, and;

- the appearance of acronyms is improved (Check Format decreases their type size by approximately 10%).

Launching Check Format
Pull down the Edit menu and do the following:

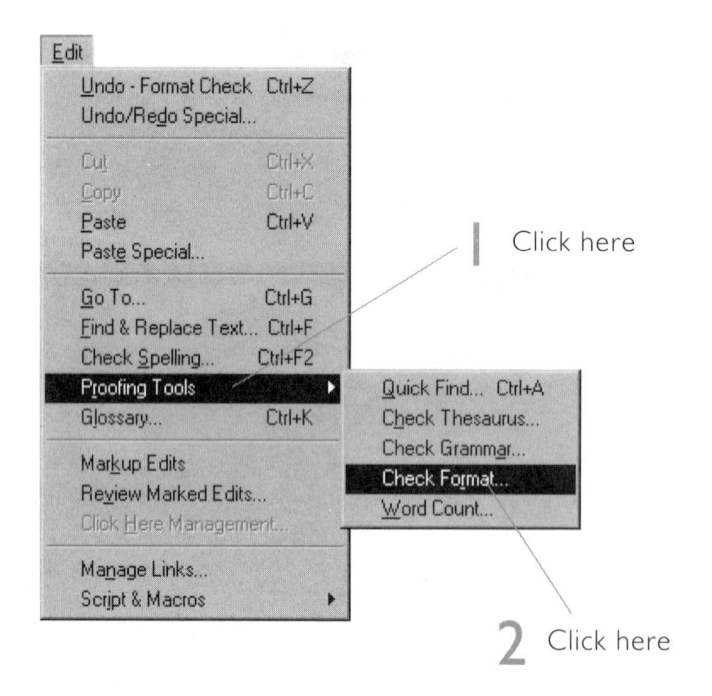

1 Click here

2 Click here

...cont'd

For how to customise your use of Check Format, see page 154.

You can click back in the document to perform manual corrections. If you do so, click Continue to go on with Check Format.

You can also click Replace All to have *all* formatting errors (irrespective of the rule) corrected (but those you skipped earlier are ignored).

When Check Format has finished, it launches a message:

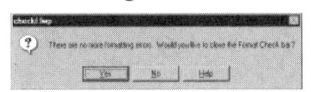

Click Yes to close Check Format.

Using Check Format

Word Pro now launches its Check Format bar, and the first instance of suspect formatting is highlighted:

Check Format Bar

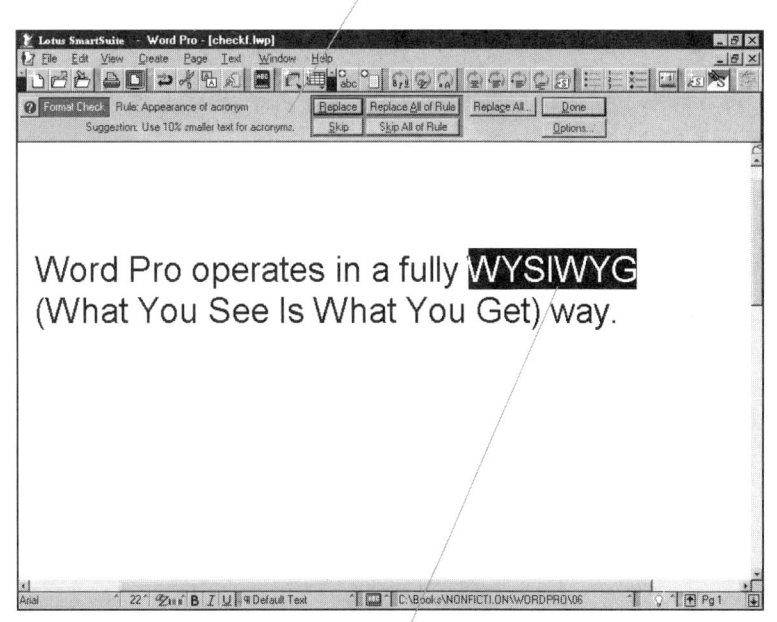

Check Format has identified an acronym

Do ONE of the following:

1. click Skip if you don't want the formatting altered in this instance;

2. click Skip All of Rule to have Check Format ignore all instances of the current rule;

3. click Replace if you do want Check Format to apply its suggested change (in the illustration above, a 10% reduction in type size) in this instance only, or;

4. click Replace All of Rule to have Check Format apply changes to all instances of the current rule.

Customising Check Format

Pull down the Edit menu and click Proofing Tools, Check Format. Do the following:

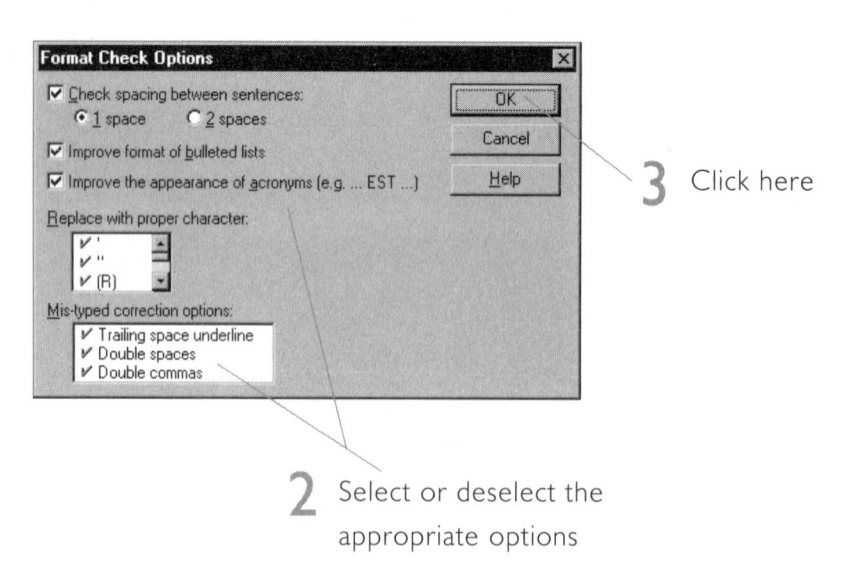

Click here

2 Select or deselect the appropriate options

3 Click here

154 Word Pro in easy steps

Tracking revisions

You can have Word Pro keep track of editing changes. This is almost indispensable if the documents you create are edited by other people. Even if they aren't, it's still very useful (for example, writers can alter their work and store details of the amendments within documents).

You can:

- have Word Pro show edits on-screen, with amendments and deletions denoted by specific colours and typefaces, and;

- review edits and decide whether to implement changes or revert to the original text.

Activating edit marking

Pull down the Edit menu and do the following:

HANDY TIP — **To turn off edit marking, simply repeat step 1 (but ensure the tick disappears).**

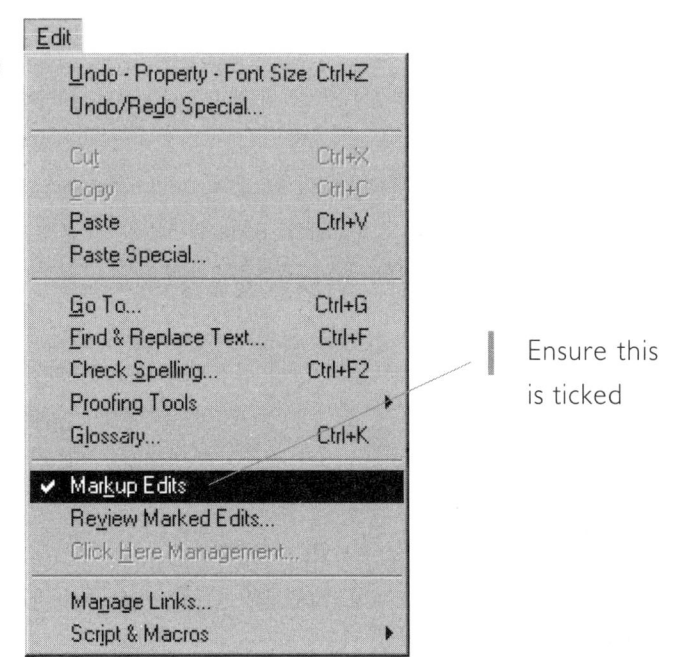

Ensure this is ticked

See page 156 for how to review mark-ups.

7 Proofing Tools

...cont'd

REMEMBER — Word Pro shows the originator of the edit here:

Edit by: Harshad / Original Version

REMEMBER — After step 1, the Find Next button becomes:

Next Edit

HANDY TIP — Additions show in blue/italic. Deletions are in red with strikethrough.

HANDY TIP — Re step 2 – you can carry out these actions instead:
  To implement all edits, click the Accept All Edits button.
  To discard all edits, click the Reject All Edits button.

Reviewing edits

After you or your team members have revised your document, pull down the Edit menu and click Review Marked Edits. Do the following:

Click here ─── Review bar

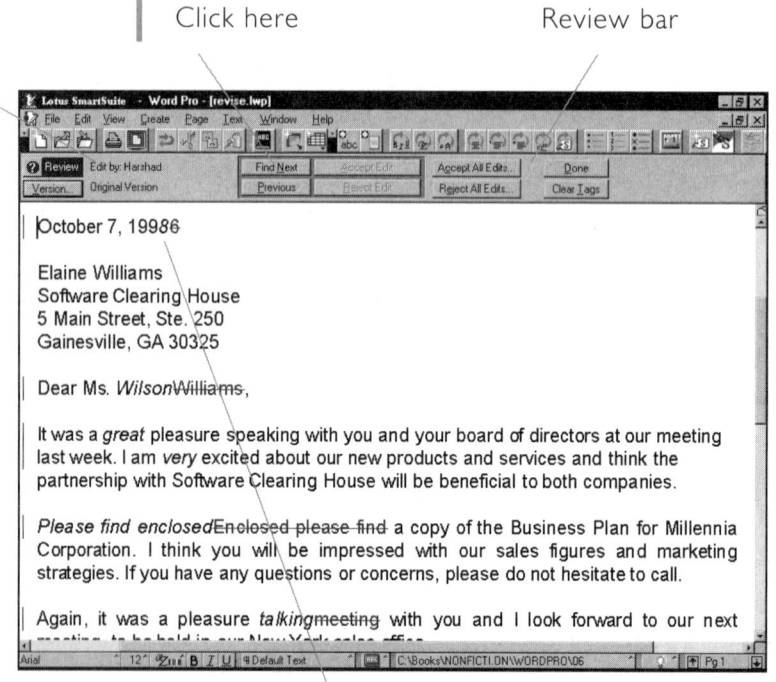

2 The cursor jumps to the first edit; click **Accept Insertion** to accept the edit, or **Reject Insertion** to discard it

Repeat step 2 as often as necessary. When you've finished proofing the document, do the following:

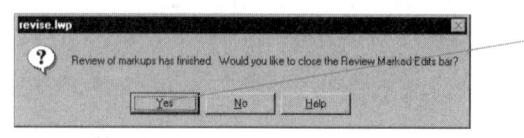

3 Click here

---

156 Word Pro in easy steps

Document versions

REMEMBER **When versioning is in force, Word Pro stores the differences between versions, rather than full copies.**

You can have Word Pro store more than one version of a file within the original file itself. This is useful if you're working as a member of a team, but also if you're working on your own. (For instance, if you're a writer working on a chapter in a book, you can store earlier versions within one overall file rather than having a series of files.)

You can:

- create new versions;

REMEMBER **When you open a Word Pro file in which multiple versions have been created, Word Pro always opens the latest version.**

- view earlier versions (but you can't edit them);
- print earlier versions;
- delete and rename versions, and;
- save earlier versions as separate files.

Creating a new version

Pull down the File menu and do the following:

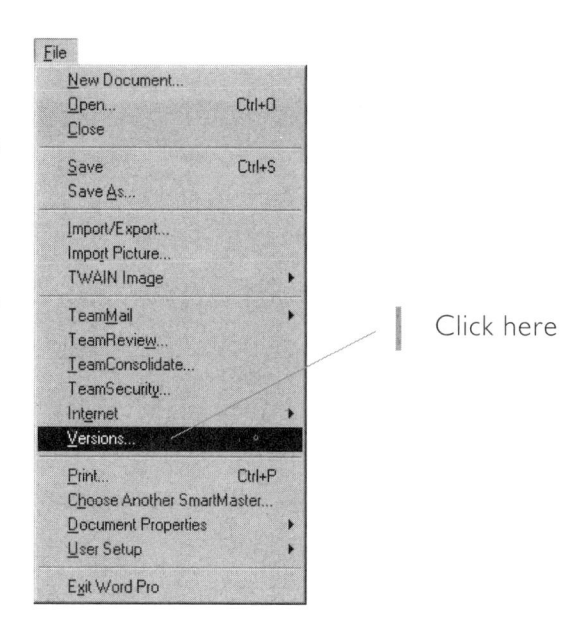

HANDY TIP **You can create a new version of a file (or work with an earlier one) where revision tracking is in force.**
  Clicking this button in the Review bar (see page 156):

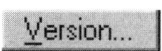

| Version... |

provides access to the 'Versions for file:' dialog. (See pages 158–160 for how to use it.)

Click here

7 Proofing Tools **157**

...cont'd

BEWARE

You must save changes made to a new version in the usual way – i.e. by pressing Ctrl+S (and completing any dialog which launches).

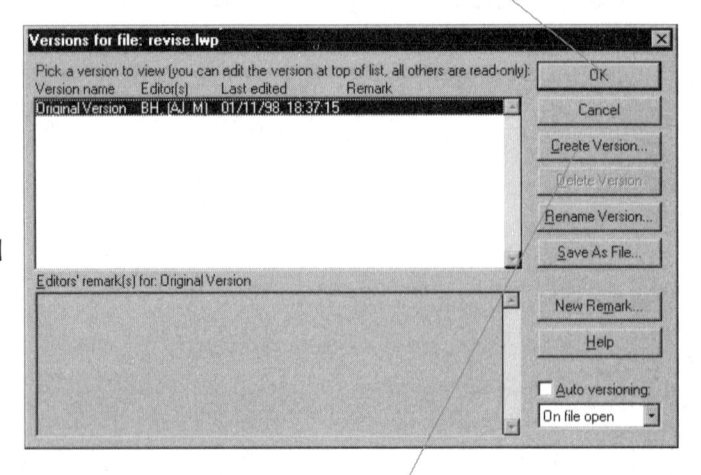

5 Click here

2 Click here

4 Click here

REMEMBER

After step 4, a warning message launches. Do the following:

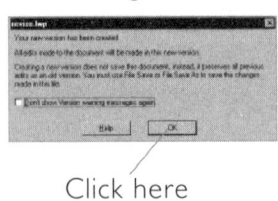

Click here

Then follow step 5.

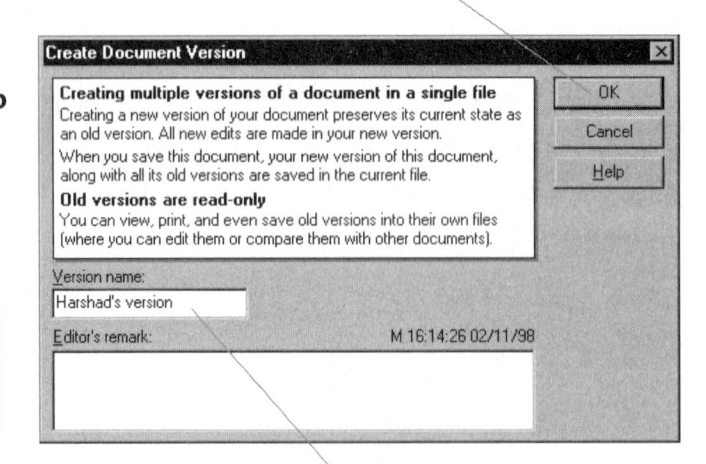

3 Name the version

158 Word Pro in easy steps

...cont'd

Viewing an earlier version
Pull down the File menu and do the following:

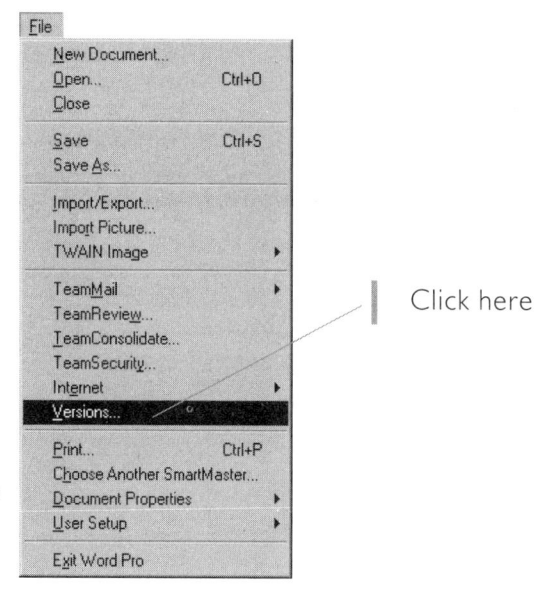

Click here

HANDY TIP

To print a version, follow steps 1-2. Then print it as normal. (See chapter 9 for how to do this.)

HANDY TIP

To save an earlier version as a separate file, follow steps 1-2. Click this button:

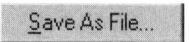

Save As File...

Now follow steps 1-4 on page 38.

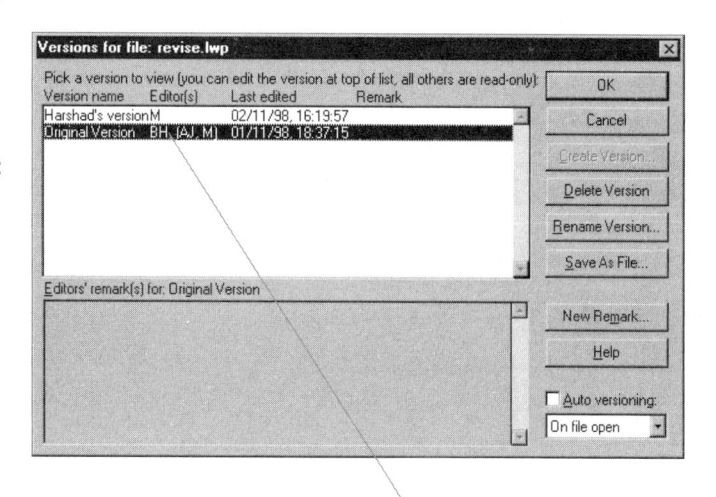

2 Double-click a version

7 Proofing Tools **159**

...cont'd

Deleting versions

Pull down the File menu and click Versions. Now do the following:

After step 2 on the right, a warning message appears. Do the following:

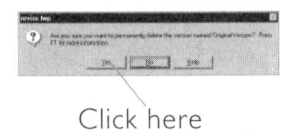

Click here

Then follow step 3.

3 Click here

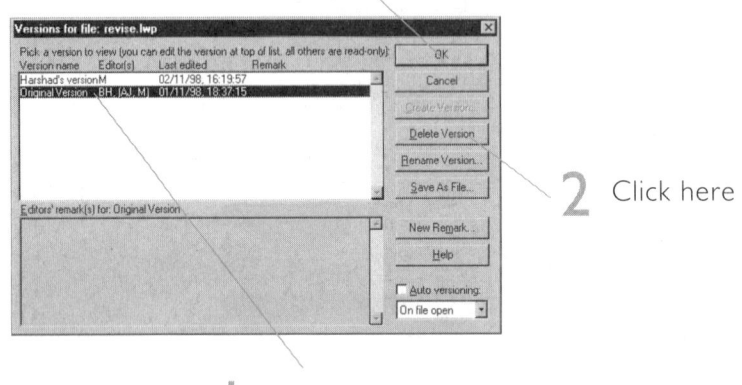

2 Click here

Select a version

Renaming versions

Pull down the File menu and click Versions. Now do the following:

After step 2 on the right, a dialog appears. Do the following:

B Click here

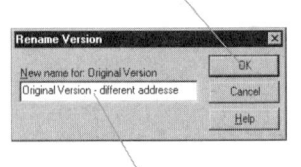

A Type in a new name

Then follow step 3.

3 Click here

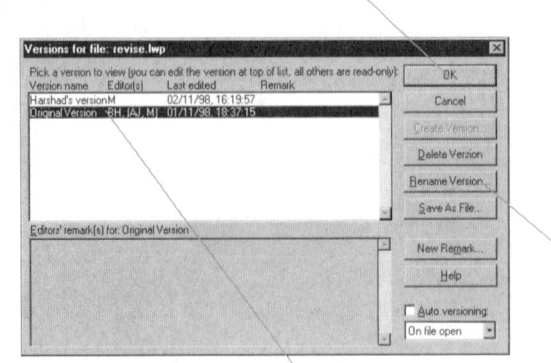

2 Click here

Select a version

Chapter Eight

Working with Pictures

This chapter provides details of graphics formats which Word Pro recognises, then shows you how to improve the visual impact of your documents by inserting pictures into them. You'll also manipulate inserted pictures in a variety of ways (to maximise their impact), then format the surrounding frame and save the enhancements as a frame style. Finally, you'll apply the style to other pictures, to ensure a consistent look in your documents.

Covers

Working with pictures – an overview | 162

Brief notes on picture formats | 163

Inserting pictures | 164

Manipulating pictures – an overview | 166

Rescaling pictures | 167

Bordering pictures | 168

Moving pictures | 169

Using frame styles | 170

Working with pictures – an overview

You can have text flow around pictures – this is called 'text wrap'.

Right-click the picture frame. In the shortcut menu, click Frame Properties. In the Frame Properties Infobox, click the Placement tab. Choose from these wrap options:

	Behind
	Above & below
	Both sides
	On left side
	On right side
	On widest side

You can wrap text around irregularly shaped frames.

Click Irregular wrap in the Placement tab of the Frame Properties Infobox.

Word Pro lets you add colour or greyscale pictures to the active document. Pictures – also called graphics – include:

- drawings produced in other programs;
- clip art, and;
- scanned photographs.

Use pictures – whatever their source – to add visual impact to documents. But use them judiciously: too much colour can be off-putting.

Pictures are stored in various third-party formats. These formats are organised into two basic types:

Bitmap images

Bitmaps consist of pixels (dots) arranged in such a way that they form a graphic image. Because of the very nature of bitmaps, the question of 'resolution' – the sharpness of an image expressed in dpi (dots per inch) – is very important. Bitmaps look best if they're displayed at their native resolution. Word Pro can manipulate a wide variety of third-party bitmap graphics formats. These include PCX, TIF and GIF.

Vector images

You can also insert vector graphics files into Word Pro documents. Vector images (e.g. CGM) consist of and are defined by algebraic equations. Less complex than bitmaps, they contain less detail but are resolution-independent. Vector files can also include bitmap information.

Irrespective of the format type, Word Pro can incorporate pictures with the help of special 'filters'. These are special mini-programs whose job it is to translate third-party formats into a form which Word Pro can use.

Brief notes on picture formats

Graphics formats Word Pro will accept include the following (the column on the left shows the relevant file suffix):

BMP The native Windows bitmap format. Frequently used

CGM Computer Graphics Metafile. A vector format frequently used in the past, especially as a medium for clip-art transmission. Less often used nowadays

CDR Files produced by version 3 of the popular drawing package CorelDRAW! from Corel Corporation. (Some later versions of CorelDRAW! will happily export files to version 3's format)

EPS Encapsulated PostScript. Perhaps the most widely used PostScript format. PostScript combines vector *and* bitmap data very successfully. Incorporates a low-resolution bitmap 'header' for preview purposes

GIF Graphics Interchange Format. Developed for the on-line transmission of graphics data across the CompuServe network. Just about any Windows program – and a lot more besides – will read GIF. Disadvantage: it can't handle more than 256 colours. Compression is supported

PCD (Kodak) PhotoCD. Used primarily to store photographs on CD

PCX An old stand-by. Originated with PC Paintbrush, a paint program. Used for years to transfer graphics data between Windows applications

TIF TIFF, or Tagged Image File Format. If anything, even more widely used than PCX, across a whole range of platforms and applications. (The illustrations in this book are TIF files)

Inserting pictures

REMEMBER

Word Pro creates special 'snapshot' files for inserted pictures. These enable it to display pictures rapidly in open documents.

HANDY TIP

You can also insert video (.avi files) and audio (.wav files) clips into any Word Pro document. To do this, pull down the Create menu and click Object. In the Create Object dialog, select 'Object from a file'. Click the Browse button and use the Create Object From File dialog to locate the clip. Click Open. Back in the Create Object dialog, click OK.

HANDY TIP

Make sure Preview is selected for an indication of what a picture will look like when inserted.

You can insert pictures in two ways:

- directly – Word Pro inserts the picture and then surrounds it with a suitably-sized frame, or;

- indirectly – you define the frame first (with the mouse, or by entering precise measurements) and then have Word Pro insert the picture into it.

The direct route

First, position the insertion point at the location within the active document where you want to insert the picture. Pull down the File menu and click Import Picture. Carry out the following steps:

2 Click here. In the drop-down list, click the drive/folder combination that hosts the file

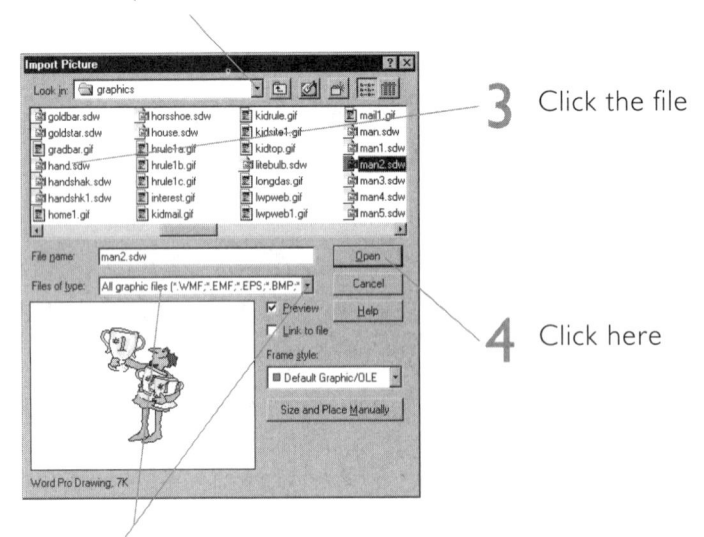

3 Click the file

4 Click here

1 Make sure the relevant file type is shown. If it isn't, click the arrow and select it from the drop-down list

...cont'd

HANDY TIP

If you don't want to define the frame manually but do want to create a frame with precise dimensions, ignore steps 1–2.

Instead, specify the frame's width and height here: then click OK.

Finally, carry out the procedures on page 164 to insert a picture.

The indirect route

Pull down the Create menu and click Frame. Carry out the following steps:

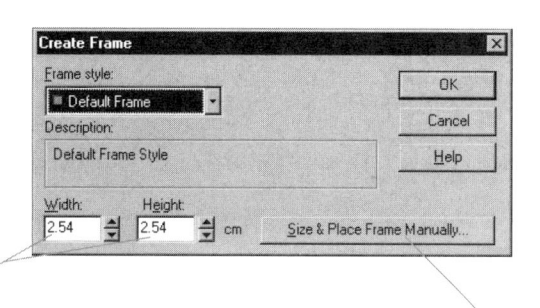

Click here

2 Use the Create Frame cursor to drag out a frame

REMEMBER

As well as the new cursor, Word Pro also displays a box showing the frame dimensions:

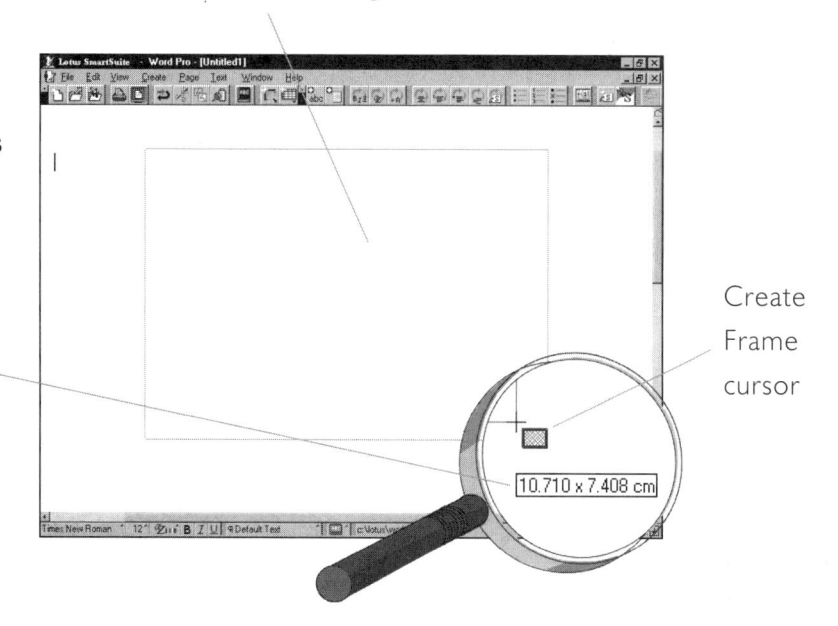

Create Frame cursor

Release the mouse button. Now carry out the procedures on page 164 to insert a picture into the frame you've just defined.

8 Working with Pictures **165**

Manipulating pictures – an overview

HANDY TIP

To add a caption to a picture, do the following.
Select its frame. Pull down the Frame menu and click New Caption. In the Create Frame Caption dialog, select the Caption tab. Select a caption type in the 'Caption type:' field and complete the rest of the dialog. (To set layout options, click the Layout tab and complete this, too.)
Finally, click OK.

Once you've inserted pictures into a Word Pro document, you can amend them in a variety of ways. You can:

- rescale them;
- apply a border;
- move and/or rotate them;
- apply a caption, and;
- format the image's frame and save the changes as a style.

Selecting an image

To carry out any of these operations, you have to select the relevant picture first. To do this, simply position the mouse pointer over the image and left-click once. Word Pro surrounds the image with eight handles (and also with a frame – see the REMEMBER tip). Handles are positioned at the four corners, and midway on each side. The illustration below demonstrates these:

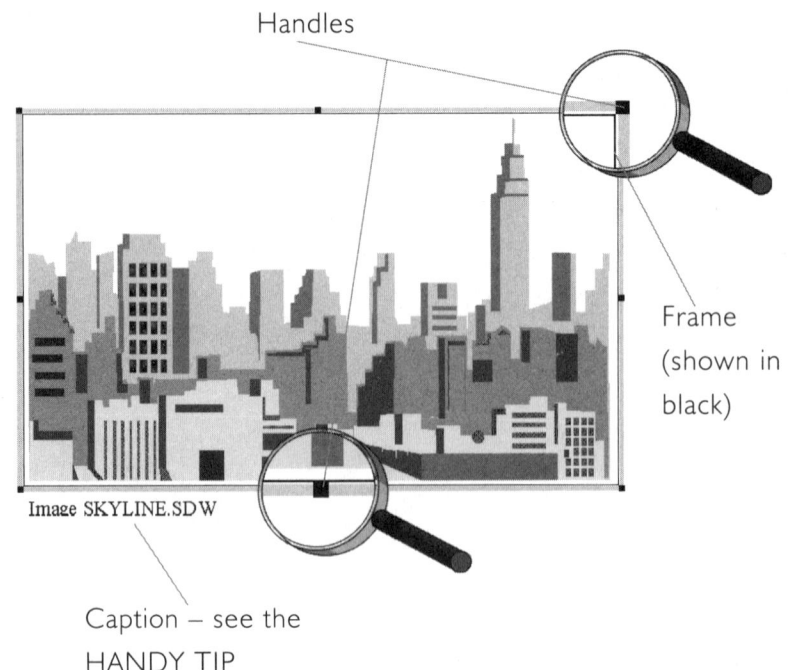

REMEMBER

By default, Word Pro surrounds inserted graphics with a frame (although it can be invisible – see page 168 for how to achieve this). Frames make pictures easier to manipulate, and even have their own Frame Properties Infobox.

Handles

Image SKYLINE.SDW

Frame (shown in black)

Caption – see the HANDY TIP

Rescaling pictures

There are two ways in which you can rescale pictures:

- proportionately, where the height/width ratio remains constant, or;

REMEMBER

By default, Word Pro rescales images proportionately. To warp a picture, do the following *before* you rescale it.

With the image selected, click Frame Properties in the Frame menu. In the Frame Properties Infobox, click this tab:

- disproportionately, where the height/width ratio is disrupted (this is sometimes called 'warping' or 'skewing').

To rescale a picture, first select it. Then move the mouse pointer over:

- one of the corner handles, if you want to rescale the image in any direction, or;

- one of the handles in the middle of the sides, if you want to rescale it laterally.

In either eventuality, the mouse pointer changes to a double-headed arrow. Click and hold down the left mouse button. Drag outwards to increase the image size or inwards to decrease it. Release the mouse button to confirm the change.

Now deselect Scale proportionately.

HANDY TIP

To select more than one picture/ frame, hold down the Shift key as you click them.

The Word Pro image from page 166, this time skewed from the right inwards

8 Working with Pictures **167**

Bordering pictures

By default, Word Pro applies an even border to inserted pictures (this is actually a frame style – see page 170). However, you can change this. You can specify:

- the border type and thickness;
- whether the bordered image should have a drop shadow;
- how many sides the border should have, and;
- the border colour.

REMEMBER

To apply a background to a picture, perform step 1. Do the following:

Background color:

Click here; select a colour in the list

Applying a border

Select the image whose border you want to amend. Pull down the Frame menu and click Frame Properties. Follow steps 1–6, as needed (if you carry out step 6, also follow 7).

HANDY TIP

Re step 2 – click either of the following icons:

if you want to border all four sides of the picture AND apply a drop shadow.

HANDY TIP

Re step 2 – click the following icon:

none

if you want the picture border to be invisible.

1 Click this tab

2 Select a border icon (to specify the extent)

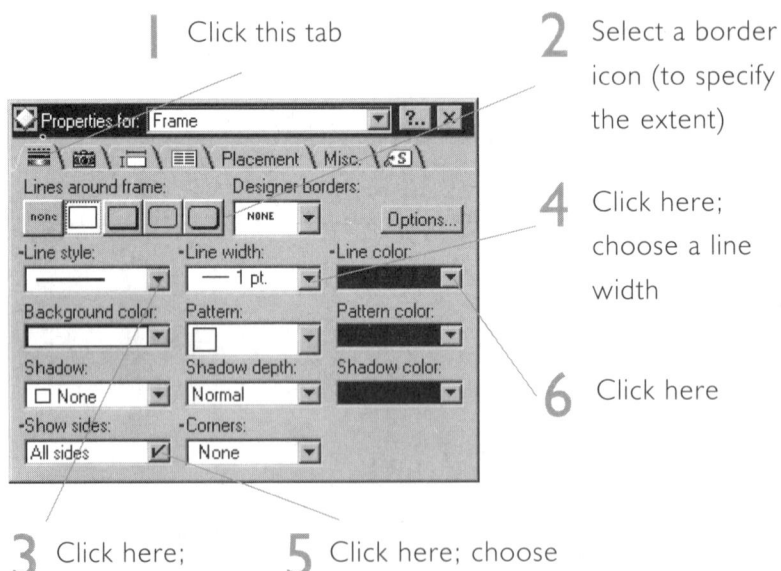

4 Click here; choose a line width

6 Click here

3 Click here; choose a style

5 Click here; choose which sides display

7 Choose a colour

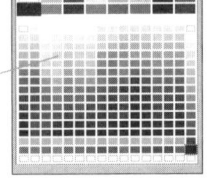

168 Word Pro in easy steps

Moving pictures

REMEMBER

You can rotate BMP **or** TIF **pictures.**
Right-click the picture frame. In the shortcut menu, click Frame Properties. Click this tab:

Click the Rotate Image box (if this is greyed out, see the HANDY TIP below), and select Other. Type in a % and click OK.

You can easily move pictures from one location on the page to another.

First, click the image. Move the mouse pointer over it; it changes to an open hand. Left-click once and hold down the button. Drag the picture to its new location.

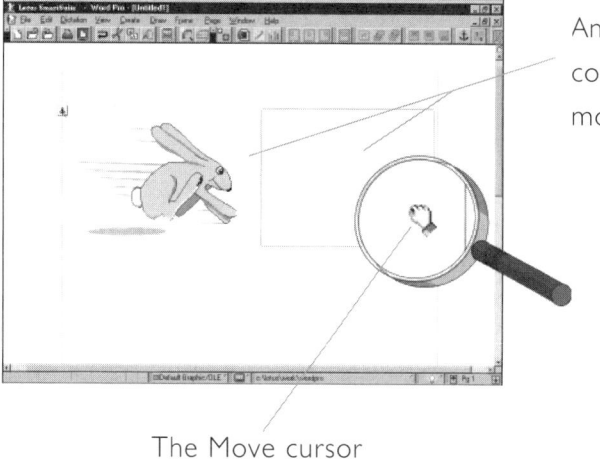

An image in the course of being moved...

The Move cursor

HANDY TIP

Only BMP **and** TIF **files can be rotated.** However, you can convert other formats into BMP.
Right-click the picture frame. In the shortcut menu, click # Object, Convert (where # is the picture format). In the Convert dialog, select Bitmap in the Object type field. Click OK.

Release the mouse button to confirm the move.

Problems with Move operations?

If you find that dragging pictures has little or no effect, select the image. Pull down the Frame menu and click Frame Properties. Carry out the following steps:

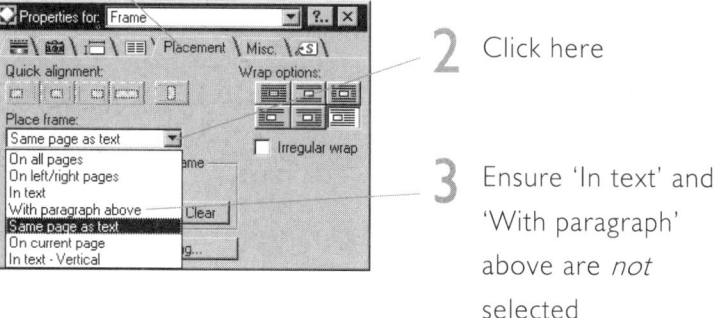

1 Click this tab

2 Click here

3 Ensure 'In text' and 'With paragraph' above are *not* selected

8 **Working with Pictures** **169**

Using frame styles

You can create and apply styles to frames. This is useful if you're working with a document which contains multiple pictures and want them to share a common formatting.

> **REMEMBER**
> Word Pro comes with two default frame styles. One of these – Default Frame – applies an automatic border:

Applying a frame style

Select a frame and press Alt+Enter. Do the following:

1 Click the Style tab

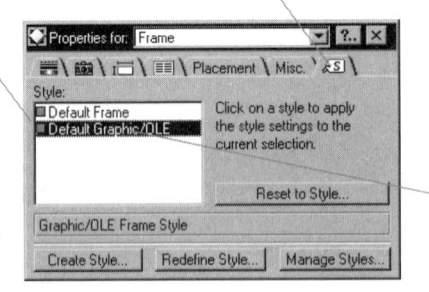

2 Click a style to apply it

> **REMEMBER**
> You can tell frame styles from other style types: they're preceded by this icon:

Creating a frame style

To create a frame style, do the following:

A. apply any or all of the formatting enhancements discussed in this chapter to a frame;

B. right-click the frame and choose Frame Properties in the menu, and then;

C. click this button: Create Style... in the Infobox and complete the Create Style dialog.

> **REMEMBER**
> To complete the Create Style dialog, perform steps 3–5 on page 114.

Amending a frame style

Do the following:

A. apply formatting enhancements to a frame which has had the style you want to redefine applied to it;

B. right-click it and choose Frame Properties in the menu;

C. follow step 1 above. Click this button: Redefine Style... , and then;

D. click OK in the Redefine Style dialog.

> **HANDY TIP**
> You can rename, copy and delete frame styles. To do any of these, carry out the relevant actions on pages 119–122.

Printing

Chapter Nine

This chapter shows you how to select the correct printer and/or printer driver, then specify the correct setup options. You'll then set Word Pro's print options and print out your documents. Finally, you'll print to Net-It Now! SE (if it's installed on your system) to produce format-rich, Web-compatible files.

Covers

Printing – an overview | 172

Print setup | 173

Customised printing | 174

Printing with Net-It Now! SE | 176

Printing – an overview

There are two basic aspects to printing:

1. ensuring that you've selected the right printer and printer setup, and;
2. selecting the correct print options within Word Pro itself.

Printer setup options

The options you can apply here depend on:

- the type of printer you're using, and;
- the options built into its driver (the software that 'drives' the printer). For example, most printer drivers allow you to specify whether or not you want pictures printed. Additionally, they often allow you to specify the resolution or print quality of the output.

Print options

Word Pro's own print options include specifying:

- the number of copies you want printed;
- whether you want the copies 'collated' (see the HANDY TIP);
- which pages you want printed – either a single page range (e.g. 6–11) or multiple ranges (e.g. 3–5 AND 7–11);
- whether pictures should print;
- whether Word Pro should print the selected pages in reverse order;
- whether Word Pro should restrict its print-run to odd or even pages only;
- whether crop marks print (see the REMEMBER Tip), and;
- whether Word Pro should apply impositioning. Impositioning allows you to print booklets. When the printed pages are folded in half and stapled together, Word Pro ensures that the pages are consecutive.

HANDY TIP

The following example illustrates collation in action:
If you're printing three copies of a 40-page document, Word Pro prints:
- pages 1–40 of the first document, followed by pages 1–40 of the second and pages 1–40 of the third

rather than:
- 3 copies of page 1, followed by 3 copies of page 2, followed by 3 copies of page 3 – and so on...

REMEMBER

Crop marks are fine lines which emphasise the corners of the printed page. They help commercial printers produce accurate colour output.

Print setup

BEWARE

You can have a printer driver installed *without* having a physical printer – see page 176 for how to print to Net-It Now! SE.

HANDY TIP

For how to send the files produced by Net-It Now! SE to your Intranet or Web site, consult your network administrator or service provider.

REMEMBER

Re step 2 – you can also access printer settings by clicking this button:

Properties

In the Print dialog – see page 174 for how to launch this.

Most Word Pro documents need to be printed eventually. Before you can begin printing, however, you need to ensure that:

- the correct printer (if you have more than one installed) or printer driver is selected, and;
- the correct printer driver settings are in force.

Word Pro calls these collectively 'Print Setup'.

Irrespective of the printer selected, the settings (step 2 below) vary in accordance with the job in hand.

Selecting the printer and/or settings

Just before you're ready to print a document, pull down the File menu and click Document Properties, Print Setup. Now do the following:

1 Click here; select the printer you want from the list

3 Click here

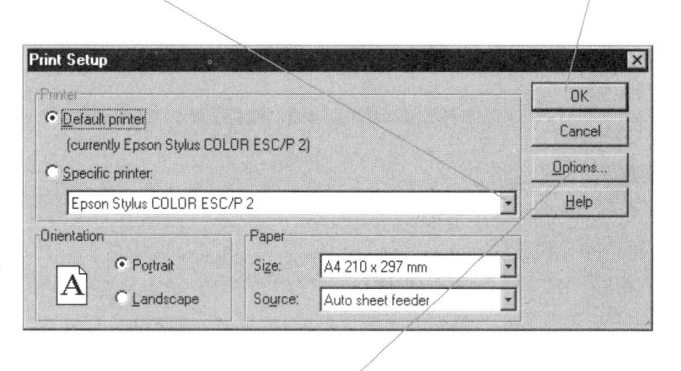

2 To adjust the printer settings, click here and complete the dialog which launches (for how to do this, see your printer's manual)

9 Printing 173

Customised printing

Once the active document is how you want it (and you've customised the print setup), the next stage is to print it out. Word Pro makes this process easy and lets you set a variety of options before you do so.

Starting to print

Pull down the File menu and do the following, as appropriate.

BEWARE

Re step 2 – the Collate option is only available in multi-page documents.

HANDY TIP

Re step 3 – this prints a *single* page range. To print multiple ranges, click the Select Pages button. Do the following:

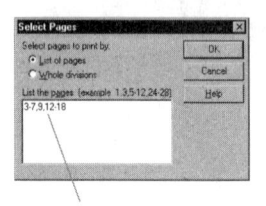

Type in page ranges (e.g. 3–7, 9, 12–18) and click OK. Now follow step 5 to begin printing.

1 Click here

5 Click here to initiate printing

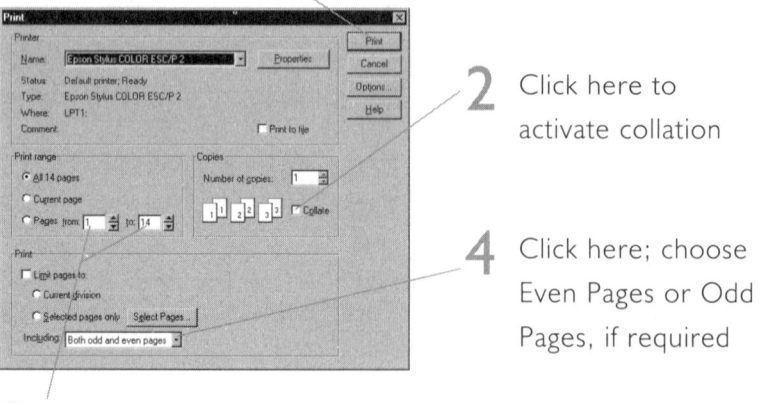

2 Click here to activate collation

4 Click here; choose Even Pages or Odd Pages, if required

3 Type in start and end pages

After step 5, Word Pro starts printing the active document. (But see page 175 if you want to set further options first.)

174 Word Pro in easy steps

...cont'd

Advanced print options

The Print dialog (see page 174) provides access to another dialog which you can use to set advanced print options. These include:

- reversing the print order (printing the last page first, etc.);

- excluding pictures (useful when you're printing a draft version of documents for proofing purposes);

- printing the documents as a booklet (useful if you're printing a magazine, brochure or leaflet, etc.), and;

- printing crop marks.

Carry out step 1 on page 174. Then click this button in the Print dialog:

    Options...

Perform the following steps:

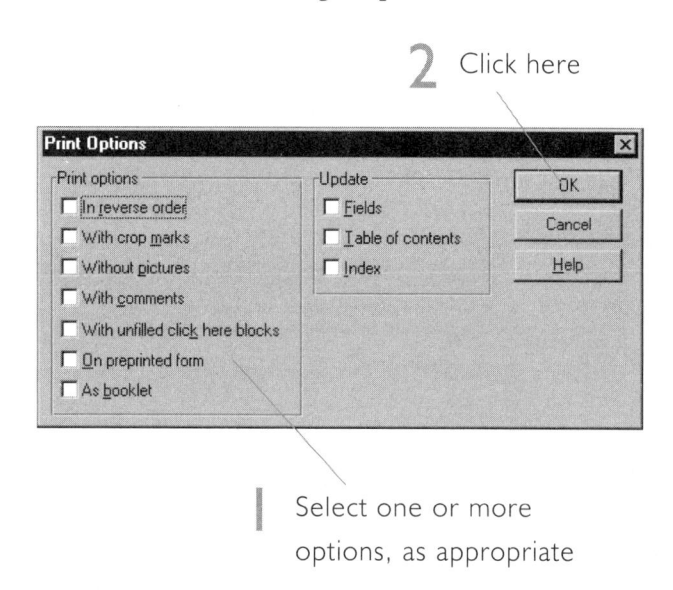

2 Click here

Select one or more options, as appropriate

Now carry out step 5 on page 174.

Printing with Net-It Now! SE

HANDY TIP

Note the following about printing to Net-It Now! SE:

- the files produced are in a special format known as jDoc;
- Word Pro formatting is reproduced very faithfully, and;
- jDoc files can be read by anyone with a Java-enabled browser.

You can use a program which comes with SmartSuite – Net-It Now! SE – to convert Word Pro documents into a format which can be used on Intranets or the World Wide Web. You do this by 'printing' to a special print driver.

Using Net-It Now! SE

Follow step 1 on page 174. Do the following:

1 Click here; select Net-It Now! SE

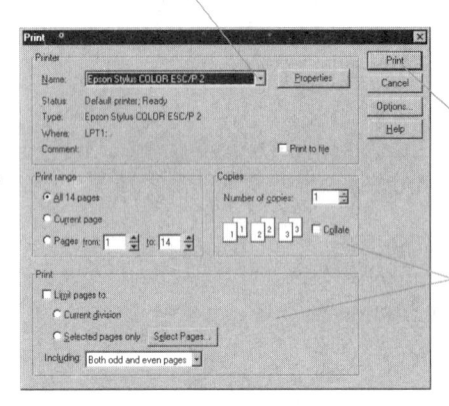

3 Click here

2 Complete the relevant options (see steps 2–4 on page 174)

HANDY TIP

Re step 2 – if necessary, perform the relevant procedures on page 175, too.

4 Type in a destination drive/folder for the resultant jDoc files

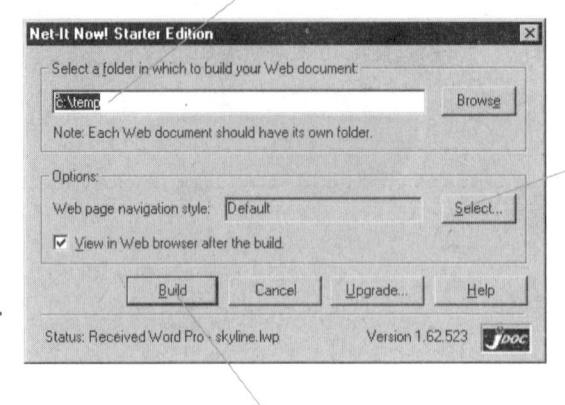

5 (Optional) click here; in the dialog, select a Web format and click OK

BEWARE

Net-It Now! SE only directly supports 3 fonts:

- Times New Roman;
- Arial, and;
- Courier New.

However, it will either convert other fonts to:

- one of the 3 it recognises, or;
- a bitmap.

6 Click here

176 Word Pro in easy steps

Chapter Ten

Using ViaVoice

This chapter shows you how to use ViaVoice to dictate text directly into Word Pro. You'll prepare ViaVoice for use by setting up your microphone and running the enrolment process. Then you'll launch ViaVoice and begin dictating text. Next you'll play back what you've dictated and convert written text to speech. Finally, you'll customise ViaVoice to suit your own requirements.

Covers

ViaVoice – an overview | **178**

Microphone Setup | **179**

Enrolment | **180**

Launching ViaVoice | **182**

Dictating text | **183**

Correcting errors | **184**

Vocalising text | **185**

Customising ViaVoice | **186**

ViaVoice – an overview

SmartSuite Millennium comes with a special edition of IBM ViaVoice which is designed to work seamlessly with Word Pro. ViaVoice lets you enter text by dictation, without typing (but see below for system requirements, which are especially stringent).

Installation

ViaVoice comes on its own CD. If you're installing it now, insert the CD and follow the on-screen instructions. Note, however, the following:

- When the installation process is well advanced, ViaVoice offers to close down and restart your computer.

- If you accept this option, a User Wizard launches just before Windows is fully re-launched. This notes your name and runs the Microphone Setup wizard. It also gives you the opportunity to carry out the enrolment process.

- If you don't accept this option, you'll have to run the Microphone Setup wizard and enrolment later (see pages 179 and 180–181 respectively) before you can use ViaVoice at its most effective.

> **REMEMBER**
>
> ViaVoice already knows English, but it needs to learn to recognise your individual speech patterns. You achieve this by reading out prepared phrases; this is enrolment.

Requirements

The requirements for installing ViaVoice and using it with Word Pro are:

- a 150 Mhz Pentium processor with MMX;

- 32 Mb RAM (48 Mb for Windows NT);

- 125 Mb hard disk space;

- a good-quality sound card, and;

- a CD-ROM drive.

Note, however, that ViaVoice will run on systems with a *slightly* slower processor. However, you should ensure that you've carried out the full enrolment process as this optimises performance.

Microphone Setup

To launch a standalone version of Microphone Setup, click the Windows Start button:

Start

HANDY TIP — **You may have already run** Microphone Setup during installation. If so, ignore steps 1-4.

In the menu which launches, click Programs, IBM ViaVoice - UK English, Tools, Microphone Setup. Now perform the following steps:

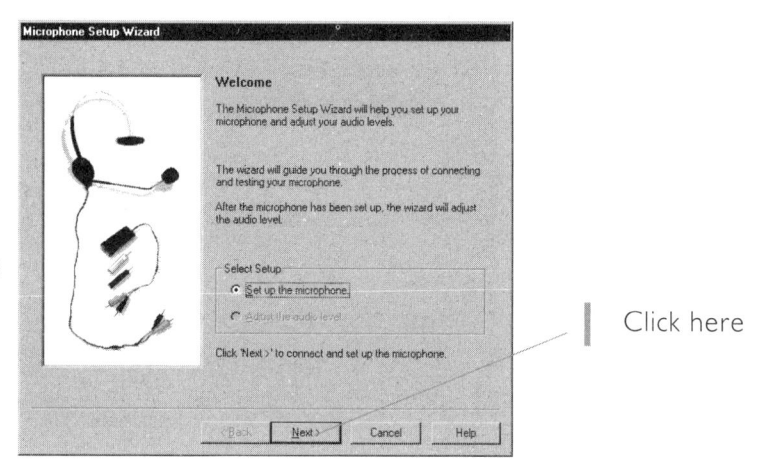

REMEMBER — **The choice you make in step 2 determines** which dialogs appear after step 4.

1 Click here

REMEMBER — **Complete the further dialogs which** launch after step 4. ViaVoice tests your audio setup and helps you adjust your headset and insert the relevant microphone jacks. You'll also repeat specific words so ViaVoice knows your microphone is working correctly.

2 Select a speaker type

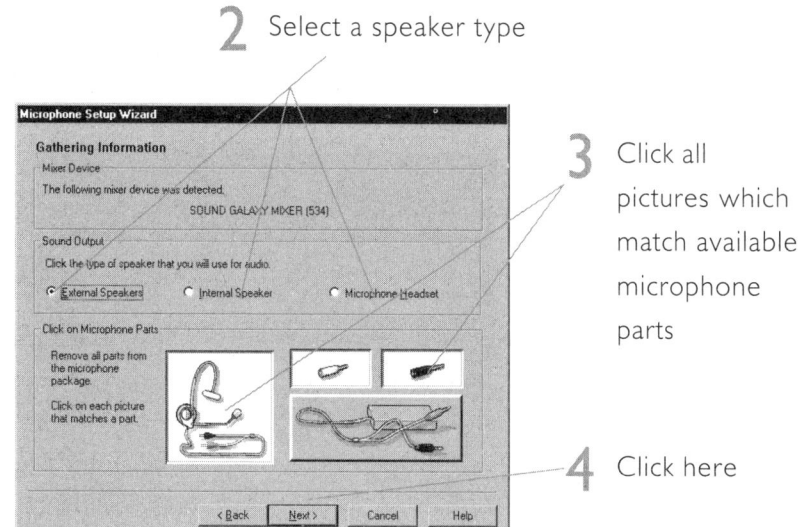

3 Click all pictures which match available microphone parts

4 Click here

10 Using ViaVoice **179**

Enrolment

HANDY TIP — **You may have already performed enrolment during installation.**

If so, ignore steps 1-6 on this and the opposite page.

HANDY TIP — **If you've created multiple users,** select the relevant one before carrying out step 1.

REMEMBER — **You should carry out enrolment in the same conditions** which will apply when you dictate text. For example:

- your microphone should be in the same position, and;
- the ambient noise level should be more or less identical.

If your voice changes for any reason (e.g. you have a cold), you should perform enrolment again.

To launch a standalone version of Enrolment, click the Windows Start button:

Start

In the menu which launches, click Programs, IBM ViaVoice - UK English, Tools, Enrolment. Now perform the following steps:

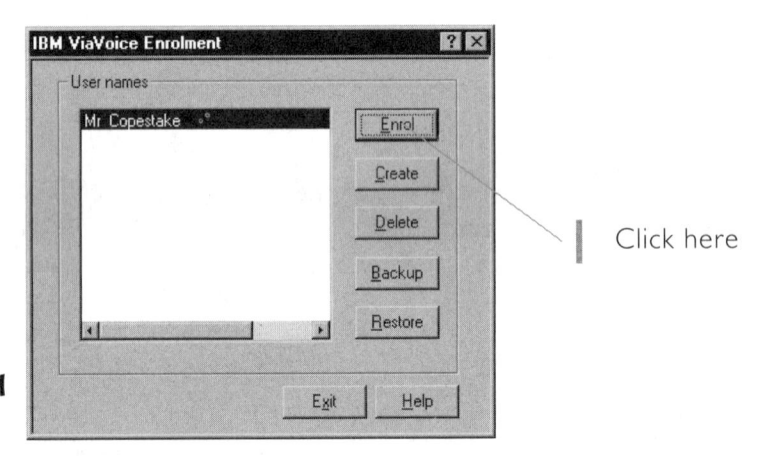

1 Click here

2 Select an enrolment (if this is the first time you've run the enrolment process, choose First Enrolment)

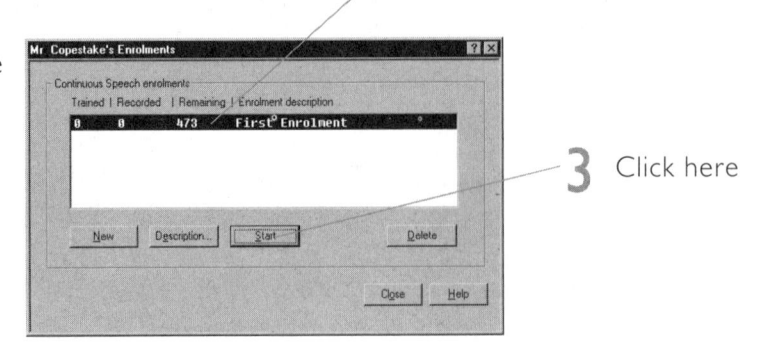

3 Click here

180 Word Pro in easy steps

...cont'd

HANDY TIP

Follow step 4 for help with how to speak when using ViaVoice.

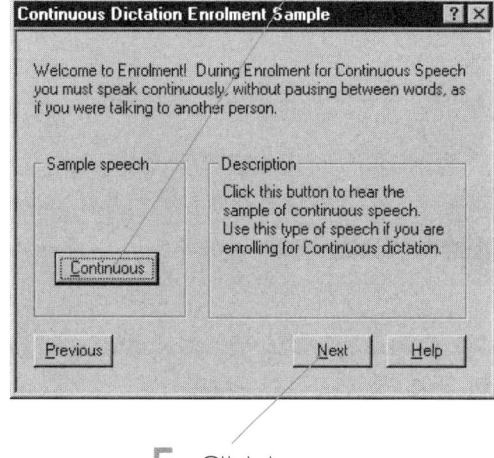

4 Click here to play back sample speech

5 Click here

6 Click here

REMEMBER

After step 6, ViaVoice displays a succession of simple phrases here: repeat each one. ViaVoice analyses it and moves on automatically to the next.
  Continue to the end – the entire enrolment process should take over an hour.

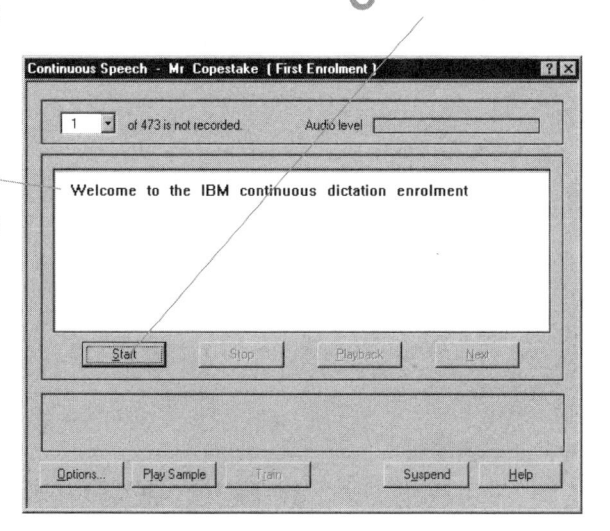

10 Using ViaVoice **181**

Launching ViaVoice

REMEMBER

To close down ViaVoice when you've finished dictating, pull down the Dictation menu and click Stop ViaVoice.

To begin dictating in Word Pro, pull down the Dictation menu and do the following:

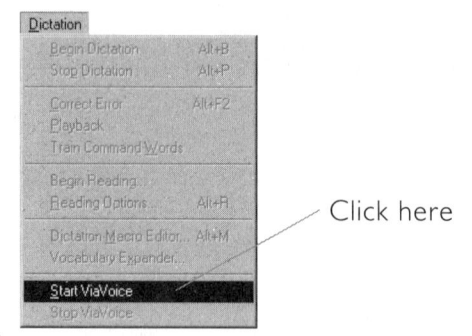

— Click here

REMEMBER

The Speech Centre displays helpful messages about speech features and helps you interact with Word Pro.

For example, clicking this button:

is an alternative route to the menu shown on page 186.

The Word Pro screen now changes (a lengthy process) and the Speech Centre displays:

Speech Centre

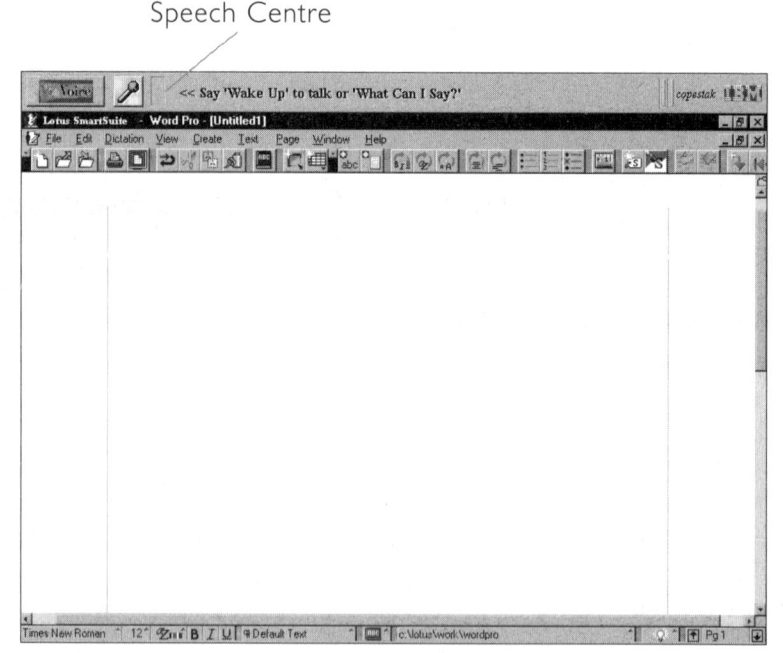

REMEMBER

When you're dictating in ViaVoice, you can't carry out standard keyboard editing.

ViaVoice provides a spoken welcome.

182 Word Pro in easy steps

Dictating text

Beginning to dictate
Place the insertion point at the relevant location within the active document and say 'Wake Up' into the microphone, followed by 'Begin Dictation'. ViaVoice responds by displaying 'Begin Dictating' on the screen:

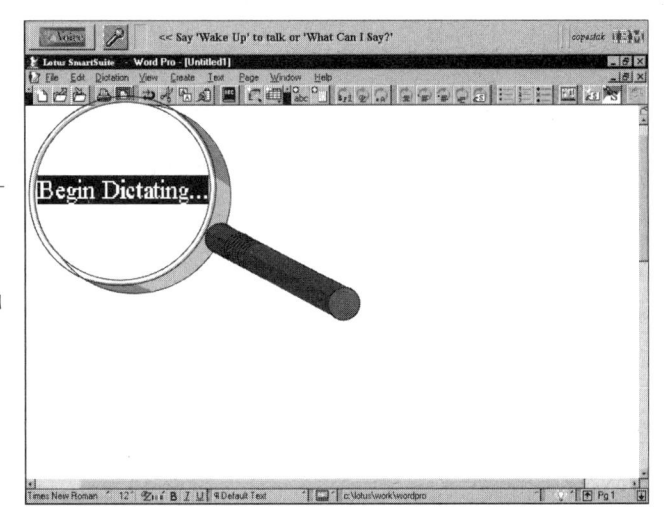

You can also use two keyboard shortcuts:
- *To begin dictation* – Alt+B
- *To turn off dictation* – Alt+P

Before you start to dictate, ensure the Microphone icon in the Speech Centre: is green. If it isn't, click it.
If you want to turn off the microphone, click the button again.

Dictate the text you want to insert, but bear in mind the following:

1. ViaVoice is a continuous-speech dictation program, so speak in complete phrases with no undue pauses between individual words.

2. Speak clearly and in a measured way, and don't over-enunciate words.

3. As far as possible, avoid interrupting sentences as this makes ViaVoice hesitant.

Terminating dictation
When you've finished dictating, say 'Stop Dictation' into the microphone.

Say: 'What Can I Say?' **into the microphone (before you begin dictating) for a list of available verbal commands.**

Correcting errors

HANDY TIP

Re step 1 – you can also use a keyboard shortcut instead. Simply press Alt+F2.

Sometimes, ViaVoice will insert the wrong word. To correct it, ensure dictation has been terminated (for how to do this, see 'Terminating dictation' on page 183). Carry out the following steps:

1 Right-click on an incorrect word

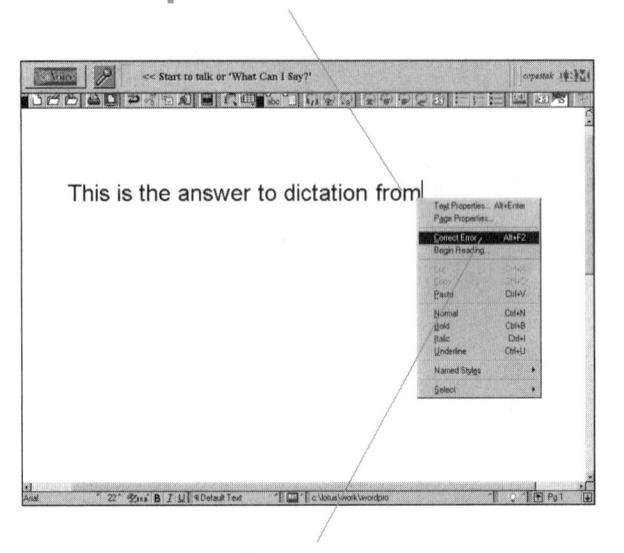

2 Click here

REMEMBER

ViaVoice learns from errors you correct in this way, and future recognition is improved.

As a result, if (when you review your work) you find text which ViaVoice transcribed correctly but which you want to change anyway, do the following:

A. disable ViaVoice, and then;
B. use normal editing techniques to correct the errors.

Now do ONE of the following:

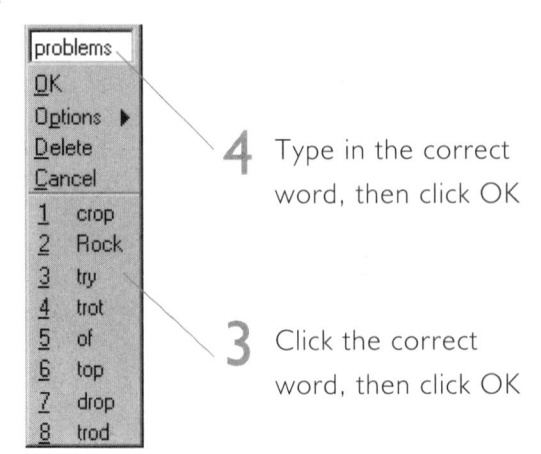

4 Type in the correct word, then click OK

3 Click the correct word, then click OK

184 **Word Pro in easy steps**

Vocalising text

You can have ViaVoice read back text in two ways:

- You can have text you've just dictated read back (here, ViaVoice is simply playing back your dictation).
- You can select written text and have ViaVoice vocalise it.

When ViaVoice is vocalising text, a small window with an animated face appears:

Playing back dictation

Select text you've dictated. Pull down the Dictation menu and do the following:

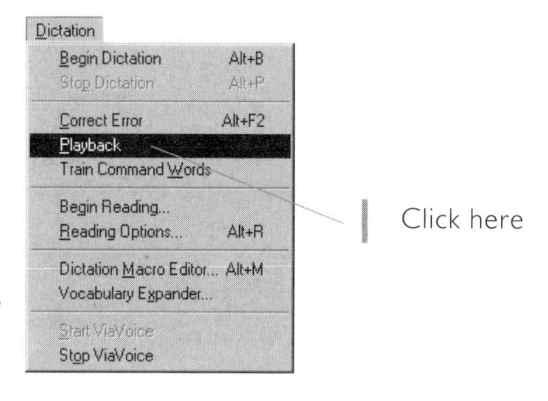

Click here

The window closes when ViaVoice reaches the end of the text.

Vocalising text

Select the relevant text. Pull down the Dictation menu and do the following:

Click here

To set text-to-speech conversion options (e.g. to specify the voice used), click the Options button below the animated face (see the HANDY TIP above). Make the relevant changes in the Virtual Voices Control Properties dialog. Click OK.

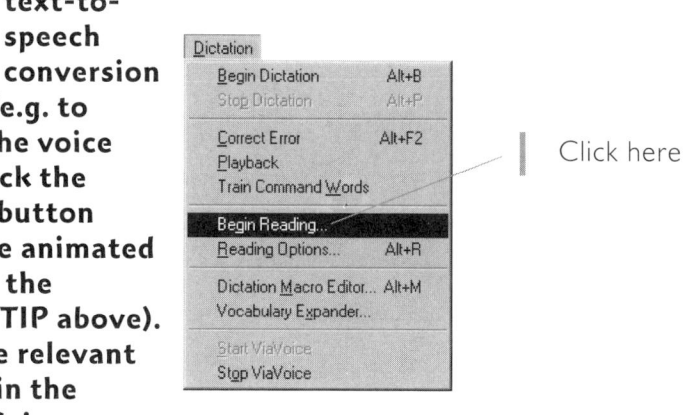

10 Using ViaVoice **185**

Customising ViaVoice

HANDY TIP

To create a new user, make sure ViaVoice has not been launched. Click User Options in the shortcut menu. Click this button:

`Add User...`

in the IBM ViaVoice Options dialog. The User Wizard launches. Complete this as appropriate, clicking Next in each screen to move to the next.
   Finally, click Finish.

You can customise the following aspects of the way ViaVoice works:

- whether the Speech Centre displays, and where, and;
- the user settings.

Customising the Speech Centre

After you've initiated dictation, by default the Speech Centre displays at the very top of the screen. ViaVoice calls this Taskbar view. There are two other settings:

Minimal view — The Speech Centre does not display

Docked view — The Speech Centre displays under Word Pro's Menu bar

To change the view, right-click this icon:

in the Windows System tray (on the right of the Task bar). A shortcut menu appears – do the following:

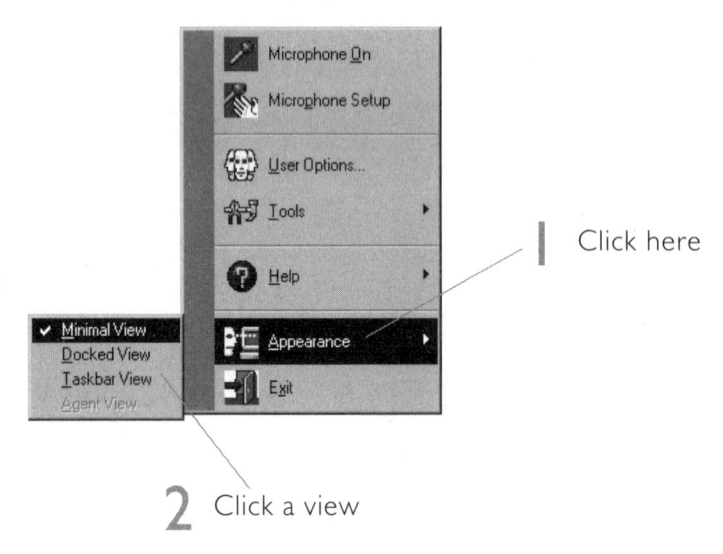

REMEMBER

To apply another user, click User Options in the shortcut menu. Do the following in the IBM ViaVoice Options dialog:

The user is:
`Mr Copestake`

Click here; select a user in the list
Click OK.

Click here

2 Click a view

186 Word Pro in easy steps

Index

A

Ask the Expert. *See* Help, Ask the Expert

B

Bitmap images 162, 176
Bookmarks
  Inserting 90
  Linking to 44–45, 89–90
Bullets
  Adding to text 67–68

C

Check Format
  Customising 154
  Launching 152
  Using 153
Clear Screen 11
Closing 8
Collation 172
  Caveat 174
Columns. *See* Text, Columns
  Adding to footers 85
  Adding to headers 80
Crop marks 172
Cycling (through Word Pro options) 12

D

Document views 30
  Switching between views 31
Drop caps 65–66

F

Fast Format 63–64
Files 21–38
  Converting to a Web-based format 42–43, 176
  Converting to jDoc format 176
  Opening 26
    From the Internet 27
  Saving 38
    To the Web 46
  Versions
    Creating 157–158
    Deleting 160
    Printing 159
    Renaming 160
    Saving as separate files 159
    Using while revision tracking 157
    Viewing 159
Fonts. *See* Text, Fonts
Footers
  Bordering 83
  Colouring 83
  Columns 85
  Editing 82
  Inserting 81
  Inserting page numbers in 88
  Watermarks 84
Frame styles
  Applying 170
  Copying 170
  Creating 170
  Default 168
  Deleting 170

Differentiating   170
Redefining   170
Renaming   170
Frames   66. *See also* Pictures/graphics, Frames

G

Go To dialog
  Using page definitions in   29

H

Headers
  Bordering   78
  Colouring   78
  Columns   80
  Editing   77
  Inserting   76
  Inserting page numbers in   88
  Margins   77
  Watermarks   79
Help
  Ask the Expert   19
  Bubble tips   20
  Contents   17–18
  Index   17–18
  QuickDemos   20
HTML Export Assistant   14, 42–43
Hyperlinks
  Activating   45
  Amending   44, 89
  Deleting   44, 89
  In action   41
  Inserting   44, 89, 147

I

Infoboxes
  Launching   16
  Overview   15
Internet
  Creating Web documents
    using SmartMasters   40–41
    using HTML Export Assistant   42–43
  Hyperlinks   44–45
    Converting URLs to hyperlinks   147
  Net-It Now! SE   176
  Tools SmartIcon bar   14
  Uploading files to an FTP server   146

J

jDoc. *See* Files, Converting to jDoc format

L

Layout view   30
Leading   60
Lines
  Numbering   69

M

Margins
  Defined   91
  Specifying
    In documents   91
    In footers   91
    In headers   91
Moving around in documents   28
  With the Go To dialog   29

N

Net-It Now! SE 176
New documents, creating
  Blank documents 24
  Web documents 41
  With SmartMasters 23
Numbers
  Applying to lines 69

P

Page formatting 73–110
  Page backgrounds 96
  Page bordering 94
  Page layouts
    Inserting and applying a new page style 110
    Inserting and editing a new page style 109
  Page numbers
    Inserting into body text 86–87
    Inserting into footers 88
    Inserting into headers 88
  Page orientation 92
  Page sizes
    Choosing 92
    Customising 93
  Page Sorter view 30–31
  Page styles
    Amending 103
    An overview 100
    Applying 102
    Assigning to function keys 107
    Copying 105–106
    Creating 101
    Deleting 104
    Distinguishing from other style types 104
    Renaming 105
  Pages
    Applying a drop shadow to 95
    Applying backgrounds to 96
    Applying patterns to 97
    Applying watermarks to 98
    Inserting new pages 99
Picas 59
Pictures/graphics 161–170
  Applying backgrounds to 168
  Applying captions to 166
  Bitmapped 162
  Bordering 168
  Converting to BMP 169
  Format details 163
  Frames
    Invisible frames 168
    Styles 168–170
  Inserting
    Via a dialog 164
    Via the mouse 165
  Manipulating 166
  Moving 169
  Overview 162
  Rescaling 167
  Rotating 169
  Selecting 166
    More than one 167
  Shadowing 168
  Skewing 167
  Snapshot files 164
  Vector images 162
Points 59
Printing
  Overview 172
  Print options 174–175

Setup options   173
  To Net-It Now! SE   176
Proofing tools   125–150
  Check Format   152–154
  SmartCorrect   147–151
  Spell-checking   127–139
    Customising   133–138
    Grammar checker   141–146
    'On-the-fly'   128–130
    Separately (after document finalised)   131–132
  Thesaurus   139–140

Q

Quick Find   36
  Caveat   37

R

Redo   34
Revisions
  Activating tracking   155
  Combining with file versions   157
  Deactivating tracking   155
  Reviewing edits   156
Ruler
  Applying tabs with   56

S

Screen   10
  Hiding components   11
  Showing components   11
SmartCenter   9
SmartCorrect
  An overview   147
  Customising   151
    Adding new entries   150

    Deleting entries   150
  Using   148–149
SmartIcons
  Customising   14
  Hiding   12–13
  Revealing   12–13
  Web authoring tools   14
SmartMasters   23
  Creating Web documents   40–41
Special characters   22
Starting   8
  With SmartCenter   9
  With SuiteStart   9
SuiteStart   9

T

Tabs   53. *See also* Text, Paragraphs, Applying tabs to
Text
  Colours   51
  Columns
    An overview   70
    Applying   71–72
  Dictating. *See* ViaVoice
  Drop caps   65–66
  Entering   22
  Fonts
    Attributes   52
    Changing   50
  Formatting   47–72
    An overview   48–49
    Changing with Fast Format   63–64
    Character v. Paragraph   48–49
    Verifying with Check Format. *See* Check Format
  Grammar-checking
    An overview   141
    Customising   145–146
    Launching   142

    Using   143–144
  Line spacing
    An overview   60
    Changing   61
  Lines
    Numbering   69
  Paragraphs
    Aligning   58
    Applying bullets to   67–68
    Applying tabs to   55–57
    Bordering   36
    Indenting   53–54
    Spacing   59
  Proofing. *See* Proofing tools
  Replacing   37
  Searching for   35
    With Quick Find   36
    With wildcards   35
  Searching for synonyms
    From within a document   139
    From within the Thesaurus   140
  Special characters
    Hiding   57
    Inserting   22
    Viewing   57
  Spell-checking
    An overview   127
    Customising   133–138
    Launching   131
    On-the-fly   128–130
    Separately (after document finalised)   131–132
    Using   132
  Type sizes   50
  Using SmartCorrect with. *See* SmartCorrect
  Wrapping round pictures   162
Text styles   111–124
  Amending   118
  Applying   115–117
  Assigning function keys to   123–124
  Character   113
  Copying   120–121
  Creating   114
  Deleting   119
  Differentiating   119
  In new documents   113
  Overview   112
  Paragraph   113
  Renaming   122
Text wrap   162
Thesaurus   139–140

U

Undo   33
  Caveats   33
  Multiple undo's   34
  Setting no. of levels   33

V

Vector images   162
Versioning. *See* Files, Versions
ViaVoice   177–186
  Closing   182
  Dictating into   183
  Enrolment   180–181
  Errors (correcting)   184
  Installation   178
  Launching   182
  Microphone setup
    Running   179
  Overview   178
  Playback options   185
  Requirements (system specification)   178
  Speech Centre
    Customising   186

Functions of　182–183
　Terminating dictation　183
　Text
　　Playing back　185
　　Verbalising　185
　Users
　　Adding new　180, 186
　　Changing　186

W

Watermarks　79
　Adding to footers　84
　Adding to headers　79
　Adding to pages　98
Wildcards　35
Word wrap　22
World Wide Web　39–46
　Creating Web documents
　　using SmartMasters　40–41
　　using HTML Export Assistant　42–43
　　Net-it Now! SE　176
　Hyperlinking　44–45
　Opening files from the Web　27
　Saving files to the Web/Uploading to an FTP server　46
　Web authoring SmartIcons toolbar　14

Z

Zoom settings　32